FRANKENSTEIN
CREATION AND
MONSTROSITY

Critical Views

FRANKENSTEIN CREATION AND MONSTROSITY

Edited by Stephen Bann

REAKTION BOOKS

Published by Reaktion Books Ltd
11 Rathbone Place
London W1P 1DE UK

First published 1994

Designed by Humphrey Stone
Jacket and cover designed by Ron Costley
Photoset by Wilmaset Ltd, Birkenhead, Wirral
Printed and bound in Great Britain by
The Alden Press, Oxford

British Library Cataloguing in Publication Data

Frankenstein, Creation and Monstrosity. –
(Critical Views Series)
I. Bann, Stephen II. Series
823.7
ISBN 0–948462–59–0
ISBN 0–948462–60–4 (pbk)

This volume was published with the aid of a subsidy
from the Centre for Modern Cultural Studies,
University of Kent at Canterbury.
The Centre was established by the Faculty
of Humanities in 1990.

Contents

Photographic Acknowledgements

The editor and publishers wish to express their thanks to the following for supplying photographic material and/or permission to reproduce it: The British Film Institute Stills Library, London: p. 92, p. 119, p. 120, p. 129 and p. 130; The Templeman Library, University of Kent at Canterbury: p. 81, p. 83, p. 85 and p. 86; and The Wellcome Institute Library, London: p. 75.

Notes on the Editor and Contributors

STEPHEN BANN is Professor and Director of the Centre for Modern Cultural Studies at the University of Kent at Canterbury. His recent books have included *Utopias and the Millennium* (co-edited with Krishan Kumar), published by Reaktion Books, 1993, and a translation into English of Julia Kristeva's *Proust and the Sense of Time* (1993). He has recently completed *Under the Sign: John Bargrave as Traveller, Collector and Witness* and *Romanticism and the Rise of History*.

ELISABETH BRONFEN is Professor of English and American Studies at the University of Zürich. Her recent publications include *Over Her Dead Body: Death, Femininity and the Aesthetic* (1992) and, co-edited with Sarah W. Goodwin, *Death and Representation* (1993). She has written articles in the areas of psychoanalysis, contemporary culture and gender studies, and is currently working on a new book, *The Knotted Subject: Hysteria and its Discontents.*

CROSBIE SMITH is Reader in the History of Science at the University of Kent at Canterbury, and Director of the new Centre for History and Cultural Studies of Science. He is co-author of *Energy and Empire: A Biographical Study of Lord Kelvin* (1989).

LUDMILLA JORDANOVA is Professor of History at the University of York. Her training is in the natural sciences, history and philosophy of science, and art history. Her publications include *Languages of Nature: Critical Essays on Science and Literature* (editor and contributor, 1986), and *Sexual Visions: Images of Gender in Science and Medicine between the Eighteenth and Twentieth Centuries* (1989).

LOUIS JAMES is Professor of Victorian and Modern Literature at the University of Kent at Canterbury. His books include *Fiction for the*

Working Man (1963), *Print and the People* (1976) and *Jean Rhys* (1979). He is working on a study of melodrama and society in the Victorian period.

MICHAEL FRIED is Professor of Humanities and the History of Art at Johns Hopkins University. He has published extensively on modern art and criticism, and is the author of *Absorption and Theatricality: Painting and Beholder in the Age of Diderot* (1980), *Realism, Writing, Disfiguration: On Thomas Eakins and Stephen Crane* (1987) and *Courbet's Realism* (1990). His study on Manet is forthcoming.

MICHAEL GRANT is Lecturer in Film Studies at the University of Kent at Canterbury. His recent publications include 'Subject and Person', 'The Miracle', 'Realism and the Defence of Consciousness: On the Work of Raymond Tallis' and 'Davie and Wittgenstein: The Music of Language' in *PN Review* between 1992–4. He has recently edited the *Selected Poems* of John Riley, to be published in Manchester in 1995.

JASIA REICHARDT is a writer on art and an exhibition organiser whose principal interests lie in the borderlines between different fields of science and the humanities. Her books include *Cybernetics, Arts and Ideas* (1971), *The Computer in Art* (1971) and *Robots – Fact, Fiction and Prediction* (1978); she curated the 1968 exhibition 'Cybernetic Serendipity' at the ICA. She is currently adviser to the ARTEC biennale in Japan, preparing an exhibition called AUTOMATIC MUSIC THEATRE, and working on a history of art and technology in the 20th century.

ROBERT OLORENSHAW is Director of International Relations at a Paris-based public relations consultancy. He also lectures on wine at the Office International du Vin. He is currently writing a book on the English novel.

JEAN-LOUIS SCHEFER lives in Paris and has published extensively on Renaissance and modern art. His works include *Scénographie d'un tableau* (1969), *L'invention du corps chrétien* (1973) and *Le Deluge, La Peste, Paolo Uccello* (1976); this last is to appear in an English translation in 1995. He is currently researching the artistic and cultural significance of the doctrine of the Eucharist in the Western tradition.

Introduction

STEPHEN BANN

Editors often have the sense that they must try to compensate, in their introductory remarks, for the diverse and heterogenous contributions that they have brought together into a single (as one might say) corpus. The 'myth of life', as Roland Barthes once put it, lurks within the continuity of the reading experience: this may be particularly true of the novel, as in Barthes's analysis, but it also applies in a modified form to our expectations of what may lie between two covers, in the form of an edited series of essays.[1] In particular, a collection which addresses itself to one single text, by one individual author, might be thought to have a self-contained, even an organic unity. The range of critical approaches to a literary text is not so hugely diverse as to cancel out this factor of convergence.

So we might think. But the text in question is Mary Shelley's *Frankenstein*. On the literal level, here is a story about a scientist who conceives the superhuman project of bringing together the fragments of dead bodies so as to imbue them with life (Dr Frankenstein: 'I had worked hard for nearly two years for the sole purpose of infusing life into an inanimate body'[2]). The success, and the failure, of this Promethean enterprise impel Mary Shelley's powerful narrative. But on a less literal level, what the author has put together is not so much a series of narrative segments, as a congeries of scientific and philosophical problems. These combine uniquely in the carefully wrought discourse of the novel. But any attempt to prise them out from it, and test them in the light of kindred ideas, risks doing violence to the imaginative core that has been fused together in the heat of the literary creation.

This is, however, a risk that the contributors to this volume are happy to accept. In fact, it is the very propensity of *Frankenstein* to generate myths and also, as in the specific case of artistic or scientific 'creation', to enable their deconstruction that is being celebrated here. *Frankenstein* offers a pretext (and here, by a creative play on words, let us take that word to mean not merely an excuse, but a preliminary or founding text) for explorations that reach far into the collective memory store of Western culture. Having originally intended to write 'modern Western culture' at that point, I am reminded, of course, that it is precisely this element of modernity that *Frankenstein* puts into question. It is not only a text which hands on, to drama and the cinema as well as to the story-telling tradition, the infinitely suggestive combined themes of creation and monstrosity. It is also the vehicle for a surprising *ricorso* – a return to issues that seemed have been washed away by the tide of Enlightenment. 'Natural magic' returns to the centre of the stage as the scientific implications of Dr Frankenstein's achievement come under review. A stage beyond, at the end of the century, lies the other founding fiction that has inundated our screens with images – Bram Stoker's *Dracula*; of this it could be said with even greater force that the tale that enriches the future also plunges us back into the study of the remote, pre-Modern past.

Critics of literature, drama and the cinema have combined here to mark different points in the historical trajectory of *Frankenstein*: its efficacy can be detected in the 'rewriting' carried out by novelists, dramatists and film directors, while at the same time (it is claimed) Mary Shelley herself 'rewrites' the texts inherited from her immediate family. Historians of science contributing to the collection begin from a different disciplinary orientation, evidently, but the issues they address frequently turn out to be similar, or identical with those raised by their colleagues. *Frankenstein* is not simply about creation and monstrosity; it is also about the representation of the monster, and his creator. That a specific 'image' of the scientist who performed the feat should have been established by the text is not irrelevant to the way in which contemporary scientists constructed an identity for themselves at this important juncture in the development of the life sciences. Equally, we could say that the 'image' of the monster that appears, first of all, in the popular dramatic productions of the 19th century and acquires definitive form, for the 20th century, in the person of Boris Karloff, is integrally linked to our concept of the man/machine relationship in an age of automation: only very recently has the 'robot' begun to lose its anthropomorphic characteristics, and its mythic links with the transgressive notion of creating life.

All of these aspects are carefully investigated in the essays that follow. I shall return at a later stage to a more detailed summary on the interconnected arguments of the individual essays. But there is a further role that this introduction can play. Precisely because *Frankenstein* embodies a relentless drive towards representation, and indeed visualization – precisely because the monster in James Whale's film through its very success tends to crowd out any other possible image – it is worth focusing for a while on another monster, whose protracted birth-pangs were roughly contemporary with those of Dr Frankenstein's monster. Such a focus helps us to occupy, in a sense, a mid-point between scientific experiment and literary creation, and to appreciate that it is not at all artificial to bring both practises into the same spectrum. Quite the opposite, it can be shown that the issue of monstrosity, however rigorously scrutinized from the scientific point of view, habitually escapes into the province of the literary text. This, however, does not imply an escape into the irrational and fantastic, but a deeper engagement with the culture that has engendered it.

The issue of monstrosity, as it begins to develop in the early modern period, is caught up from the start in the shift between paradigms of knowledge that differentiates that age from the Renaissance. As Michel Foucault emphasizes in *Les Mots et les choses* (translated as *The Order of Things*), the collocation of elements from different parts of the natural world can be placed under the sign of 'convenientia', or resemblance, and as such, testifies to the principle of universal congruence observed in nature as a whole. There are, for example, as many fishes in the sea as there are animals on the land, and this type of basic analogy justifies, by extension, the fact that moss-like plants grow on shellfish, or in the antlers of stags.[3] Yet this generously inclusive principle surely cannot account for the early seventeenth-century fascination, not with existing cross-overs between the realms of nature, but with the design and creation of new, ingenious examples.

One of the most indefatigable creators of monsters in this period was the Dutch silversmith Arent van Bolten. An album of his work dating from *c.*1595 to *c.*1603 (now in the British Museum) contains innumerable monsters and grotesque decorations. Even more interesting than these inventive drawings, however, is the small collection of bronzes that have been attributed to him as a result of their close similarity to designs in the album. In one case, for example, we have the intriguing spectacle of 'a monster with a reptile's head, a bird's body (the wings replaced by snails' shells), an erect curly tail, and the long legs of a bird of prey'.[4] Little is known about the collectors of this type of object. But it is probably right to stress that the bronze monster entered the contemporary 'cabinet of curiosities' not simply as index of the wonderful diversity of nature, but as a pointer to the new, inquisitive scrutiny of the world. Scientists were beginning to study the world as 'an entity embracing countless objects, and not as a universe of predictive or mysterious portents'.[5]

Let us assume that the aesthetic achievement of the bronze monster tickled the fancy of those engaged in the more sober pursuits of observation and classification. The corollary also appears to hold: that is, the attempt to make sense of the myriad forms of the natural world sometimes necessitated a leap into creative mythmaking. David Freedberg has drawn attention to the remarkable interest of one of the first major treatises on the classification of citrus fruits: Giovanni Battista Ferrari's *Hesperides, sive De malorum Aureorum cultu* (1646). Whenever Ferrari was baffled by the 'fanciful forms' assumed by certain examples of the fruit, he did not simply admit defeat, but shifted the register of discussion. 'Where the laws of nature could not be bent to embrace its variety, Ferrari told a story to explain it. The poetic imagination, harnessed by the rules of rhetoric, became a heuristic tool to supplement empirical logic and the limited evidence of the eyes.'[6]

Ferrari did not simply compile myths in order to explain monstrosities: he also commissioned leading artists to illustrate them. Hence we have Sacchi's version (engraved by Bloemart) of 'The Transformation of Harmonillus', in which the eponymous young man, victim of a jealous matron, is espied with his hand already turning into a form of citrus-tree. The purpose is to explain the particular monstrosity of the 'digitated' or finger-like form taken by certain citrus fruits (in Ferrari's terms: *Maleum citreum multiforme seu digitatum*).[7] The result, however, is not presented as a frivolous excursion from the business of scientific classification, but as a legitimate and serious supplement.

It could be argued that evidence of this kind simply points to a transitional, or unresolved, quality in seventeenth-century speculations about the natural world. Krzysztof Pomian has defined 'curiosity' as an 'interim rule' between religion and science.[8] Phenomena of the type described might appear to be symptomatic of this state of being neither one thing nor the other. Surely the collector of curiosities must have been aware that the bronze monster served no real purpose in the classification of species? Surely the expert on citrus fruits, however knowledgeable about the *Metamorphoses* of Ovid and the artistic tradition used to validate his poetic interpretations of the natural world, must have had some sense that the digitated form required a more reasonable explanation?

On this issue, the important thing is surely to avoid imposing our own

1. True and False Griffins.

John Ruskin, *True and False Griffins*, drawing engraved by R.P. Cuff,
from *Modern Painters*, III (1856).

prejudices about the antagonism between science and representation.
This may not only be an erroneous reading of the texts of the early
modern period. It may also be a barrier to our understanding of some of
the most profound currents of thought in the century that saw the
publication of *Frankenstein*, and is next in place to our own. Take, for
example, the assumptions about the link between creation and monstrosity implicit in John Ruskin's celebrated distinction between 'True
and False Griffins'. The 'Griffin' does not exist in the natural world, being
a fanciful beast composed from the head and wings of an eagle, and the
body and paws of a lion. But such a beast does exist in the tradition of
artistic representation, from the classical period, through the Middle
Ages and beyond. Moreover, for Ruskin, the fabulous nature of the
monster in no way prevents the artist from realizing a 'truth' that goes far
beyond mere representational effect. This resides, quite simply, in the fact
that some (but not all) griffins are conceived and realized in their
wholeness, rather than being merely the sum of their component parts:

You know a griffin is a beast composed of lion and eagle. The classical workman
set himself to fit these together in the most ornamental way possible. He
accordingly carves a sufficiently satisfactory lion's body, then attaches very
gracefully cut wings to the sides. . . .
  Let us see what the Lombardic workman saw [the griffin] doing.

Remember, first, the griffin, though part lion and part eagle, has the united *power of both*. He is not merely a bit of lion and a bit of eagle, but whole lion incorporate with whole eagle. So when we really see one, we may be quite sure we shall not find him wanting in anything necessary to the might either of beast or bird.[9]

Ruskin's conviction that 'the imagination is *always* right' goes far beyond the simple assertion that there is an artistic truth that is not subject to rational calculations. It goes far beyond the preference for one kind of rhetoric over another: the trope of 'wholeness' (synecdoche) over the addition of parts (metonymy). For what is being vindicated is the psychological truth of an aesthetic effect that is also, and crucially, the result of patient and clear-sighted observation.

How then does the unhappy Dr Frankenstein measure up to the example of the 'Lombardic workman'? The answer, on the most obvious level, is that the scientist, like the classical artist, misconceives his task as one of adding 'graceful' and 'satisfactory' parts one to another: 'life' must then be infused as an external animating principle, rather than as an aesthetic property of 'wholeness' that irradiates the concatenated forms. On a secondary level, of course, we could go on to consider in parallel terms the achievement, over a long term, of Mary Shelley herself, who is not a scientist but an artist. What remains imperfect and hideous in the make-up of the monster is recuperated aesthetically through the design of *Frankenstein* the text. And if, in Ruskin's terms, the truth of the monster lies pre-eminently in the fact that, through the artist's intermediacy, we can 'really see' it, then Mary Shelley's power of imagination is indeed justified: she created a monster who demanded to be seen, whose effective visualization, in the form of the horror-film, elevates the scientist's botched job into an aesthetic wholeness.

This would be one of the paradigms that we could use to illuminate the dynamic of creation and monstrosity that passes through Mary Shelley's *Frankenstein*. Ruskin's 'True and False Griffins', reminiscent though they are of the aberrant species validated by the early modern scientist's leap into poetic metamorphosis, demonstrate in an even more categorical way that the monster can be redeemed by the imagination: indeed, that the metamorphoses of art do not simply take over where the classificatory system is found wanting, but have an integral role in organizing and intensifying perceptions of the natural world. In a word, the artist teaches us to see the world. But there are other paradigms that must also be taken into account in considering the cultural resonances of *Frankenstein*. Ruskin's Griffin had been created in the Middle Ages, and he salutes retrospectively the Lombardic artist's divinatory powers. But who was creating monsters in early nineteenth-century England? Who really had the job of sticking the bits together and imbuing them with life? One person, at any rate, comes to mind, and his achievement, both in discursive and in practical terms, forms a curiously illuminating counter-point to Mary Shelley's imagined world.

In 1812, 1816, 1820 and 1824, the young Yorkshireman Charles Waterton, of an aristocratic but somewhat decayed Catholic family, undertook a series of prolonged journeys throughout South America, the record of which was eventually published in 1826, and rapidly established his notoriety. The very first of these journeys, undertaken with the support of the great naturalist Sir Joseph Banks, had as its primary aim the collection of the highly poisonous substance later to be known as curare, which was prepared from certain types of native creeper by the Amazonian tribes. On his first return to London, around the year 1814, Waterton took part in an unprecedented experiment with the repatriated poison, which we could anachronistically call a trial in anaesthesia:

A she-ass received the wourali poison in the shoulder, and died apparently in ten minutes. An incision was then made in its windpipe, and through it the lungs were regularly inflated for two hours with a pair of bellows. Suspended animation returned. The ass held up her head, and looked around; but the inflating being discontinued, she sunk once more in apparent death. The artificial breathing was immediately recommenced, and continued without intermission for two hours more. This saved the ass from final dissolution; she rose up and walked about. . . .[10]

As the description makes clear, the fascination of this experiment lay, for Waterton, in the interpolation of a new, problematic zone between life and death: the poison is deadly, and has already killed more than one ass, in a matter of minutes, but, at the very point where this particular animal appears to be dead, the operation of the bellows sustains life and ensures eventual survival. Surgical technique has intervened to blur the forthright opposition between the living and the dead.

Waterton's major scientific concern in his South American journeys was not, however, with the collection of curare, but with the location of the most perfect specimens that he could find of the native birds and beasts. These he transported home with great care, and mounted for exhibition, using a wholly new approach to the science, or art, of taxidermy. In his essay 'On preserving Birds for Cabinets of Natural History' he gives scrupulous attention to what he calls the mechanical and scientific requisites for this demanding task: the new taxidermist must arm himself with a penknife, a needle and thread etc., and he must have a steady hand; but he must also evince 'a complete knowledge of ornithological anatomy'. 'You must pay close attention', he writes, 'to the form and attitude of the bird, and know exactly the proportion each curve, or extension, or contraction, or expansion of any particular part bears to the rest of the body'.[11] One might conclude that the new taxidermist's assignment is precisely to obviate those effects of distortion and disproportion which the previous manner of mounting ornithological specimens had incurred. Unlike Dr Frankenstein (though admittedly with only one carcass to deal with at a time), he learns to predict the effects of his handiwork. Nor is the idea of creation, with all its transgressive implications, absent from his activity. 'In a word', he continues, 'you must possess Promethean boldness, and bring down fire, and animation, as it were, into your preserved specimen'.[12]

Waterton leaves us in no doubt of the ultimate test that he expects his stuffed birds and animals to survive. Thoroughly despising as he does the paltry efforts of earlier taxidermists, whose specimens have uniformly shrunk and shifted into grotesque and distorted attitudes, he uses an audacious new method of removing all the bones and remodelling the skin from the inside, having previously made it malleable through soaking it in the chemical preparation of 'corrosive sublimate'. In this way he attempts to shock his audience into exclaiming, in front of the new creations: 'That animal is alive!'[13] Yet how does he justify this overweening ambition to restore and perpetuate life – not temporarily, as with the she-ass, but for a period that is to last indefinitely into the future, since (as he puts it) the tropical bird will 'retain its pristine form and colours for years long after the hand that has stuffed it has mouldered into dust'?[14]

Part of the answer to this question is that he makes use, like the seventeenth-century naturalist Ferrari, of the supreme repository of myths about the death and resurrection of bodies in the natural world: Ovid's *Metamorphoses*. 'Mox similis volucri, mox vera volucris', he quotes:[15] 'Soon he is like a bird, soon a true bird'. The taxidermist's capacity to transform a puny corpse into a beautiful and quasi-eternal bird (like Keats's nightingale) is equated with the pagan poet's celebration of the mythic density of nature, where, from the flowers to the stars, individual appearances reflect the stories of unhappy, or unlucky, lovers rescued from the mortality of the flesh. But is there not an anxiety underlying this technical assurance? When Waterton names the god who epitomizes the power of nature to take on a myriad successive forms, and proclaims that 'the sun of Proteus has risen to our museums',[16] is he not fearful that his power to simulate life might have other implications, especially for a good Catholic?

This is not just an idle enquiry, since Waterton's Catholicism was more than a personal faith. As recusant Catholics, members of his family had been forbidden from holding public office since the Reformation, apart from a brief spell under Mary Tudor, and Waterton himself maintained a contemptuous distaste for the Hanoverian monarchy. Even, and perhaps especially, when he visited South America, his conviction that the world was still dominated by the legitimate struggle of the Roman Church to reassert its universality, was never far from his concerns. Portugal had expelled the Jesuits from her colonial possessions, as well as from mainland Europe; Waterton, who had been educated at the Jesuit school of Stonyhurst in Lancashire, deplored the decision, and vituperated those of his countrymen who, like the poet Southey, acclaimed their expulsion as a triumph of enlightenment:

When you visit the places where those learned fathers once flourished, and see, with your own eyes, the evils their dissolution has caused . . . what will you think of our poet laureate, for calling them, in his 'History of Brazil', 'Missioners, whose zeal the most fanatical was directed by the coolest policy?'[17]

It would indeed be difficult to think of anyone less attuned to the liberal and free-thinking milieu of Percy and Mary Shelley than the man who took care, after his second lengthy journey to South America, to write long, personal letters to Pope Pius VII about 'The State of Religion' in those climes. Waterton's present-day reputation has been based, first of all, on his acclamation by Edith Sitwell as an 'English eccentric', and second on his being regarded as a pioneer of the ecological approach, since he turned his estate near Wakefield into a nature reserve.[18] But when Gerald Durrell congratulates him for '[turning] the grounds of Walton Hall into a sanctuary', it is doubly significant that the contemporary naturalist should use this particular term. For Waterton's religious ideology and his original attitude to the natural world were, in fact, indissolubly intertwined. The animal against which he declared unremitting war, within the precincts of Walton Hall, was the 'Hanoverian rat' – so called because of a rumour that the first specimens had been brought over to Britain in the same boat as George I: it was Waterton's considered view that this species was responsible for the virtual extinction of the native English brown rat – a plausible theory that, in his case at least, could be described as overdetermined. Indeed Waterton's attitude to the natural world, and the reserve which he went to considerable trouble to create, can be seen to reflect theological and geopolitical, rather than ecological, ideas at work: his task was not to prefigure an 'earthly paradise' of liberated species, but to fence off an area that, with great ingenuity, could be preserved from the threat of encroaching irreligion. The diminishing estates of Walton Hall, where the Catholic faith had been kept alive in spite of persecution, were surrounded by a high wall within which the children of nature could live in uncontaminated innocence.

This almost Manichean view of the world accounts no doubt for the fact that Waterton did not simply stuff and exhibit superb specimens of birds and animals (they have fulfilled his ambitions by remaining pristine right up to the present day); he also took time off to create monsters. And, in his case, monstrosity is precisely the other face of the as yet uncorrupted natural world. Working with bits and pieces of animals and birds, he does not seek to give them the compelling wholeness of the 'True Griffin'; on the contrary, he underlines their heterogeneity so as to bring out the devilish character of the institutions of the modern world. He puts together the head of an eagle owl, together with the legs of a bittern and the wings of a partridge, in order to signify: 'Noctifer, or the Spirit of the Dark Ages, unknown in England before the Reformation'. He uses a tortoise, with a seemingly human face, on a porcupine's body, to convey the political message of 'John Bull and the National Debt'. Strange lizards, in threatening attitudes, surround and surmount the caricatural image of a country overburdened by its newly acquired debts and obligations.

Waterton's satirical creations recall the bronze monsters of the early seventeenth century to some extent, just as they evoke the iconographic traditions of religious painting, from the grotesques in the margins of medieval manuscripts to the works of Bosch. The difference, of course, is that these are genuine specimens, bizarrely adapted to their new role. And what can pass without comment when the taxidermist utilizes mere reptiles and birds, acquires a different degree of seriousness when he moves out of the animal kingdom to evoke, through unpromising materials, the features of the human face. 'John Bull' is already partially humanized, but the specimen to which he gives the fullest degree of humanity (and whose prominence as an illustration to the *Wanderings* caused the greatest public offence) is the one he christens the 'Nondescript'. This is Waterton's most memorable monster, all the more

Charles Waterton, *John Bull and the National Debt*, preserved porcupine
with human face and tortoise shell, assailed by preserved lizards
and other creatures. Wakefield Art Galleries and Museums.

Charles Waterton, *The Nondescript*, c. 1824, skin of howler monkey converted
into a bearded man. Wakefield Art Galleries and Museums.

effective for not being harnessed to any stated religious or political programme.

The Nondescript is, as its title suggests, not burdened by an intrusive significance. Waterton affects to describe it in the text of his *Wanderings* as the head and shoulders of an entirely new species, whose 'features are quite of the Grecian cast'; however, he lets out on the side the information that this sagacious face was, in fact, produced from the hindquarters of a monkey. Anticipating the disarray of his readers, he uses the example to put crucial questions about the implications of his practice: 'if . . . we argue that this head in question has had all its original features destroyed, and a set of new ones given to it, by what means has this hitherto unheard-of change been effected?'[19] The answer has to be that it is Waterton's own skill in taxidermy that has produced this surprising *volte-face*, and the consequences are far-reaching:

If I have succeeded in effacing the features of a brute, and putting those of a man in their place, we might be entitled to say that the sun of Proteus has risen to our museums. . . . If I have effected this, we can now give to one side of the skin of a man's face the appearance of eighty years, and to the other that of blooming sixteen. We could make the forehead and eyes serene in youthful beauty, and shape the mouth and jaws to the features of a malicious old ape.[20]

Waterton's Nondescript is not burdened with the same satirical connotations as his other composite figures. Admittedly, he allowed it to be thought that the features were modelled on those of a customs officer, one Mr Lushington, who had obstructed the passage of his specimens at Liverpool (he was, as Waterton's most recent biographer puts it, 'a paradigm of bureaucratic principle, and a most Hanoverian rat'[21]). But he also encouraged the rumour that it was a new wild animal discovered in the South American forests. In effect, this floating significance was all that could be sustained while Waterton was approaching a threshold beyond which his devout conscience would not allow him to stray: here he was not simply creating monsters, the sanctioned other side of the Christian body, but opening up a dizzying prospect in which youth and age, beauty and malice, the face and the hindquarters, became freely convertible into one another, dependent only on the infinite plasticity of the taxidermist's skill.

So Waterton's experiment arrives at a dead end, while Mary Shelley's fictional hypothesis continues to generate new forms and new interpretations. Yet the very fact that Waterton, in the stubborn traditionalism of his Catholic faith, occupied a part of the political spectrum so far away from the Shelleys, opens up another dimension no less relevant to this collection of essays. In his journeys through South America, Waterton was in the habit of encouraging strange visitors: 'I have often wished to have been once sucked by a vampire. . . . Many a night have I slept with my foot out of the hammock to tempt this winged surgeon . . . but it was all in vain.'[22] This commendably rational attitude to the creatures of the forest was not, however, maintained in his accounts of the miracles of the Catholic faith. On a visit to Naples in 1840 he witnessed one of the most celebrated of these: 'Everything else in the shape of adventures now appears to me trivial and of no account', he exclaims; 'the liquifaction of the blood of St Januarius is miraculous beyond the shadow of a doubt'.[23]

If it is paradoxical to be at the same time sanguine about the vampire bat, and credulous with regard to St Januarius, then Waterton incarnates paradox. A more plausible approach would be to reiterate the point that what Waterton does in the interests of 'nature', when he rings his park with a high wall, is bracketed within the concerns of a religious position all the more staunchly held for being, historically, under threat. The Waterton of Catholic recusant stock reminds us in the very euphoria of his scientific explorations how archaic is his map of the world, or at least how resistant to the universalizing power of Enlightenment. Appropriately, this collection ends with a shift of attention from Mary Shelley to Bram Stoker, whose *Dracula* is hardly less influential, and fertile in progeny, than *Frankenstein*. In the recent new edition of *Dracula*, modern myth-making is amply satisfied by an introduction that focuses almost exclusively on Stoker's psychosexual dispositions, and regales us with accounts of his correspondence with Walt Whitman and his subservient love of the actor Henry Irving.[24] The case of Charles Waterton reminds us – and the last essay in this collection makes it transparently clear – that tracing holy rings is an activity deserving of a different kind of cultural explanation: that Carpathian vampires are indeed more able to strike home than the shrinking bats of Guiana.

The practice of Charles Waterton, taxidermist, aptly illustrates the way in which the themes of creation and monstrosity are intertwined in the culture of the nineteenth century. It also indicates the trajectory leading from *Frankenstein* to *Dracula*, which is the direction followed by a number of essays in this collection. Jean-Louis Schefer chooses to place his major emphasis on the later text, equating the issue of monstrosity with the long-term history of the Christian doctrine of the Eucharist and seeing the figure of Dracula himself as a figure of the Profanation of the

Host, symptomatically generated at the borderline between Eastern and Western Christianity. Robert Olorenshaw looks more specifically at the way in which Mary Shelley's novel accommodates the monstrous within the form of narrative, and goes on to investigate the particular engagement of Bram Stoker with registering the materiality of writing. This is also the central theme of Michael Fried's analysis of a latter-day creation allegory: H. G. Wells's *The Island of Dr Moreau*. The form that is ultimately taken by the scientist's monstrous creatures, as they regress to sub-human status, is the form assumed by written characters on the horizontal page.

A second thread in this collection is provided by the various investigations of the visual form adopted by monstrosity, in the tradition deriving from *Frankenstein*. If the monster can achieve a disquieting existence in terms of the material form taken by literary creations, he can also assume a vivid and memorable presence through being realized in visual and scenographic terms. First of all comes the theatre. As Louis James shows, the dramatic iconography of the 'Wild Man' in nineteenth-century theatre is powerfully affected by the popularity of representations of *Frankenstein*. Michael Grant takes up the story in the present century, when the cinema has showed itself to be the ideal medium for the dissemination of the 'fantastic' tales generated in Mary Shelley's epoch. As is consistent with Schefer's reading of *Vampyr*, and his essay in this collection, Grant firmly dismisses the reductive Freudian approaches to the horror film, and argues for a less perfunctory attention to the aesthetic characteristics of the Horror Film. Jasia Reichardt shares with him the image of Boris Karloff, as the definitive monster of Frankenstein. But her comprehensive visual survey of the forms taken by machines embodying artificial intelligence raises the interesting question: will the monster perish, together with all types of anthropomorphic projection, as the new machines shun all reference to the external characteristics of the human body?

This is a question addressed more to the scientist than to the creator of novels or films. Yet, as Mary Shelley's text shows, the scientist cannot exist without a self-validating image, and is obliged to choose between different paradigms of what constitutes the scientific. Ludmilla Jordanova examines the carefully constructed persona of Dr Frankenstein from the point of view of the image that such 'unveilers of nature' entertained of their own professional commitment. Crosbie Smith looks at the more general traits that identify the unhappy scientist's view of the natural world, and concludes that Frankenstein is reaching back beyond the

Enlightenment to the tradition of 'natural magic', with its roots in the Middle Ages.

So *Frankenstein*, and the myth of creation embodied in it, not only brings us right up to date, with the questions pertaining to artificial intelligence. The implications of the text also lead us far back, to those 'Middle Ages' that Schefer describes as 'a vast reservoir of fantasies' irrigating the institutions of the modern world. It is left to Elisabeth Bronfen, in the opening essay, to argue persuasively for a more immediate source for the ideas governing *Frankenstein* in the revolutionary writings of Mary Shelley's mother, Mary Wollstonecraft, and her father, William Godwin. And this is also the place to acknowledge that the original idea for a collection of essays based on this text came from Ralph Cohen, whose Center for Literary and Cultural Change at the University of Virginia is dedicated to similarly wide-ranging investigations of the contribution of literature to knowledge.

I

Rewriting the Family:
Mary Shelley's 'Frankenstein'
in its Biographical/Textual Context

ELISABETH BRONFEN

Sigmund Freud suggested that the progress of society depends on the opposition between successive generations. 'The liberation of an individual, as he grows up, from the authority of his parents', he argued, 'is one of the most necessary though one of the most painful results brought about by the course of his development'. Given that this essential liberation is to some extent achieved by every human being by the time the onset of adulthood has been normalized, Freud's concern is for those neurotics whose condition is determined 'by their having failed in this task'.[1] He applies the term 'the neurotic's family romance' to a peculiarly marked imaginative activity engendered by a child's dissatisfaction with the curtailment of parental affection. For in a later stage in the development of her or his estrangement from her or his parents, the neurotic uses the activity of daydreaming as a 'fulfilment of wishes and a correction of actual life' in response to parents she or he feels to be unsatisfactory. In the course of such phantasies the actual insufficient parents are replaced by others 'who, as a rule, are of higher social standing'.[2] These phantasies exalt the paternal and maternal figure, or, at a later point, denigrate them. As imaginative activities they are an expression of revenge and retaliation, however, that in fact preserves the child's original affection that has been thwarted by the actual events of life. Ultimately these phantasies are an expression of nostalgia and regret, for 'the happy, vanished days when his father seemed to him the noblest and strongest of men and his mother the dearest and loveliest of women'.[3]

Harold Bloom, in turn, resorts to Freud's concept of 'family romance' so as to describe the succession between two generations of poets.[4] In his theory of literary influence, Bloom argues that all poets are intimidated by the strength of their predecessors – and this serves as a source of poetic anxiety that he calls an anxiety of influence. Only by reading their predecessors incorrectly – for which Bloom coins the term creative misreading – can authors carve out for themselves an imaginary space within which they can survive and produce. By virtue of misreading they can repress their true legacy, namely the fact that they owe their creativity to a parent-poet, and this act of repression serves as a second source of anxiety. At the same time, one could add, misreading acknowledges a literary parentage, even as it follows the pattern sketched by Freud. In the act of exalting or denigrating one's literary predecessors, what occurs is a form of re-creation of the parent-poet.

In the following pages I suggest taking Bloom far more literally than he intended, so as to look at the way that Mary and Percy Shelley's self-conception as authors emerged in a response that significantly merges the spiritual with the actual parents. Though the argument can be made for Percy Shelley as well, I focus on the way Mary Shelley's biography and, especially, her textual creation, *Frankenstein*, can be interpreted as a form of misreading and rewriting of the texts by her parents, Mary Wollstone-craft and William Godwin. At the same time I will extend Bloom's term, 'anxiety of influence', so as to emphasize the fact that, as the second generation structures its life, it imitates the writings of the first. What occurs in the process is the recreation of parents in response to a sense of insufficiency that is worked out quite literally by virtue of an imaginary activity. The parents are exalted in a two-fold manner. They are stylized into literary figures, engendering the imaginative or poetic activity of their children, and, as the literary predecessors that they are, idealized. Godwin and Wollstonecraft as texts are thus transformed into figures of the all-sufficient father and mother they never were in life (due to the restrictions exerted by the former and the early death of the latter). One of the crucial questions thus becomes, whether, as a result, the children implement in a consistent way that which their parents only theorized, or whether in this act of self-fashioning they wilfully misunderstood their parents' texts. For what is significant about the Godwin–Shelley family is the fact that here the second generation *does not* repress the importance of their pre-decessors. Rather, both Mary and Percy seem to have assigned a fetish-like quality to the writings of their parents, as these take on a prototypal function.[5] Furthermore, the repressed ideas of the first generation seem to return and, in the gesture of repetition, become lived reality for the second generation. The children take their bearings precisely from the way they rewrite the lives of their parents, in an act, however, that also refashions these paternal biographies.

For the particular family of authors and texts I have chosen, what links the succession of family generations and textual production is an opposition typical for the Romantic period, namely a polarization between solitary artistic activity and natural procreation. At stake is the question of influence and transmission, as well as the mutual inter-dependance between the question of origins and that of reproduction, between genesis and propagation. Given that my concern is the con-flation of two opposites, i.e., the enmeshment of actual and spiritual parentage, my discussion of this interrelation between family and text will itself undertake a heterodox theoretical approach. My reading of *Frankenstein* as Mary Shelley's version of her family romance will collapse a *biographical* approach with the already well-established *thematic* discussion of this gothic tale as an example of the conflict between the ethics of creation and the phenomen of monstrosity.[6] Within my discussion of the paternity/maternity of Shelley's text, the issue of biography, I will argue, should not be located outside the text but also be sought internal to its structure.

I will begin with a brief sketch of the biographies of my four subjects, always bearing in mind the way the second generation misreads and *mis*-reproduces the writings of the first, in its imaginative effort to recreate its own family romance. The mother in this narrative is Mary Wollstone-craft (1759–97), a courageous, passionate and unconventional feminist, author of *A Vindication of the Rights of Woman* (1792), in which she pleaded for women's rights for self-determination and equality in intellectual, public and private realms. After working as a governess she moved to London, to live there as an independent author. She was the friend of progressive thinkers like Tom Paine and William Blake. She fell in love with Henry Fuseli and, given her ideas about free love, wanted to live with him and his wife in a *menage à trois*. In 1792 she travelled alone to Paris, where she was at first an ardent supporter of the French Revolution. Two years later she returned to England with her illegitimate daughter, Fanny Imlay, politically and personally disappointed. The infidelities of her American lover, Gilbert Imlay, twice drove her to attempt suicide.

In 1797 she married William Godwin (1756–1836) – the paternal figure in the narrative – a radical political thinker, who had been ordained as a dissenting minister in 1778 but a few years later gave up the clerical profession. Like Wollstonecraft he moved to London to live as an independent writer, and was active in the same intellectual circles. Owing to his polemical *Enquiry Concerning Political Justice* (1793) he was for several years a celebrity, but afterwards fell into obscurity and debt. During his marriage with Mary Wollstonecraft he felt that for the first time in his life he was learning how to combine radical intellect with emotions. Mary died ten days after giving birth to a daughter, also called Mary. The intense grief Godwin experienced while mourning compelled him to represent his wife in two very different texts. The first rendition is found in his extraordinarily candid *Memoirs of the Author of 'A Vindication of the Rights of Woman'* (1798), in which he disclosed the full unconventionality of his late wife to what was becoming an increasingly conservative audience. The opinion of that audience, which was derived from readings of his text, held that she was an 'unsex'd female' (i.e., liberal or rather immoral in her sexual behaviour), and this negative image was transmitted well into the twentieth century.

Whatever public opinion may have been, over the years Godwin himself increasingly idealized her: Mary's portrait hung in the entrance to his home; and in the novel *St Leon* (1831) he offers a second rendition of Wollstonecraft, here in the figure of Marguerite.[7] In contrast to his earlier depiction of her liberal love-life, she is now presented as the resilient and practical wife, the site of harmony in a strife-ridden family. In the introduction to *St Leon* Godwin calls his narrative a recantation of his extreme rejection of sensibility in his earlier work, the *Enquiry Concerning Political Justice*. He now argued that the legacy of his deceased wife was his own recognition that 'domestic and private affections' (p. x) are inseparable from any profound and active sense of justice.

The story about the second generation begins some sixteen years after the death of Mary Wollstonecraft, with the appearance in the Godwin household of Percy Bysshe Shelley (1792–1822) – a rebellious, eccentric, genius, who was forced to leave Oxford University because of a pamphlet he had written on atheism. He was already married to the sixteen-year-old Harriet Westbrook when he informed Godwin that he considered Godwin to be his spiritual father and gave him his poem *Queen Mab* to read, claiming it was a poetic translation of the *Enquiry Concerning Political Justice*. What is interesting about this philosopher/father and poet/son couple, however, is not only the fact that for the older man the young poet seemed to incarnate the lost 'spirit of 1793'. The relationship between the two can, in fact, be seen as a hypertrophic family romance, a superlative elevation of the paternal figure, namely in the translation of written text into life. Godwin had already perceived Shelley's poem

H.W. Pickersgill, *William Godwin*, 1830. National Portrait Gallery, London.

(British School), *Mary Wollstonecraft*, c. 1792.
Walker Art Gallery, Liverpool.

Reginald Easton, *Mary Wollstonecraft Godwin, later Shelley*,
miniature made posthumously. Shelley Relics, Bodleian Library,
University of Oxford.

Amelia Curran, *Percy Bysshe Shelley*, 1819.
National Portrait Gallery, London.

Queen Mab as a misreading of his theory of political justice. And when the poet eloped with his daughter Mary to Italy, doing so explicitly in the light of Godwin's own treatise against marriage, the father was outraged and wanted to cast off his daughter.[8]

Paralleling Shelley, the daughter Mary (1797–1851) had, in her turn, largely fashioned herself in the image of her dead mother. She constantly read Wollstonecraft's texts and diaries, and did so, furthermore, at her mother's grave in St Pancras – which was also the place where Shelley declared his love to her.[9] During their flight through France, accompanied by Mary's half-sister Claire, Mary and Percy realized the *menage à trois* Wollstonecraft had once imagined for herself, Fuseli and his wife. Paradoxically, against the prohibition and displeasure of the old Godwin, Percy and Mary legitimized their actions by continually rereading the writings of the young radicals Wollstonecraft and Godwin. Percy's courtship of Mary and their extramarital cohabitation in Switzerland one year later thus marks both the return of the radical French philosophy before 1795 and a concrete, lived realization of Godwin's and Wollstonecraft's political treatises.

Given such behaviour, one could argue that the second generation understood parents as predecessors that encouraged, confirmed and justified their way of living. While the first generation seems to have modified its radical theories when it came to living, the second generation allowed the past to return, but in a far more radical transformation of theory into practice. The relationship between Mary and Percy not only imitates the parents' but transforms into lived reality what they merely *intellectually* conceived as a possibility. In fact, shortly before her suicide in 1816, Harriet Westbrook, who had remained Percy's wife throughout, attributed her husband's infidelity to his *reading* of Godwin's *Enquiry*; 'the very great evil that book has done', she wrote, 'is not to be told'.[10] In the same year, Mary, pregnant for the third time, not only used Harriet's death but also, in turn, her renewed *reading* of Wollstonecraft's *Vindication of the Rights of Woman* to justify to Percy their need to enter into marriage. By this means she hoped to legitimize her children and be recognized again by her father. 1816 is also the year in which she began writing *Frankenstein, or, The Modern Prometheus*.

Having presented this brief biographical sketch, I now turn to the relationship between the genesis of texts and the generation of a family in some of the writings of these four authors. While in the biographical sketch I was concerned with an extratextual sequence of events, I now concentrate on an intratextual comparison of texts, in order to explore how the question of parental legacy is related to the situation in which certain texts can, or perhaps even must, be generated. To do so I first, briefly, present the theme of monstrosity at stake in Godwin's novel *St Leon*. In a second step I will concentrate on an interpretation of Mary Godwin Shelley's *Frankenstein* (1818, second edition revised 1831), with Godwin's novel, Shelley's poem 'Alastor, or, The Spirit of Solitude' (1816) and the 'Tale of Jemima' in Wollstonecraft's novel *The Wrongs of Woman* (1798) serving as the intertextual / biographical context for my discussion.[11]

Given that *St Leon* is a *roman à thèse*, it is worth pausing for a moment to summarize Godwin's political philosophy. Godwin connects cultural determinism with extreme liberalism and individualism. For him all forms of social institutions represent a corruption of the citizen and pervert his ability to form judgements, because they create prejudices. Owing to these prejudices man does not perceive himself, his fellow men and the events of his life as they are, but rather experiences them only as preconceived opinions. Only a non-institutional sympathy can allow one to comprehend the true complexity of the Other. The ideal social community is one in which individuals can work together without constraint, because they mutually sympathize with and love one other, with each one recognized to be an individual. The central tragedy of human existence consists in the solitude that prejudices call forth, a solitude making it impossible to enjoy the happiness of friendship. For Godwin man is naturally good and potentially perfectible. The crucial trait for perfectibility is individual judgement, for through this ability man can liberate himself from institutionally engendered prejudices, such as marriage, virtue and rank, and see things as they really are.

St Leon represents the fictional memoirs of a French aristocrat who comes to possess both the philosopher's stone and the elixir of life; the former allows him to artificially generate gold, the latter to gain immortality. For this superhuman knowledge, however, he pays by being excluded from a happy family existence. The explicit concern of these memoirs is a repeated self-accusation, that he willingly destroyed his perfect wife – epitome of true, untainted human nature – and gave up the perfect relationship he had with her. In these memoirs he represents his life as a succession of events; and each experience of a mutually sympathetic family security is disrupted by the striving for institutional-ized values like ambition, fame and wealth, all stamped by prejudice. The resulting inhuman loneliness is invariably recuperated into the renewed formation of bonds of sympathy only to lead, once again, to their disruption. Bonding and disruption structure the text. Thus, for example, he marries the virtuous Marguerite de Damville. However, rather than cultivating domestic affection in the midst of his family, he forgets his family and turns to gambling instead, hoping to gain wealth and glory. He loses his entire inheritance and his family name is erased from the annals of France. While he succumbs to a form of brain-fever, his wife organizes their retreat to Switzerland, nurses him and generates a second intact, now rural family. However, St Leon once more introduces alienation and mistrust into the idyllic family recreated by his wife. After a period of dreadful poverty he succumbs to a new urge for wealth and fame and accepts the clandestine knowledge – the philosopher's stone and the elixir of life – from a mysterious stranger. He acquires knowledge and limitless power, but this pact with the Devil is an exclusive one that is directed against the natural family and renders him socially monstrous.

We are thus presented with the following opposition: the maternal legacy, a family bond of love, peace and mutual sympathy, simplicity and openness in communication; and the paternal legacy, the lost aristocratic title, a striving for fame and wealth, which can be repeatedly regained by virtue of a demonic secret. By accepting this forbidden knowledge Reginald St Leon renounces his family forever, as well as the ability to pass on his genealogy. Marguerite turns from him, wounded by the loss of his trust, and dies soon after. She calls him a 'monster' because he now no longer has an equal among human men and is thus cut off from 'cordiality and confidence'.[12] His oldest son, Charles, deserts his father. His daughters return to the family estate, to live there without the father who has contaminated their family name. Alone, St Leon travels throughout Europe, without family or family name, seeking for a friend 'with whom I can associate on equal terms'.[13]

At the end of the narrative a confrontation between St Leon and Charles de Damville takes place that represents the confrontation between these two legacies. On the one hand there is the father, who has taken on the unnatural fatal legacy of the stranger, the artificial generation of gold and of life, and connected with this an unconditional solitude, and on the other there is the son, who, by taking on the name of his mother, passes on her values – an honourable sincerity and candour and the rejection of all unnatural, demonic legacies. In his marriage to Pandora, Charles will generate a new family, based on trust, in the image of his mother and bearing her name. In other words, the maternal legacy, the natural family, a community based on sympathy and unconditional affection, can be transmitted in the worldly realm. The paternal legacy, perverted owing to a striving for fame, and then owing to the artificial legacy of superhuman knowledge, is rejected by the son and the only proponent of this legacy, Reginald St Leon, is cut off from the community of fellow humans.

But – and this is what makes Godwin's text so fascinating – the narrator, Reginald St Leon, does ultimately create an affective alliance through the implied community with his reader, whom he addresses directly, so that the reader takes on the function of the sought-after friend. Though he will not disclose the secret knowledge imparted by the stranger, he does confess all the circumstances of his life. St Leon addresses the reader, not merely to warn him against the fate that has befallen him but also – and therein lies a seminal contradiction – to praise his son. In so doing, however, he guarantees a double paternity, namely that of his corporeal son and that of his text: 'That the reader may enter the more fully into *my* sentiment of congratulation upon the happiness of *my* son, and rise from the perusal of *my* narrative with a more soothing and pleasurable sensation, I will recapitulate [his good] qualities. . . . *I* was the hero's *father!*' (italics mine).[14] As the signature used to sign these memoirs, the name St Leon is, after all, preserved. While Charles does not recognize that Reginald is his father, and to the end remains unwilling to re-acknowledge him as his father, St Leon, in turn, uses his memoirs to proclaim his paternity *in writing*, a paternity he was unable to insist on in his last oral confrontation with his son. In his direct address to the reader he implicitly uses these memoirs to acknowledge his son, and thus, by virtue of the power of his text, to reassure himself of his family bonds.

Thus Godwin's novel preserves a contradiction. These fictional memoirs are meant as the political philosopher's warning against the loss of friendship and family. In the figure of Marguerite, an idealization of Mary Wollstonecraft, he represents his ideal community. But at the same time, the poet Godwin cannot completely escape from the fascination that resides with the solitary artist figure. Along with the vice of prejudice, his St Leon also incorporates that which Godwin praised as the highest virtue – individual judgement. At the onset of his tale he writes that 'In the progress of my story, my motive for recording it will probably become evident',[15] and what becomes evident is an oscillation between the warning against the Devil's pact, which the solitary artist undergoes, and a proud appraisal of self-representation – paternal authorship – made possible through a community with one's reader.

The *notion*, that a prerequisite for creativity is *necessarily* the *betrayal of family bonds*, however, induces *unmitigated* anxiety in Godwin's daughter Mary – and, so as to delineate this anxiety produced by the paternal text in the daughter, I move to my interpretation of *Franken-stein*, one divided into four parts – the author's introduction, Walton's tale, Frankenstein's tale and the monster's tale.

In her introduction to the third edition (1831) of *Frankenstein*, Mary Shelley, describing the genesis of her tale, asserts that she was 'from the first very anxious that I should prove myself worthy of my parentage'.[16] At the same time, she also wanted to participate in the rivalry between Byron and Shelley, who in the summer of 1816 set up a competition for the best ghost story. Thus from the very beginning, writing for Mary means affirming her parents as author–predecessors, and acknowledging that, in her position as wife to Percy, she could be on an equal footing with her husband. As the 'devout but nearly silent listener'[17] of the conversations between Byron and Shelley about the origin of life, she comes upon the idea that 'perhaps the component parts of a creature might be manufactured, brought together, and endued with vital warmth'. That night she has the vision of a 'pale student of unhallowed arts' that bestows life on a 'hideous phantasm of a man . . . to mock the stupendous mechanism of the Creator of the world'. Hoping that, if left to itself, this artificial life would once again lose its spark and subside again into dead matter, he falls asleep, but as he opens his eyes again his horrible creation stands next to him 'looking on him with yellow, watery, but speculative eyes'. Mary Shelley adds 'I opened *my eyes* in terror. The idea so possessed my mind that a thrill of fear ran through me'.[18] So as to protect herself from being haunted by this hideous phantom she decides to write her gothic tale.

I focus on this passage not only because it can be read as a rewriting of Shelley's 'Alastor', as I will delineate in detail further on, but also because it reveals a problematic analogy between the author, Mary Shelley, and her protagonist, Dr Frankenstein. In the same gesture that allows Frankenstein to materialize his hideous phantasm of an artificial man, Mary Shelley uses her novel to realize the phantom of her nightly vision. In contrast to her protagonist, who turns away from his creation, she, however, ends her introduction with the wish 'I bid my hideous progeny go forth and prosper. I have an affection for it'.[19] With this analogy she already articulates the moral concern of her novel – the necessity to acknowledge one's own progeny.

Significant also is the fact that Mary Shelley considers the act of creation reactive rather than originary – 'in the power of moulding and fashioning ideas suggested to it'.[20] With this she articulates another analogy to Frankenstein's act of patching together dead body-parts, and I use the following analogy as the point of departure for the rest of my discussion. Mary's text is a *hideous progeny* in that it reduplicates on a textual level Frankenstein's artificially re-generated body of dead component parts. I will suggest that some of the *component parts* of her artificially created being refer back to writings of other members of her family. In this effort I confirm her own notion that invention does not 'consist in creating out of void, but out of chaos; the materials must, in the first place be afforded'.[21] I use her term chaos to refer to those texts of her parents and her husband that were already existing in her imagination, and which she moulded and refashioned, as Frankenstein does the dead body parts. Her own novel can, then, be seen as a misreading and rewriting of these predecessors.

In the midst of my reading one must, however, bear in mind that the self-description Mary Shelley presents in the introduction to the edition of 1831 was written ten years after the death of her husband. She harbours an affection for her thirteen-year-old text because it was 'the offspring of happy days, when death and grief were but words',[22] when she was not alone (and in this lament we find an echo of St Leon's, Frankenstein's and the monster's complaint). The realization of her nightly vision into a gothic tale serves as therapy against the anxiety the dream induced *and* as a recognition of the legacy of authorship handed down to her by her parents and her husband. It also bears, however, not only an anxiety of influence – given that she called her early writings close imitations, 'rather doing as others had done than putting down the suggestions of my own mind'.[23] It also harbours an 'anxiety of creation'.[24] For in her misreading of her predecessors, her moulding and refashioning of their texts, the materialization of phantasies gives birth to monsters.

Moving into the novel *Frankenstein* itself, we find the frame narrative – Walton's letters to his sister Margaret – in order to interpret these in comparison with the frame narrative of *St Leon*, for which I have already indicated the coexistence of two affective bonds, namely between St Leon and the reader, and between Charles the son and Pandora the wife. Walton, a failed poet, seeks to explore the North Pole in order to become famous as the first man ever to have set foot on the land of 'eternal light ... surpassing in wonders and in beauty every region hitherto discovered'.[25] But realizing this dream means separating himself from his family. Like St Leon he complains, significantly in his written correspondence with his sister, 'I bitterly feel the want of a friend . . . who could sympathize with me'.[26] In other words, the prerequisite for discovering new territories is the epistolary relationship with his natural companion, his sister. While he needs her letters, and her as addressee, he also needs to assure himself that his filial bond is unstable. He repeatedly emphasizes that he doesn't know when, or in fact whether, he will see her and his homeland again. His fourth letter to Margaret marks a turning-point. Walton explains he must write down the strange events of the last days, although 'you will see me before these papers can come into your possession'.[27] He writes because, or rather although, he is about to come home. His crew has forced him to turn back, and even while this means relinquishing his chance of fame, he submits himself to the general well-being and abandons the expedition.

Walton describes how, with his ship surrounded by ice, barely able to float, he saved the dying Frankenstein and discovers in him the long sought-for friend, albeit under the sign of belatedness – 'I *should have* been happy to have possessed [him] as the brother of my heart'.[28] Like the stranger in *St Leon*, Frankenstein is a 'divine wanderer'[29] who could transmit to him some secret knowledge. In contrast to Godwin's protagonist, however, Mary Shelley's Walton is not allowed to receive the clandestine knowledge from the stranger. In diametric opposition to St Leon, he is given the biography of the stranger (about which Godwin's stranger had been completely silent), but *precisely not* the legacy of the power that comes with the stranger's superhuman knowledge. While Godwin represents a form of boundary transgression – St Leon takes on the position of the stranger – Shelley maintains the opposition between Walton and Frankenstein, and with it the prohibition to transgress the boundary of human knowledge. Frankenstein offers a threefold justification for his confession: he wants to save Walton from the madness of scientific obsession, which has ruined his life; he hopes that a memory of the evil results of his experiment will not die with him; he wants to emphasize the fatality of his failure. What Shelley leaves out as she creatively misreads her father's gothic tale is any positive evaluation of the individual judgement of the explorer and his happy serenity. While in her father's text, the frame narrator and the solitary scientist were one and the same figure – Reginald St Leon – she splits the frame narrator and the solitary scientist into two characters, Walton and Frankenstein. While in *St Leon* the protagonist, who has separated himself from his fellow men, is also the frame narrator who can enter into a worthy community with his reader, Shelley not only draws her overreacher exclusively in pejorative colours,[30] for Frankenstein is also denied such an imaginative community, and dies pitifully, owing to his scientific obsession. The story he tells is meant to serve as a warning for his spiritual brother, Walton, and Walton himself can pass on Frankenstein's tale only after he has been forced to return to the community of his family. In contrast to St Leon, Walton does not narrate this tale in such a way as to lend the same status to his solitude as to an existence within a family. Rather, he narrates because the fulfilment of his solitary creativity, the discovery of a wonderful land, has been denied him. At the end of Mary Shelley's novel we don't find two distinct affective bonds, but rather the preservation of the natural family – Walton and his sister Margerite – against the complete destruction of the artificial family generation, Frankenstein and his monster.

The next layer of the text is the first diegetic narrative, Frankenstein's confession. This, too, can also be seen as Mary's rereading of *St Leon* in so far as it reflects on the opposition between the solitary artist and the security of the family, though far more intensively than the extradiegetic frame of Walton's letters. Here, too, the son breaks his bonds with his socially respected and responsible parents, turns against the living spirit of love, incorporated in his bride Elizabeth, and against a moral relation to the world, as this is represented by his friend Henry Clerval. Because he wants to penetrate the hidden laws of nature, he departs from his father's house and moves alone to Ingolstadt. Though he finds a spiritual father in the chemistry professor Waldman, he generates his own superhuman knowledge in complete solitude, without the help of any stranger. This condensation of the stranger and St Leon into one figure, Frankenstein, points to another form of enmeshment of characters, intended by Mary Shelley to give expression to her radical critique of the egotism she found at the heart of the romantic spirit. Not only is her father's stranger, with his clandestine knowledge, already part of the creator Frankenstein: the creator and his hideous progeny are also two parts of the same being. What this creature literally embodies is, as Margaret Homans calls it, the 'monster of narcissism'.[31]

Mary Shelley's critique of the Romantic spirit allows me to discuss *Frankenstein* as a rereading of another text – Percy Shelley's 'Alastor, or the Spirit of Solitude', written in 1815.[32] The title refers to the poet's own spectre: 'the alastor or avenging demon of his self-chosen solitude'.[33] In this poem the poet's search for the secret origin of all powers of nature is enmeshed with his search for a sensual fullfilment, and in so doing he finds himself confronted with a fatal aporia. The limited object of desire, the ideal woman, is meant to harbour within itself the unlimited, immeasurable idea of the poet. Percy Shelley begins with an address to nature: 'And my heart ever gazes on the depth / Of thy deep mysteries. I have made my bed / In charnels and on coffins . . . / . . . to render up the tale / Of what we are'. In a similar manner Mary Shelley has her Frankenstein search for the origin of life in the hiding-places of nature – in the vaults, charnel-houses, graves and dissecting rooms. Percy's address frames his narrative around the death of the solitary poet, who, like Walton, seeks 'strange truths in undiscovered lands'. (l. 77). His self-generated inspiration endows him with a first dream vision: 'he saw / The thrilling secrets of the birth of time' (l. 128). Because of the persuasive power of his inspiration, he remains blind to the love an Arab girl feels for him. Instead, the object of his desire becomes a veiled woman, whom he sees in a second dream, and whose voice seems to echo his own, indeed who seems to incarnate a counterpart to himself, 'Herself a poet' (l. 161). Once he has awakened from the dream of their erotic fusion, his life consists only in pursuing 'beyond the realms of dreams that fleeting shade' (l. 206). Now irrevocably driven from all worldly bonds with other maidens, he seeks this 'spectral form' (l. 259) – this self-generated feminine image of himself – until in a glade, high in the mountains, he is able to experience a materialization of his vision: 'A spirit seemed / To stand beside him . . . when his regard / Was raised by intense pensiveness . . . two eyes, / Two starry eyes, hung in the gloom of thought, / And seemed with their serence and azure smiles / To becken him' (ll. 479–92).

Mary Shelley's translation of this sequence (both in the author's introduction and in Victor Frankenstein's confession) exhibits several significant differences. Her scientist also experiences a form of inspiration, regarding the question of birth: 'I succeeded in discovering the cause of generation and life . . . I became myself capable of bestowing animation upon lifeless matter'.[34] After this first inspiration he too is haunted by a dream, namely the wish to create a being in the image of himself, though this being does not appear to him during a trance but rather as a scientific project. Intoxicated by his success he imagines that 'a new species would bless me as its creator and source . . . many happy and excellent natures. . . . No father could claim the gratitude of his child so completely'.[35] Like Alastor in relation to the adoring maidens, Frankenstein now becomes blind toward nature and toward his family. However, while Alastor perceives his ideal being to be lost, Frankenstein conceives of his ideal as realizable. In a significant manner, Mary Shelley merges the dream with the experienced real presence of the phantom. While Alastor wakes up, only to realize that his 'fleeting visitant' can never become incarnated, Mary's scientist falls asleep after he has successfully fulfilled his dream image only to recognize its monstrosity: 'I saw the dull yellow eye of the creature open . . . now that I had finished, the beauty of the dream vanished, and breathless horror and disgust filled my heart'.[36] Even after Frankenstein has awoken, these eyes stare at him, and in counterdistinction to Alastor, who realizes that his phantom lady has fled, he himself flees before his idea made flesh. One could see Mary's rereading of Percy's 'Alastor' as a deconstruction, for she shows that in the act of realization, the alastor becomes a demon. Percy's poet can preserve his desire by virtue of deferral, and Alastor dies peacefully, with the image of his phantasm before his internal eye. That in *Frankenstein* the desired object made flesh turns out to be a monster, and is accordingly repudiated by its own father, can be interpreted as Mary's critique of romantic desire. For her, as Margaret Homans argues, 'Romantic desire does not desire to be fulfilled, and yet, because it seems both to itself and to others to want to be embodied, the Romantic quester as son is often confronted with a body he seems to want but does not'.[37]

In *St Leon* Reginald falls into fever fits whenever *failure* sets in. In Mary Shelley's tale, in contrast, *successful* artificial paternity makes Frankenstein ill. Because the monster is not allowed to be the object of his desire, he turns away from his studies and returns to his natural family. But here, as in *St Leon*, a reintegration of the solitary artist is no longer possible. However, while St Leon's efforts are thwarted by virtue of the prejudices of his fellow men, Frankenstein fails due to his own prejudices – he didn't acknowledge his unnatural child, seeks to repress it, and this repressed matter literally returns, and systematically kills off all his family members: his brother William, his bride Elizabeth, his father, his friend Henry. Like St Leon, Frankenstein remains, in the end, utterly alone, possessing 'no right to share man's intercourse'. This destruction of all relationships is also a significant rereading of Percy's 'Alastor', for while in the poem the revenging demon of the non-realized vision merely destroys the poet, Mary designs a sequence of events, in which the realized monster precisely does not kill the guilty progenitor, but rather his innocent family relatives. Frankenstein's self-accusation can be read as yet another example of the way Mary's rewriting of the texts of her father and her husband offers an extremely *unambiguous* reading, so that she can formulate an *unequivocal* message. For here Frankenstein equates the monster with 'my own spirit let loose from the grave and forced to destroy all that was dear to me'.[38] What she thus compellingly impresses upon us, is that the urge for artistic creativity *is always* irrevocably intertwined with the urge to destroy.

I will now briefly present the tale embedded within Frankenstein's tale – the confession of the monster – as Mary's rereading of a novel by her mother, *The Wrongs of Woman, or Maria, a Fragment*.[39] In *Frankenstein*, the monster levels a twofold accusation against his father: that he did not carry out his duty toward his progeny, and that, owing to his inability to create a *beautiful* creature, he has condemned his progeny to an unbearable solitude. What Mary borrows from her mother's text is the idea that the evil and the desire to destroy is not innate but rather only engendered once a basically good creature is expelled from his family and his society.

The monster's model, Jemima, in *The Wrongs of Woman*, is a hardhearted guard in an insane asylum, and she relates her life story to Maria, who has been falsely committed there, as a sign of her rediscovered ability to feel sympathy for another fellow human. In her tale Jemima relates how, after the death of her mother, she was humiliated by her stepmother and cast out by her father. She attributes all her sorrows, her crimes and her degradations – theft, prostitution, accessory to murder, abortion, beggary – to the lack of maternal affection: 'I had no one to love me; to enable me to acquire respect. I was an egg dropped on the sand; a pauper by nature hunted from family to family, who belonged to nobody – and nobody cared for me'.[40] Because others feel contempt for her, she despises herself and her surroundings. An aging *libertin* takes her in, educates her, and, for the first time in her life, offers her human affections. Yet, just as she about to integrate herself into his bourgeois world, he dies, and she is once more cast out, this time by his family. Her lot is now doubly hard to bear, because her education has made her self-conscious and she can now reflect on the injustice of her fate.

For her monster's tale Mary Shelley borrows this image of the naturally good creature that has been forced into doing evil owing to environmental prejudices. The transformation she depicts is, however, far more cruel, for in contrast to Jemima, her monster is initially merciful, charitable and looks at the world in wondering joy, as he moves from 'family to family' having been cast out by Frankenstein. As long as the members of the De Lacey family – with whom he lives, and for whom he clandestinely undertakes chores – can't see him, they believe him to be a benign spirit. As the monster, however, compares himself to this ideal family, he realizes his alterity: 'But where were my friends and relations?

No father had watched my infant days, no mother had blessed me with smiles and caresses'.[41] Like Jemima, the monster educates himself by reading, and the self-consciousness he thus gains makes his alienation appear to him all the harsher. He presents himself to the family, at first to the blind father, who can't see his hideous appearance and, thus not being prejudiced, recognizes in his voice that he is in truth sincere. The children, in contrast, blinded by the prejudice against what is physically different, react in horror and cast him out. Having been scorned and rejected by this family, which for him had embodied kindness, goodness and beauty, the monster is now overcome with rage and a desire for destruction.

Mary Shelley is thus far more radical than her mother in her depiction of how evil is only engendered through social prejudice. For in contrast to Jemima, who must witness a scene of affective bonding before she can shed tears of sympathy, the monster at first harboured 'thoughts . . . filled with sublime and transcendent visions of the beauty and the majesty of goodness'.[42] These come together in his love for the De Lacey family. His crimes are more horrible than Jemima's because of his original knowledge of his own 'excellent qualities', while Jemima only discovers her charitable nature after she has experienced Maria's kindness. At the same time, Mary Shelley deconstructs the utopic vision of her parents, for she shows that the existence of the ideal community depends on the unconditional exclusion of what is radically Other. Even after hatred has taken over the monster's mode of being, she continues to show moments of goodness in his behaviour – he does, after all, request a companion from his father, with the words 'let me see that I excite the sympathy of some existing thing. . . . My evil passions will have fled, for I shall meet with sympathy'.[43] While it is precisely through the experience of *such mutuality, such sympathy* that Jemima loses her evil passion, Frankenstein, afraid of an entire race of monsters, denies such an experience of love of another to his creature. In response, the monster internalizes the prejudices of others and in the core of his being becomes as ugly and as malignant as, up to that point, only his external appearance was. Mary Shelley's vision is thus far more unremitting than that of her parents. In her text, the reintegration of a pariah is as impossible as the withdrawal of an offence to its desire for affection.

I have already suggested that in the introduction to the 1831 edition Mary Shelley offers an analogy between herself and Victor Frankenstein, for, given that she calls her novel her 'hideous progeny', she too obliquely articulates an 'anxiety of authorship'. As my reading has shown, the monster's tale draws another analogy to Mary Shelley's biography, now, however, in the sense of an 'anxiety of monstrosity'. Through her birth she became responsible for the death of her mother, her stepmother disapproved of her and Mary was able to win her affection only after William Godwin's death. Her father disowned her after her clandestine flight with Percy Shelley, and was unwilling even to acknowledge his first grandson, named after him. Due to the unconventionality of her life with Shelley, she was marginalized by English society. She came to feel that her depression caused by her dead children, Shelley's infidelities, and their poverty was a confirmation of her own monstrosity. Thus *Frankenstein* articulates her extremely ambivalent relation to the legacy of her parents. She realizes that to write like her parents is concommitant with a monstrous externalization of her inner phantasies. In an effort to assure herself that she will not be rejected by her reading public, she diffuses this anxiety by appending the author's introduction in the later republication of her novel. What *Frankenstein* also articulates is her realization that the materialization of the liberal political ideas of her parents produced an unbearable social solitude. For in her novel she gives expression to a far more unequivocal argument against solitary artistic practice than one can find in the writings of William Godwin or Percy Shelley. Mary does borrow from her mother the idea of sympathy as the crucial bond among members of a community, but instead of a radical break with conventions she ultimately makes a plea for a radical conformation to social conventions. In other words, in this novel, which at once establishes and deconstructs intertextual family bonds, in the sense that Mary Shelley uses her text to recognize the spiritual legacy of her politically radical parents, she also makes an extraordinarily conservative plea for real family bonds. At the age of nineteen she seems to have had a premonition of the catastrophe of her own life, the loss of her family as a site for 'domestic affection'.[44] Percy Shelley dies four years after the appearance of her novel, only one of her children survives, and for many years Sir Timothy Shelley keeps her from gaining her rightful inheritance. In her own life she was forced to learn that the intellectual legacy of her parents was inextricably interwoven with the monstrosity of being socially outcast.

In a last effort of rewriting of her life, Mary Shelley was, however, able to a degree to sublate the conflict between family and authorship, which had accompanied her so painfully throughout her relatively long life. If she called her first novel 'my hideous progeny', this designation is equally befitting of her son Percy Florence, who, together with his wife, Lady

Jane Shelley, sought to cleanse the public image of his family. In their subsequent refashioning, Shelley's first wife, Harriet, is systematically defamed as a faithless and psychically unstable woman. Documents that could harm the family reputation were removed from the family archives and burned, for example the correspondence between Wollstonecraft and Fuseli.[45] Percy Shelley himself was raised to the status of a saint, and a room in the house was furnished as a shrine to honour the poet.

Mary Shelley herself collaborated in this exonerating act of refashioning. So as to assure the inheritance of the Shelley estate for her son, she had ceded to Sir Timothy's prohibition against writing a biography of her dead husband. In her memoirs of Godwin, published in 1831, the spiritual bond to Shelley is never mentioned. When in 1838 she received her father-in-law's permission to publish a collected edition of her husband's poetry, she appended her own 'Notes' so as to offer the biographical context from which Shelley's creative genius was shown to have emerged. But these 'Notes', in fact, serve the purpose of transforming her disruptive life into a conventional bourgeois marriage, and in this recuperative gesture Mary effaced all traces of any spiritual debt to Wollstonecraft and Godwin. She recreated, one could say gave birth, to the poet Shelley a second time, now in the image of Victorian expectations – this too an example of 'hideous progeny'. In these seemingly biographical 'Notes', the political urgency of Percy's poetry, as well as any personal weaknesses in the poet's character, are covered up: neither Godwin, nor Harriet, nor Claire Clairemont are mentioned, and their extramarital cohabitation in Switzerland, as well as the many marital crises, are withheld. The revolutionary, the atheist, the renegade is transformed into an alienated, inspired prophet, and his poetry is described as a shield against his disappointment in life. With this fictionalizing biographical rewriting Mary assured her husband an irrevocable position in the pantheon of English poets and integrated him effortlessly into the mainstream of Victorian national culture, namely as the myth, in Matthew Arnold's words, of the 'beautiful and ineffectual angel'.

These appended critical and biographical notes are the epitome of Mary Shelley's family romance, the imaginative re-creation of the domestic happiness of family bonds, meant to elevate a husband, by whom she has been disappointed, who had proven insufficient. As Muriel Spark notes, this rewriting of Shelley's life was both a torment – Mary notes in her journal 'I am torn to pieces by memory' – as well as a clever way to circumvent the prohibition of her father-in-law, Sir Timothy, and write a biography of the poet.[46] Yet these 'Notes', creatively misreading her biography as well as the spiritual bonds between her husband and her parents, are also, in Freud's definition of the family romance, nostalgic, for they express her longing for the happy, vanished days when her husband seemed to her both the noblest and the dearest person in the world, when her family bonds offered her a sense of plenitude. Yet the crucial point in my reading of *Frankenstein* – where I sought to straddle a biographical with a textual reading, so as to suggest that the monstrosity of this text resides precisely in the way it is a composite textual body of its author's family's writings and her own imaginative rewriting of her family – resides precisely in the way this novel questions the idea of any original sense of plenitude. These 'Notes', one could say, serve a similar purpose, for they not only function as the imaginative counterpart to Mary Shelley's novel, fashioning an image of domestic happiness where *Frankenstein* traces the slow destruction of the family. They also, in turn, deconstruct their own interest in the conservative image of the family which they (along with the author's introduction of 1831) are meant to afford. For what Mary Shelley obliquely illustrates, even as she makes concessions to comply with the conventions of her time, is that the intact image of the family she offers, like her hideous progeny *Frankenstein* that offers an image of its dissolution, can only be a textual body – always a phantasy, a replacement.

2

Frankenstein and Natural Magic

CROSBIE SMITH

Victor Frankenstein warns Captain Robert Walton of the dangers of a quest for god-like knowledge and power:

I see by your eagerness, and the wonder and hope which your eyes express, my friend, that you expect to be informed of the secret with which I am acquainted; that cannot be: listen patiently until the end of my story, and you will easily perceive why I am reserved upon that subject. I will not lead you on, unguarded and ardent as I then was, to your destruction and infallible misery. Learn from me, if not by my precepts, at least by my example, how dangerous is the acquirement of knowledge, and how much happier that man is who believes his native town to be the world, than he who aspires to become greater than his nature will allow.[1]

John Baptista Porta instructs his readers on 'what manner of man a Magician ought to be' (1658):

Now it is meet to instruct a Magician, both what he must know, and what he must observe; that being instructed every way, he may bring very strange and wonderful things to pass. Seeing Magick, as we shewed before, is a practical part of Natural Philosophy, therefore it behoveth a Magician, and one that aspires to the dignity of that profession, to be an exact and very perfect Philosopher. . . . If you would have your works appear more wonderful, you must not let the cause be known: for that is a wonder to us, which we see to be done, and yet know not the cause of it: for he that knows the causes of a thing done, doth not so admire the doing of it; and nothing is counted unusual and rare, but only so far forth as the causes thereof are not known.[2]

'In a fit of enthusiastic madness I created a rational creature', the dying Victor Frankenstein confessed to Walton.[3] Mary Shelley's celebrated text was largely structured by powerful tensions between the surface 'rationality', associated with Enlightenment ideology, and the deeper and darker side of nature and human beings beloved by the Romantic poets with whom the young novelist shared a common culture. Within the text, the character of Victor embodied these tensions. Brought up in an enlightened family whose hallmarks were stability and happiness, Victor himself slipped inexorably into a very different state, one characterized by instability, misery and, above all, by secrecy. No longer a wholly 'rational creature', Victor's confessions revealed a dangerous and even demonic side to man in which natural philosophy, that supposed triumph of the Age of Reason, was recruited for secret and sinister ends.

Recent *Frankenstein* scholarship has increasingly recognized the fruitfulness of interpreting the novel in its historical contexts. We are indebted especially to Marilyn Butler for her superb edition of the 1818 text and for her demonstration of Mary Shelley's significant 1831 transformation of Frankenstein himself into a character with greater appeal to contemporary Christian audiences.[4] In this essay I also adopt a contextual approach, and focus on the issues raised by the themes of natural magic and natural philosophy that run through the novel. By setting the text against a broad context of 'Enlightenment' ideology, I argue that the persistent subversion of that ideology by Frankenstein's personal inclination towards natural and even demonic magic, adapted to his 'Romantic' character, underpinned a major textual preoccupation with questions of human knowledge and power.

Earlier studies of *Frankenstein* have sometimes drawn attention to the conspicuous lack of scientific detail culminating in the celebrated scene in chapter IV:

It was on a dreary night of November, that I beheld the accomplishment of my toils. With an anxiety that almost amounted to agony, I collected the instruments of life around me, that I might infuse a spark of being into the lifeless thing that lay at my feet. It was already one in the morning; the rain pattered dismally against the panes, and my candle was nearly burnt out, when, by the glimmer of the half-extinguished light, I saw the dull yellow eye of the creature open; it breathed hard, and a convulsive motion agitated its limbs.[5]

In Mario Praz's introductory essay to his anthology *Three Gothic Novels* (Walpole's *The Castle of Otranto*, Beckford's *Vathek*, and *Frankenstein*), it is claimed that although Mary Shelley's novel surpassed the others 'in its capacity of stirring our sense of horror', it nevertheless had a 'fundamental weakness which seriously hampers the suspense of disbelief', namely, that the author neither described 'the materials of the experiments' nor 'the manner of the unholy operations'.[6] In contrast, the famous 1931 film offered its audiences far more scientific detail, mainly in the form of late nineteenth-century electrical apparatus, than did the original text, while simultaneously introducing human witnesses into Frankenstein's laboratory.

A contextual approach directs attention to the cultural construction of all such artefacts as 'the suspense of disbelief' and away from a concern with universalist, timeless judgements like those of Praz. By investigating the image of the natural philosopher in historical context, we can begin to understand that the character of Frankenstein plays a very distinctive role, one which might be described as that of an 'extraordinary' rather than conventional man of science.[7] I therefore argue that Mary Shelley's central character does not conform to the image of orthodox practitioners of science in the late eighteenth century and early nineteenth, still less to that of the modern scientist. Most obviously, Frankenstein's obsession, his isolation, his individualism and his egoism are strongly suggestive of Romantic images of the mad genius, the creative artist, and the natural philosopher *qua* natural magician. Above all, as the opening quotation from Porta shows, secrecy acted to preserve that sense of wonder and mystery which the rationality of the Enlightenment had seemed, in the eyes of the Romantics, to threaten and destroy.

NATURE IN THE 'AGE OF REASON': VICTOR'S GENEVESE YEARS

Eighteenth-century Enlightenment philosophers promoted the broad assumption that Nature was ordered and rational. Natural history, concerned with the *classification* of plants, of animals, of human beings, of stars, revealed the systematic arrangements within Nature. These patterns of order sometimes formed the basis for the famous 'design argument' in British natural theology (design *in* Nature demonstrates the existence and wisdom of God), and sometimes the basis for a de-Christianized deism that recognized an omniscient Designer.[8]

Natural philosophy, the study of the *laws* by which Nature acted or moved, complemented natural history. Investigations of the principles of regularities or uniformities of Nature, rather than Nature's hidden and ultimate causes, became standard for academic natural philosophers of the Age of Reason, with 'reason' itself being redefined as Natural Law. The Laws of Nature themselves, such as Newton's Law of universal gravitation, stood as the exemplars of Reason. Any further attempts to probe the causes 'behind' the law were then assigned to an ancient metaphysics (such as that of natural magic) and thus to *forbidden* territory.[9] Combining natural history (the arrangements) with natural philosophy (the laws of operation) yielded Nature's *economy*. In fact, Nature consisted of many economies or systems – the solar system, for example, or the plant economy. All of these natural economies, characterized by orderly arrangements and governed by immutable laws, acted in harmony with one another.

By the late eighteenth century, these various economies of Nature shared a common characteristic. They were all 'equilibrium systems', exemplified by the simple case of the lever or balance. The important feature was that in such systems slight disturbances would be compensated and adjusted in such a way that the equilibrium (or average) position was restored. Thus the phrase 'balance of Nature' was not just an empty cliché, but one that was related to actual systems in Nature.[10] Examples are numerous: Lavoisier's chemical equations that balanced quantitatively; D'Alembert's and Lagrange's reduction of the whole of the science of dynamics to that of statics or equilibrium through a so-called 'principle of virtual velocities', which was also exemplified in the Law of the lever; and Laplace's and Lagrange's new model of the solar system, in which planetary perturbations (thought by Newton to require God's restoring power) were shown to be periodical and self-restoring, such that the solar system would never fall into disorder.[11]

It followed that each system was a perfect system, operating like a perfect machine and capable of self-restoration. Such natural systems could thus form a model for the reform of other systems that showed anything but perfection, especially human institutions and societies. Nature stood as the exemplar of perfection amid human imperfection, but doctrines of the 'perfectibility of man' meant that human beings could at least aspire to such perfection by reforming or even overthrowing unnatural tyranny and authoritarian systems in favour of free individuals in a new state of nature, with each individual pursuing life, liberty and happiness and thereby maximizing the sum total of human happiness.[12]

These doctrines presupposed that man, thus set free, would act as a rational creature, seeking to optimize his own interests but not at too great an expense to other rational creatures. In John Locke's words (*pace* Hobbes), 'the state of Nature has a law of Nature to govern it, which obliges everyone . . . that being all equal and independent, no one ought to harm another in his life, health, liberty or possessions'.[13] A perfect human economy would also act like a balanced machine, and small variations would only lead to fluctuations around a natural mean.

The notion of a balanced economy of nature, however, carried with it something more than benevolent harmony: Nemesis, the goddess of retribution. Traditional views persisted in the work of, for instance, the celebrated eighteenth-century botanist–classifier Carl Linnaeus (1707–78). *Divine nemesis* would act to prevent a loss of equilibrium in Nature's economies. All levels of Nature and society needed to be maintained within their 'proper limits' so as to prevent evil – entailing chaos and disorder – triumphing over good, the latter understood in terms of order, balance and happiness.

The clergyman Thomas Robert Malthus (1766–1834) offered a similar perspective around 1800. The sexual appetites of living creatures led to a tendency towards ever-expanding populations according to a geometrical increase. But the arithmetical increase in food supply provided a natural check on any given population, such that a balance was always maintained with respect to a given species. The benefits to the whole economy of nature were obvious: no single species could overrun the world. But the price paid in terms of suffering, starvation and death by individuals (especially human individuals) by allowing free reign to their populating urges could be very high indeed. This kind of nemesis derived principally from God through the system established by Him for ordering Nature and society. But more radical 'secular' philosophers tended to view the laws of Nature as sufficient guides to morality. Violation of natural law and disobedience to her systems would bring Nature's retribution on the 'evil-doer'.[14]

From the opening of the very first chapter of Victor Frankenstein's personal account, readers learn that his family origins combined all the values of enlightened Swiss respectability and stability:

I am by birth a Genevese; and my family is one of the most distinguished of that republic. My ancestors had been for many years counsellors and syndics [legislators]; and my father [Alphonse] had filled several public situations with honour and reputation. He was respected by all who knew him for his integrity and indefatigable attention to public business. He passed his younger days perpetually occupied by the affairs of his country; and it was not until the decline of life that he thought of marrying, and bestowing on the state sons who might carry his virtues and his name down to posterity.

And, as Victor added later, the 'republican institutions of our country have produced simpler and happier manners than those which prevail in the great monarchies that surround it'.[15] Victor's father, then, was a man of impeccable republican credentials, a man prepared to sacrifice self-promotion and self-gratification for the public good. Even marriage was to serve the interests of the state by allowing the perpetuation of virtue, embodied in the name of Frankenstein, to posterity. Indeed, the Frankensteins were construed as guardians of virtue rather than individuals employing, as Victor would employ, virtue as a means to power and self-aggrandisement.

Alphonse Frankenstein displayed those very qualities of nobility and honour in the events that led to his marriage to Caroline Beaufort, daughter of an old merchant friend. Beaufort's slide from prosperity into poverty prompted the merchant, following honourable settlement of his debts, to retreat into a wretched state of isolation from society. Sacrificing all self-interest in the search for his friend, Alphonse arrived too late to save the old man from death, but 'came like a protecting spirit to the poor girl, who committed herself to his care'.[16] Following marriage to Caroline, Alphonse sacrificed his public employments to the call of domestic duty, devoting himself to the education of his children. Victor, the eldest child, expressed the state of family stability and happiness thus: 'No creature could have more tender parents than mine. My improvement and health were their constant care, especially as I remained for several years their only child'.[17]

Into this ideal domestic state came the abandoned Elizabeth, Victor's cousin and future fiancée. Indeed, it was Victor's mother who, desiring 'to bind as closely as possible the ties of domestic love', had decided 'to consider Elizabeth as my future wife'. The immediate result was a powerful reinforcement of domestic equilibrium and happiness:

> If the servants had any request to make, it was always through her intercession. We [Elizabeth and Victor] were strangers to any species of disunion and dispute; for although there was a great dissimilitude in our characters, there was a harmony in that very dissimilitude. I was more calm and philosophical than my companion; yet my temper was not so yielding. My application was of longer endurance; but it was not so severe whilst it endured. I delighted in investigating the facts relative to the actual world; she busied herself in following the aërial creations of the poets. The world was to me a secret, which I desired to discover; to her it was a vacancy, which she sought to people with imaginations of her own.[18]

Already, of course, Victor's listeners are given a hint that something dark lurked in Victor's nature, perhaps even within Nature itself, in contrast to the outward stability, harmony and delights of conventional and enlightened domestic society, where even the servants could share in the state of happiness. But in the meantime, 'No youth could have passed more happily than mine. My parents were indulgent, and my companions amiable'.[19]

The talented Henry Clerval, Victor's best friend, was also rescued from the perils of social isolation by the Frankenstein family: 'for being an only child, and destitute of companions at home, his father was well pleased that he should find associates at our house; and we were never completely happy when Clerval was absent'. Together with Victor's younger brothers, the domestic balance was almost perfect:

Such was our domestic circle, from which care and pain seemed for ever banished. My father directed our studies, and my mother partook of our enjoyments. Neither of us possessed the slightest pre-eminence over the other; the voice of command was never heard amongst us; but mutual affection engaged us all to comply with and obey the slightest desire of each other.[20]

Again, however, Victor was concerned to show that the origins of his later misfortunes were contemporaneous with the bright childhood 'visions of extensive usefulness', visions ultimately transmuted 'by insensible steps' into 'gloomy and narrow reflections upon self'. What Victor, with the benefit of hindsight, called 'the birth of that passion which afterwards ruled my destiny', had in his view arisen 'like a mountain river, from ignoble and almost forgotten sources; but, swelling as it proceeded, it became the torrent which, in its course, has swept away all my hopes and joys'. That source of disequilibrium was natural philosophy, 'the genius that has regulated my fate'.[21]

In its earliest form, this historical river of natural philosophy had begun when inclement weather disrupted a 'party of pleasure to the baths near Thonon', confining the Frankenstein family to the inn. Victor, then thirteen, 'chanced to find a volume of Cornelius Agrippa'. Agrippa (1486–1535) was a natural magician whose activities were to inspire the famous tale of the sorcerer's apprentice. Fired with enthusiasm, and undaunted by his father's dismissal of the work as 'sad trash', Victor returned home to devour still more of Agrippa's works, complemented by those of the alchemist Paracelsus (c. 1493–1541) and the Aristotelian natural magician Albertus Magnus (c. 1192–1280).[22]

It was thus that Victor 'entered with the greatest diligence into the search of the philosopher's stone and the elixir of life'. The latter especially drew his undivided attention, for 'wealth was an inferior object; but what glory would attend the discovery, if I could banish disease from the human frame, and render man invulnerable to any but a violent death'.

Medieval alchemy had often been concerned with the relatively ordinary practices of metallurgy and medicine. But the strong mystical dimensions, blended from several ancient cultures into Christianity, meant that there was also a concern with material and spiritual perfection. Perfection would be achieved by the liberation of material and other earthly substances from a temporal existence in which all objects, living and non-living, were subject to ageing and decay.

Gold represented perfection for metals. Base metals turned into gold would have achieved material perfection, for gold, unlike other metals, did not rust or decay. Hence came the ancient search for the so-called Philosopher's Stone, which would bring to its possessor unlimited wealth. Immortality or eternal youth would achieve material perfection for human beings. Hence, too, came the quest for the elusive Elixir of Life. Spiritual perfection, on the other hand, related to salvation of the individual soul. Consistent also with the practices of such medieval and Renaissance natural magicians, Victor did not limit his concerns to matters of health and disease: 'The raising of ghosts or devils was a promise liberally accorded by my favourite authors, the fulfilment of which I most eagerly sought'.[23]

As Victor came of age, the early streams gradually yielded to a wider and less passionate river of eighteenth-century natural philosophy. A spectacular lightning strike (lightning was traditionally associated with powers outside the ordinary course of Nature) elicited instead a very 'modern' explanation from Victor's father. Rather than offer anything like an occult or causal explanation, he followed an eighteenth-century experimental natural philosopher's practice of describing only 'the various effects of that power' and of constructing 'a small electrical machine', exhibiting 'a few experiments' and flying a kite to draw down 'electrical fluid' from the clouds.[24]

In his *History and Present State of Electricity* (1767), the English natural philosopher and chemist Joseph Priestley (1733–1804) had similarly asserted modern man's power over nature:

What would the ancient philosophers, what would Newton himself have said, to see the present race of electricians imitating in miniature all the known effects of that tremendous power, nay, disarming the thunder of its power of doing mischief, and, without any apprehension of danger to themselves, drawing lightning from the clouds into an private room and amusing themselves at their leisure by performing with it all the experiments that are exhibited by electrical machines'.[25]

Such claims tended, of course, to elevate the power of the experimental natural philosopher well beyond that of ordinary mortals, and to give him, in the eyes of his audience, something approaching god-like status.

As Simon Schaffer has shown, the concomitant physical dangers of electricity could readily be linked to the myth of Prometheus: his punishment for the presumptuous act of stealing fire from the gods. The death of the Russian-based theorist G.W. Richmann during thunderstorm experiments into electricity in 1753 thus occasioned *The Gentleman's Magazine* to comment that 'we are come at last to touch the celestial fire, which if . . . we make too free with, as it is fabled

Prometheus did of old, like him we may be brought too late to repent of our temerity'. Likewise referring to lightning experiments, the French electrician Mazéas wrote concerning 'that Wonderful Matter which Nature has kept hid from us since the Creation of the World. The fable of Prometheus is verify'd – what after this can mortals find difficult?'[26]

As a result of his father's electrical demonstrations, conveying as they did a sense of modern mastery even over Nature's most mysterious powers, Victor abandoned his allegiance to the 'old lords of my imagination'. But, thanks in part to the incomprehensibility of a local chemistry lecturer, he also discontinued his interest in natural philosophy in favour of mathematics and languages.[27]

Just prior to Victor's departure, in accordance with his parents' wishes, for the University of Ingolstadt, 'the first misfortune of my life occurred'. Disease, in the form of scarlet fever, not only introduced instability into the family but also, as his mother sickened and died, demonstrated to Victor the imperfections of the human frame:

On the third day my mother sickened; her fever was very malignant, and the looks of her attendants prognosticated the worst event. [. . .] I need not describe the feelings of those whose dearest ties are rent by that most irreparable evil, the void that presents itself to the soul. . . . [When] the lapse of time proves the reality of the evil, then the actual bitterness of grief commences. Yet from whom has not the rude hand rent away some dear connexion; and why should I describe a sorrow which all have felt, and must feel?[28]

Although temporarily restored by Elizabeth's devotion to the duty of 'rendering her uncle and cousins happy', Victor's ties to the stable social world of his family were entirely broken as he finally set out for Ingolstadt three months late. In contrast to Victor's parents, Clerval's father insisted that he 'became a partner with him in business' on the grounds that 'learning is superfluous in the commerce of ordinary life'. Safely placed in the world of trade, Clerval was thus spared the corrupting and disturbing influence of the pursuit of knowledge. And as he journeyed to Ingolstadt, Victor, separated from all his social protectors, 'indulged in the most melancholy reflections'.[29]

NATURE IN THE AGE OF ROMANTICISM: VICTOR'S INGOLSTADT YEARS AND AFTER

As Victor himself confessed, 'life had hitherto been remarkably secluded and domestic; and this had given me invincible repugnance to new countenances'. He therefore believed himself 'totally unfitted for the company of strangers'. Yet as he proceeded further, his 'spirits and hopes arose' and he 'ardently desired the acquisition of knowledge'.[30] The way therefore seemed open for the new student to forge fresh social links with peers and professors alike.

The signs, however, were inauspicious. On arrival, Victor was conducted to his 'solitary apartment'. Furthermore, he had entered Ingolstadt three months later than his peers. All of these factors would compromise his stability. Worst of all, the possibility of throwing aside subjective anxieties in the common cause of the pursuit of objective knowledge was almost immediately thwarted by his reaction against the character of the professor of natural philosophy, M. Krempe. Foolishly admitting that his reading on the subject had been limited to Paracelsus and Albertus Magnus, Victor was treated to a heated diatribe from his prospective master:

Every minute. . . , every instant that you have wasted on those books is utterly and entirely lost. You have burdened your memory with exploded systems, and useless names. Good God! in what desert land have you lived, where no one was kind enough to inform you that these fancies, which you have so greedily imbibed, are a thousand years old, and as musty as they are ancient? I little expected in this enlightened and scientific age to find a disciple of Albertus Magnus and Paracelsus. My dear Sir, you must begin your studies entirely anew.[31]

Having already abandoned his faith in ancient science, Victor's response was less a matter of disappointment at Krempe's invective, and more one of contempt for the moderns, personified in the 'gruff voice and repulsive countenance' of this 'squat little man'. Furthermore, Victor felt more strongly than ever an utter contempt for the mundane uses of modern natural philosophy. How very different 'when the masters of the science sought immortality and power; such views, although futile, were grand'. Now the 'ambition of the inquirer seemed to limit itself to the annihilation of those visions on which my interest in science was chiefly founded. I was required to exchange chimeras of boundless grandeur for realities of little worth'.[32]

The indications here of Victor's latent enthusiasm for grand visions strongly suggest that he would not conform to 'safe' Enlightenment models of 'scientific' man as a 'rational' creature who knew that the best interests, happiness, pleasure and wealth of himself as an individual, and of society as a sum of individuals, lay in obedience to Nature's laws and systems and that deviations from those conventions would only bring disorder upon society and nature, as well as inevitable retribution upon himself. Victor would slip imperceptibly from his place in 'rational society' (exemplified both by his home and by his academic masters) into a state of enthusiasm, radicalism and even madness, a state that threatened the social order itself. Such 'enthusiasts' for natural philosophy, often associated with radical religious sects, with superstition and even with magic, were commonplace in late eighteenth-century England. Given access to the powers of nature, these dangerous individuals were themselves powers for social, political and religious instability. Natural philosophy itself, which offered a route to stability and perfection, could, if left unpoliced, easily function as a path to chaos and revolution.[33]

Through the second half of the eighteenth century, the official voice of European science issued from the prestigious scientific academies. As Thomas Hankins has argued, the constructed image of establishment science had been initiated by Fontenelle (1657–1757), whose eulogies of deceased members of the French Academy of Sciences were moral biographies, emphasizing the virtues of these dead heroes of science. Such natural philosophers embodied qualities of simplicity, humility, austerity, love of nature, want of ambition and an unselfish pursuit of truth. The pursuit of natural science was regarded as the highest moral good: the motives were pure, the objectivity stood opposed to self-interest and ambition, and the virtues (such as 'duty' and 'courage') were Stoic, as in the classical world.[34]

While Victor's own father possessed such classical virtues of self-sacrifice and devotion to duty, it was evident that the mundane Professor Krempe did not at all conform to this constructed image. But Victor soon encountered another very different scientific character at the university. Neither a paragon of classical virtue nor a pedantic man of science, the charismatic professor of chemistry, Waldman, would provide the inspirational spark which ignited the obsessive genius of Victor Frankenstein.

From Victor's account, it is evident that Waldman's appearance and manner, 'expressive of the greatest benevolence', and a 'voice the sweetest I had ever heard', contrasted dramatically with his natural philosophy colleague. But it was Waldman's 'panegyric upon modern chemistry' that really fired Victor's dormant enthusiasm for natural science:

'The ancient teachers of this science [chemistry]', said he, 'promised impossibilities, and performed nothing. The modern masters promise very little; they know that metals cannot be transmuted, and that the elixir of life is a chimera. But these philosophers, whose hands seem only made to dabble in dirt, and their eyes to pore over the microscope or crucible, have indeed performed miracles. They penetrate into the recesses of nature, and shew how she works in her hiding places. They ascend into the heavens; they have discovered how the blood circulates and the nature of the air we breathe. They have acquired new and almost unlimited powers; they can command the thunders of heaven, mimic the earthquake, and even mock the invisible world with its own shadows'.[35]

In part, Waldman's powerful rhetoric reflected the dramatic impact of the 'chemical revolution', usually associated with the French chemist Antoine Lavoisier (1743–94). Towards the end of the eighteenth century, Lavoisier's identification of 'oxygen' as a constituent of the 'air we breathe' formed a centrepiece of the language of chemical elements that offered a whole new system of classification for material substances. As Waldman privately told Victor, the ancients had 'left to us, as an easier task, to give new names, and arrange in connected classifications, the facts which they in a great degree had been the instruments of bringing to light'. Furthermore, 'Chemistry is that branch of natural philosophy in which the greatest improvements have been and may be made; it is on that account that I have made it my peculiar study; but at the same time I have not neglected the other branches of science'.[36]

More broadly, therefore, Waldman's public rhetoric also presented the most triumphant vision of spectacular scientific achievements since the Scientific Revolution of the seventeenth century. First, the ascending of the modern masters into the heavens simultaneously suggested a Christ-like power *and* referred specifically to the dramatic and dangerous hot-gas balloon ascents of the late eighteenth century, notably those of Pilâtre de Rozier from 1783 (hailed by Lavoisier as the year of the first human flight) until his death two years later in a spectacular crash at Boulogne. Typically, these balloon ascents were linked to scientific investigations, for example meteorology.[37]

Second, the modern masters, from William Harvey (1578–1657) onwards, had 'discovered' how the heart pumps the blood of animals in circular and regular fashion through arteries and veins. Third, these masters (notably Lavoisier) had analysed the nature of the air that creatures breathe. Prometheus-like too, they 'command the thunders of heaven' in electrical experiments. Furthermore, in an allusion to the attempts of Priestley and others to model or imitate earthquakes using electrical discharges, the moderns had begun to 'mimic the earthquake'.[38]

Uniting animal physiology with grand electrical phenomena by means of a single natural economy, that of the atmosphere, Waldman emphasized the consequent 'new and almost unlimited powers' acquired by the chemists and natural philosophers. He thus privately counselled Victor that 'A man would make but a very sorry chemist, if he attended to that department of human knowledge alone'. In order to 'become really a man of science, and not merely a petty experimentalist', Victor would need to apply himself to 'every branch of natural philosophy'.[39]

Waldman's sympathetic and sensitive personality appealed to Victor. Rather than dismiss the ancients with contempt, the professor had referred to them as 'men to whose indefatigable zeal modern philosophers were indebted for most of the foundations of their knowledge'. Indeed, he asserted that the 'labours of men of genius, however erroneously directed, scarcely ever fail in ultimately turning to the solid advantage of mankind'. But he also pointed to the spectacular *performance* of the modern chemists, understood not as 'petty experimentalists' but as masters with a vision. Not surprisingly, Victor overcame his prejudices against modern chemists and at once became apprentice to Ingolstadt's charismatic chemist.

Waldman's private remarks on the dichotomy between a 'petty experimentalist' and a true 'man of science' were also symptomatic of a cultural shift within German-speaking lands at the close of the eighteenth century. As Schaffer has argued, 'ingenuity' was an epithet by which to characterize the inventive craft skills of seventeenth- and eighteenth-century experimenters and instrument makers. But 'genius', as a term used by Romantic natural philosophers, implied not simply a special capacity of the creative artist or philosopher, but the power which *possessed* him.[40]

In this sense, the imagery of 'genius' was related to excessive, and even divine, power: the genius was a 'modern Prometheus'. Waldman could thus refer with approval to the ancients' 'indefatigable zeal' and 'labours of genius', even though they 'promised impossibilities and performed nothing'. Victor too would soon 'read with ardour those [modern] works, so full of genius and discrimination, which modern inquirers have written' on natural philosophy and especially chemistry. It was thus that natural philosophy became the 'genius that has regulated my fate'.[41]

Although Waldman provided something of an ideal role-model for Victor, it soon emerged that 'an intrinsic love for the science [of chemistry] itself' had taken possession of the aspiring natural philosopher. If Waldman served as an ideal for Victor, the reality was that Victor's pursuit of the science 'became so ardent and eager, that the stars often disappeared in the light of morning whilst I was yet engaged in my laboratory'. After two years, throughout which he remained at Ingolstadt, he 'made some discoveries in the improvement of some chemical

CROSBIE SMITH

52

instruments, which procured me great esteem and admiration at the university'.[42]

Up to this point, Victor had been acting in relation to the Ingolstadt science professors. Now, however, he felt himself 'as well acquainted with the theory and practice of natural philosophy as depended on the lessons of any of the professors at Ingolstadt'. To paraphrase his later remarks, he could no longer rank himself 'with the herd of common projectors'. No petty experimentalist, Victor had been thoroughly grounded in the principles and practice of a unified natural philosophy embracing everything from human physiology to atmospheric electricity. And as he shifted from matters of chemistry to those of physiology, he began seeking an answer to the ancient question: 'Whence . . . did the principle of life proceed?'[43]

Motivated by 'an almost supernatural enthusiasm', yet with no fear of 'supernatural horrors', Victor had indeed been possessed by the genius of natural philosophy. His fate would therefore be controlled, not by supernatural forces or evil spirits from without, but by that enthusiasm within himself which would make him aspire 'to become greater than his nature will allow'.[44] This 'super-natural' possession, then, would be productive of all his subsequent misery and tragedy.

Moving from investigations of the structure of the human frame (anatomy) to 'observe the natural decay and corruption of the human body', Victor now sought to control the causes of imperfection in living creatures:

Now I was led to examine the cause and progress of this decay, and forced to spend days and nights in vaults and charnel houses. . . . I paused, examining and analysing all the minutiae of causation, as exemplified in the change from life to death, and death to life, until from the midst of this darkness a sudden light broke in upon me – a light so brilliant and wondrous, yet so simple, that while I became dizzy with the immensity of the prospect which it illustrated, I was surprised that among so many men of genius, who had directed their inquiries towards the same science, that I alone should be reserved to discover so astonishing a secret. . . . What had been the study and desire of the wisest men since the creation of the world, was now within my grasp.[45]

Finding 'so astonishing a power placed within my hands', Victor now 'possessed the capacity of bestowing animation' upon lifeless matter. Ultimately undaunted by the difficulties of applying that power in practice, he was none the less equivocal concerning the precise status of the project. When, therefore, he spoke of giving 'life to an animal as complex and wonderful as man', his words suggested either the creation of an animal *like* man or of man himself. But, having begun 'the creation of an human being', a desire for rapid completion of the project prompted him to 'make the being of a gigantic stature; that is to say, about eight feet in height, and proportionably large'.[46] His impatience was to cost him dear, for the less than perfect end-product would, in appearance at least, emerge as nothing less than a monster, an outcast from any natural species of being.

Driven onwards by a variety of feelings 'like a hurricane', Victor indeed seemed possessed by powers outside human nature. The visionary goals of making a new species that would 'bless me as its creator and source', and perhaps ultimately of renewing 'life where death had apparently devoted the [human] body to corruption', supported him in a task undertaken 'with unremitting ardour'. So single-minded indeed was he that he again envisaged no tensions between the divergent aims of creating a new species and the renewal of life in the existing human species. The former goal, of course, not only violated God's prerogative to have fixed all species 'in the beginning', but also promised to introduce a disturbing and inherently unnatural force into the balanced economy of living nature. The latter goal similarly challenged a traditional Christian acceptance of human imperfection, manifested in sin and suffering, disease and death, with a presumptuous conviction that nature's imperfections could be made perfect by human genius.[47]

Victor's initial goal of creating a new human being coincided in part with an Enlightenment dream of a 'new man', capable of perfection through reason and free from the inherited encumbrances of the past, such as noble rank or religious dogma. One of the most stirring and popular advocates of Reason, the Marquis de Condorcet (1743–94), believed that the 'new man' and his rights would derive from 'the single truth, that man is a sentient being, capable of reasoning and of acquiring moral ideas'. All that had to be done to initiate the process was to strip away the inheritance of status and property. In its conception, Victor's creature was to have been just such a 'new man'. But as the creature later explained to Victor, this 'new man' was likely to find himself outside existing eighteenth-century human society:

I heard [from the De Lacey family] of the division of property, of immense wealth and squalid property; of rank, descent, and noble blood.

The words induced me to turn towards myself. I learned that the possessions most esteemed by your fellow-creatures were, high and unsullied descent united with riches. A man might be respected with only one of these acquisitions; but without either he was considered, except in very rare instances, as a vagabond and a slave, doomed to waste his powers for the profit of the chosen few. And what was I? Of my creation and creator I was absolutely ignorant; but I knew that I possessed no money, no friends, no kind of property. I was, besides, endowed with a figure hideously deformed and loathsome; I was not even of the same nature as man . . . Was I then a monster, a blot upon the earth, from which all men fled, and whom all men disowned?[48]

In the process of creation, Victor had been driven by enthusiasm rather than motivated by a quest for perfection. Like Walton, Frankenstein was 'too ardent in execution, and too impatient of difficulties'.[49] Early on, he admitted that he had 'prepared myself for a multitude of reverses; my operations might be incessantly baffled, and at last my work be imperfect'. However much he might hope that his 'present attempts would at least lay the foundations of future success', the source of his less than perfect creation lay in the *unnatural* and *secretive* character of his scientific approach. His whole experimental practice seemed to violate nature and natural law:

. . . with unrelaxed and breathless eagerness, I pursued nature to her hiding places. Who shall conceive the horrors of my secret toil, as I dabbled among the unhallowed damps of the grave, or tortured the living animal to animate the lifeless clay? [. . .] a resistless, and almost frantic impulse, urged me forward; I seemed to have lost all soul or sensation but for this one pursuit. It was indeed but a passing trance, that only made me feel with renewed acuteness so soon as, the unnatural stimulus ceasing to operate, I had returned to my old habits. I collected bones from charnel houses; and disturbed, with profane fingers, the tremendous secrets of the human frame.[50]

All these activities were conducted in Victor's 'workshop of filthy creation', a 'solitary chamber, or rather cell, at the top of the house'. Victor's original natural magic had been transmuted into a form of demonic magic, less a perversion of religion than of Nature.

Victor confessed that at this stage in his work his eyes had been 'insensible to the charms of nature' and that likewise he had forgotten 'those friends who were so many miles absent'. He therefore moralized retrospectively:

A human being in perfection ought always to preserve a calm and peaceful mind, and never to allow passion or a transitory desire to disturb his tranquillity. I do not think that the pursuit of knowledge is an exception to this rule. If the study to which you apply yourself has a tendency to weaken your affections, and to destroy your taste for those simple pleasures in which no alloy can possibly mix, then that study is certainly unlawful, that is to say, not befitting the human mind. If this rule were always observed; if no man allowed any pursuit whatsoever to interfere with the tranquillity of his domestic affections, Greece had not been enslaved; Caesar would have spared his country; America would have been discovered more gradually and the empires of Mexico and Peru had not been destroyed.[51]

Very soon, however, the first signs of *nemesis* appeared. Victor began to be 'oppressed by a slow fever', and 'became nervous to a most painful degree; a disease that I regretted the more because I had hitherto enjoyed most excellent health, and had always boasted of the firmness of my nerves'. Indeed, we recall that in happier times Victor was supposedly more calm and philosophical than his cousin Elizabeth. But these symptoms were as nothing compared to the succession of nervous disorders that followed his infusion of life into the inanimate body of his unnatural and imperfect creation: 'the beauty of the dream vanished, and breathless horror and disgust filled my heart'.[52]

Initially 'disturbed by the wildest dreams', he was then confined by a nervous fever during which the 'form of the monster on whom I had bestowed existence was for ever before my eyes'. His balance temporarily restored through Clerval's efforts and by the sight of 'a divine spring', he nevertheless remained in a very unstable condition: 'When I was otherwise quite restored to health, the sight of a chemical instrument would renew all the agony of my nervous symptoms'.[53]

Throughout his tale Victor continually contrasted the tranquil face of external Nature, with its Wordsworthian capacity to restore peace and stability to the troubled human mind, and the underlying powers of that Nature which, in their intensity and in their capacity to produce instability, mirrored the dark, disturbing forces within human beings. As he returned to Geneva Victor 'contemplated the lake: the waters were placid; all around was calm. . . . By degrees the calm and heavenly scene restored me'. Yet the combination of mountain and lake prompted him to question whether the scene was 'to prognosticate peace, or to mock at my unhappiness'.[54]

As night closed around, Victor saw only 'a vast and dim scene of evil' and 'foresaw obscurely that I was destined to become the most wretched of human beings'. An electric storm of increasing violence 'appeared at once in various parts of the heavens', presaging Victor's first encounter with his creature since the fateful night: 'A flash of lightning illuminated the object, and discovered its shape plainly to me; its gigantic stature, and the deformity of its aspect, more hideous than belongs to humanity, instantly informed me that it was the wretch, the filthy deamon to whom I had given life'.[55] Victor's dark passion for natural philosophy had created this being. Now Nature herself, with passionate intensity, was angrily displaying to Victor the unnatural product of his perverted genius.

The creature, embodiment of the genius of natural philosophy, mirrored the personality of his creator with its qualities of intense passion and power. Thus with respect to the impossibility of pursuing the suspected murderer of his brother William, first casualty of the creature's revenge on its creator and on the unjust human society that had rejected him, Victor admitted that 'one might as well try to overtake the winds, or confine a mountain-stream with a straw'.[56]

Similarly, Victor described the approach to the valley of Chamounix: 'we beheld immense mountains and precipices overhanging us on every side, and heard the sound of the river raging among rocks, and the dashing of waterfalls around'. Towering over this display of Nature's passionate intensity, the Alpine pyramids and domes belonged 'to another earth, the habitations of another race of beings'. Significantly, it was within these unearthly regions that the creature had taken up habitation and from which it threatened to unleash 'the whirlwinds of its rage' upon Victor, his family and all mankind. Much later, a wind rising 'with great violence in the west', accompanied by 'restless waves' on the lake and then a sudden 'heavy storm of rain', heralded the murder of Elizabeth at the hands of Victor's creation.[57]

In contrast, the creature himself would recall an earlier stage in his existence when the coming of spring had given him new hope: 'Happy, happy earth! fit habitation for gods, which, so short a time before, was bleak, damp, and unwholesome. My spirits were elevated by the enchanting appearance of nature . . . the present was tranquil'. But the creature could find no place in this natural order, this Garden of Eden:

Like Adam, I was created apparently united by no link to any other being in existence. . . . [But Adam] had come forth from the hands of God a perfect creature, happy and prosperous, guarded by the especial care of his Creator; he was allowed to converse with, and acquire knowledge from beings of a superior nature: but I was wretched, helpless, alone. . . . God in pity made man beautiful and alluring, after his own image; but my form is a filthy type of yours, more horrid from its very resemblance. Satan had his companions, fellow-devils, to admire and encourage him; but I am solitary and detested . . . no Eve soothed my sorrows, or shared my thoughts; I was alone.[58]

Discovering that 'the unnatural hideousness' of his person was the 'chief object of horror' to human beings, he became 'an outcast in the world for ever'. The creature, 'miserable and the abandoned', was 'an abortion, to be spurned at, and kicked, and trampled on'. He therefore 'declared everlasting war against the [human] species, and, more than all, against him who had formed me, and sent me forth to this insupportable misery'. He soon identified with the violent and discordant powers of Nature, the deeper, darker and secret Nature that destroyed rational and stable order:

As the night advanced, a fierce wind arose from the woods, and quickly dispersed the clouds that had loitered in the heavens: the blast tore along like a mighty avalanche, and produced a kind of insanity in my spirits, that burst all bounds of reason and reflection. I lighted the dry branch of a tree, and danced with fury around the devoted cottage, my eyes still fixed on the western horizon, the edge of which the moon nearly touched. A part of its orb was at length hid, and I waved my brand; it sunk, and, with a loud scream, I fired the straw. . . . The wind fanned the fire, and the cottage was quickly enveloped by the flames, which clung to it, and licked it with their forked and destroying tongues.[59]

The creature had indeed become a fiend. This ritual was akin to demonic magic, destroying the cottage, that symbol of human tranquillity and harmony with nature. Although his heart had been 'fashioned to be susceptible of love and sympathy', the misery brought about by rejection and injustice produced the creature's desire for evil: 'The completion of my demoniacal design became an insatiable passion' which would only end with the death of Victor Frankenstein.[60] That death represented the conclusion to Victor's nightmare journey from the 'Enlightenment' stability of his Genevese childhood to the 'Romantic' instability of Ingolstadt and after.

Following the deaths of William and Justine, Elizabeth 'often conversed of the inconstancy of fortune, and the instability of human life'. She simultaneously renounced all belief in Enlightenment optimism regarding the progress and perfectibility of man and society: 'I no longer see the world and its works as they before appeared to me. Before [Justine's death], I looked upon the accounts of vice and injustice . . . as tales of ancient days, or imaginary evils . . . but now misery has come home, and men appear to me as monsters thirsting for each other's blood'.[61] But it was Victor himself who would embody most vividly the shift from stability to instability.

Once again, Victor's journey towards increasing mental instability often contrasted with Nature's tranquillity: 'I [was] the only unquiet thing that wandered restless in a scene so beautiful and heavenly . . . often, I say, I was tempted to plunge into the silent lake, that the waters might close over me and my calamities for ever'. Initially diverted from all such easy options by the commitment to create a companion for his creature in return for the creature's promise to leave humanity in peace, Victor was nonetheless haunted by the potential for even greater discord and misery. As he asked Walton: 'Can you wonder, that sometimes a kind of insanity possessed me, or that I saw continually about me a multitude of filthy animals inflicting on me incessant torture, that often extorted screams and bitter groans'.[62]

Setting up his laboratory on one of the remotest parts of the Orkney Islands, Victor no longer had the consolation of Switzerland's tranquil lakes: 'Its fair lakes reflect a blue and gentle sky; and, when troubled by the winds, their tumult is but as the play of a lively infant, when compared to the roarings of the giant ocean'. The ocean also acted as almost 'an insuperable barrier between me and my fellow-creatures'. In this mood of desolation Victor 'thought with a sensation of madness on my promise of creating another like him, and, trembling with passion, tore to pieces the thing on which I was engaged'.[63] From then on, creator and creature were locked in mortal combat.

Victor's continuing slide from stability to instability was hastened by his fear of being designated mad by society: 'I had a feeling that I should be supposed mad, and this for ever chained my tongue, when I would have given the whole world to have confided the fatal secret'.[64] Unable therefore to call upon human assistance, he attempted to enlist unearthly powers in a crusade against his creature:

By the sacred earth on which I kneel . . . I swear; and by thee, O Night, and by the spirits that preside over thee, I swear to pursue the daemon. . . . And I call on you, spirits of the dead; and on you, wandering ministers of vengeance, to aid and conduct me in my work. Let the cursed and hellish monster drink deep of agony; let him feel the despair that now torments me.[65]

But such rituals of demonic magic, together with his passionate denials of insanity, served only to reinforce a sense of instability. 'I am not mad', he told his father as he called the sun and the heavens to testify to his past deeds. 'I am the assassin of those most innocent victims; they died by my machinations'. Unable to find lasting tranquillity of mind, Victor himself ultimately admitted that soon 'a real insanity possessed me'.[66]

Just prior to commencing his story, Frankenstein had told Walton that he believed 'the strange incidents connected with it will afford a view of nature, which may enlarge your faculties and understanding'. Through that story Mary Shelley expressed in prose fiction a dramatic shift from late eighteenth-century Enlightenment philosophies of Nature, society and man that emphasized Nature's balance, stability and perfection, to early nineteenth-century Romantic perspectives that probed beneath the tranquil face of Nature and man to confront the dark and passionate powers therein. By the close of the story Walton could thus summarize the condition of Frankenstein, the modern Prometheus, as that of one who sometimes

commanded his countenance and tones, and related the most horrible incidents with a tranquil voice, suppressing every mark of agitation; then, like a volcano bursting forth, his face would suddenly change to an expression of the wildest rage, as he shrieked out imprecations on his persecutor.[67]

For his part Walton had introduced Frankenstein's tale with reference to his own polar voyage to a 'country of eternal light', whereby he might benefit mankind by finding 'in those undiscovered solitudes' and 'unexplored regions' a North-west passage to the Pacific or by 'ascertaining the secret of the magnet'. Clerval also, in obtaining his father's permission to have leave of absence from book-keeping to visit Ingolstadt, spoke of 'a voyage of discovery to the land of knowledge'.[68] Victor's story, then, was a voyage of discovery that imaginatively explored the mysterious and dark side of Nature and man, especially in relation to an individual's quest for god-like power and knowledge through natural philosophy. As the scientific knowledge of the nineteenth and twentieth centuries gained power and credibility, can we wonder that the story of *Frankenstein* assumed mythic status?

3

Melancholy Reflection: Constructing an Identity for Unveilers of Nature

LUDMILLA JORDANOVA

When Frankenstein finally left his secluded home for the University of Ingolstadt following his mother's death, his feelings were ambivalent – loss combined with desire:

> I . . . indulged in the most melancholy reflection. . . . I was now alone. My life had hitherto been remarkably secluded and domestic. . . . I believed myself totally unfitted for the company of strangers. . . . as I proceeded, my spirits and hopes rose. I ardently desired the acquisition of knowledge. . . . my desires were complied with. . . .[1]

Shelley's choice of the term 'melancholy' was apt, since it encapsulated ambivalence. Although it suggested sad, gloomy and mournful feelings, it also evoked a sense of pleasure, of the delicious self-indulgence of such feelings. Melancholia was a disease, a neurosis, in the terminology of William Cullen, 'characterised by erroneous judgement'. One image of melancholy, a looser term, which in the early nineteenth century carried both medical and general emotional connotations, associated it with refined, learned and civilized men. While melancholy could be patho-logical, it also expressed the superior sensibilities of an intellectual elite.[2] Frankenstein's inability to keep his intimate, domestic self in a healthy balance with his thirst for knowledge, both of which had a melancholic aspect, constitutes the central monstrosity that the novel explores.

Far from being a simple moralistic tale of masculinist, scientific overreaching, drawing on simple definitions of 'science', 'medicine' or 'surgery', Frankenstein is a remarkably precise exploration of the internal conflicts felt by practitioners in a variety of fields, which we can conveniently yoke together as 'natural knowledge', and which are examined by Shelley with acuity. These conflicts are also historically specific, since they surfaced at a time when the expectations and claims of men of science and of medicine were disproportionate to their actual status and power. This mismatch was all the more frustrating because the idiom of scientific heroism, which became increasingly widely available in the first three decades of the nineteenth century, was enticing and seductive, yet insufficiently backed up by state support and cultural rewards.[3] Instability, uncertainty, ambiguity – these are key themes of Shelley's text, and they are explored with particular power through the account of his life that Frankenstein gives to Walton. Walton's character, like Frankenstein's, is portrayed as an uneasy mix. On the one hand he is a daring explorer, a student of nature, possessed of an 'ardent curiosity' and of a desire to triumph over the elements, while on the other he is an isolated, lonely daydreamer, who is ultimately a failure. Walton and Frankenstein recognize their kinship, as the latter asks the former: 'Do you share my madness?'[4]

In order to pursue this argument I need to advance on two fronts, first by discussing the key chapters of Shelley's text, and second by analysing some of the issues portrayals of 'scientists' and 'doctors' raised in her time. Here we must note the anachronism if not of 'doctor' then certainly of 'scientist'. Although the term itself was not coined until the 1830s, there was none the less a sense well before then of men grouped together into some kind of collective, with shared concerns and values, and above all with a common epistemology.[5] This feeling of commonality, well before the word 'scientist' was current among those who produced natural knowledge, is a significant phenomenon. We might cite in support of this point the oil painting *Men of Science Now Living* (1807–8), in London's National Portrait Gallery, which was an attempt to represent a collective and national achievement by means of a group portrait assembled from existing images of those selected as worthy of inclusion.[6]

In Mary Shelley's treatment, what is common to the different pursuits Frankenstein is enthused by is their capacity to open up nature's secrets, or at least they are designed to do so. They reveal or unveil something, personified as female, and presented as mysterious, enticing and potent. I wish to concentrate on the first four chapters, in which Frankenstein narrates his life until the time he is on the brink of completing his creation. From these chapters six themes, all of overriding importance for my argument, emerge. First, seclusion and reclusiveness; these character-ize his early family life long before he undertakes his solitary work on making the 'monster'. Second, passion. Even as a child he is described as having a temper, being passionate, and throughout the account of his life his strong desires are foregrounded, above all his desire to learn the secrets of heaven and earth, to possess a kind of knowledge that is full of grandeur. These aspects of his personality were presented by Mary

Shelley as overwhelming him, as forces he could not resist or control. Third, there was an absence of satisfaction. Frankenstein was often left unsatisfied by the activities he undertook, by the knowledge available to him, and accordingly he is set apart from others, suffering an inner emptiness. Fourth, he was drawn to particular kinds of natural knowledge. It is striking that he felt attracted to domains that were marginal, contentious or on the boundaries of what could be controlled, such as alchemy and electricity, and that he changed his mind so often about what interested him. This intellectual fickleness led him to discard areas in emotive terms: 'I at once gave up my former occupations, set down natural history and all its progeny as a deformed and abortive creation'.[7] Here fields of knowledge are treated in the way his monster was to be. Fifth, Frankenstein had powerful responses – both positive and negative – to those in positions of intellectual authority over him: his father, his father's friend who explained electricity to him, and his two, very different, teachers at Ingolstadt: Krempe, who repels him, and Waldman, to whom he feels drawn. It is important to note that in the last case this included a strong *physical* reaction to their persons and demeanour. Shelley's account gives credence to the idea that the character of men of science was to be 'read' in their appearance. It was also to be 'read' in their signatures, which were often reproduced beneath their printed portraits.[8]

Finally, the history of natural knowledge is given prominence. The contentious nature of some of the areas to which Frankenstein is attracted derives from the fact that they are archaic: they belong to a past, not a present. Specific mention is made of Cornelius Agrippa, Paracelsus and Albertus Magnus. Humphry Davy's *Elements of Chemical Philosophy*, which Mary Shelley read in 1816, opened with a 'Historical View of the Progress of Chemistry'. His purpose there was to place earlier chemical traditions, including alchemy, in a broad framework, which defined how proper chemical knowledge was to be acquired, specified its usefulness to humankind, and asserted its status as part of an 'intelligent design of the system of the earth'. For Davy, history helps to reveal the stable aspect of experiment, which 'is as it were the chain that binds down the Proteus of nature, and obliges it to confess its real form and divine origin'.[9] For Frankenstein, history and experiment had released an aberrant form of nature, whose origins are profane. Furthermore, Frankenstein revealed his scepticism about the 'modern professors of natural science'.[10] It is true that this refers to his early years, but Frankenstein's evocation of a sense of there being a *history* to natural knowledge is nonetheless significant: 'I had retrod the steps of knowledge along the paths of time . . .'.[11] His sense of history was reinforced by Waldman, who 'began his lecture by a recapitulation of the history of chemistry', as did many lecturers in the eighteenth century. And what really inspired Frankenstein was Waldman's way of presenting 'the ancient teachers of science' as mere speculators, and 'the modern masters' as the real miracle-workers.[12] The appeal of performing miracles and probing secrets is still there, but now, thanks to Waldman, it is associated with the moderns. Yet, Waldman's humanity allows the historical figures others dismissed to become those who laid 'the foundations' of modern knowledge. A historical perspective allowed Frankenstein to embrace the present, which he had previously rejected. Here, as elsewhere in the book, Shelley explored different modes of knowledge, not in order to rank and evaluate them, but rather to probe their moral and psychic qualities.

One possible reading of Shelley's depiction of Frankenstein's development and inner life is as an unambiguously critical portrayal of perverted science. And it could be added that it bears no resemblance to the behaviour of medical practitioners and students of nature at the time she was writing. I want to suggest that, on the contrary, she was acutely sensitive to areas of uncertainty and ambiguity felt by those who studied medicine and/or the natural sciences and whose relations with the past of their 'disciplines' were being carefully negotiated at just this time. Many practitioners wrote histories precisely in order to work out the extent of their debt to the ancients and to their other forebears, to give a perspective to 'modern' achievements, to place themselves in a lineage.[13] This was important precisely because they felt deeply implicated by the past, which was not yet separate enough to be put aside safely, but was still sufficiently 'close' to require active management. Those who studied medicine at universities had to read some of the ancients very closely indeed; they would have been well aware of attempts to give a shape to the history of their field, which included compilations and codifications of medical writings.[14] It was because savants felt vulnerable to the suggestion that magic, and an improper concern with death and the supernatural, were still part of the scientific enterprise that they felt the need to repudiate them so firmly. Debates about physiognomy, with its troubling kinship with divination, mesmerism and the violent contests over definitions of 'quackery' can all be characterized in these terms.[15]

In the early decades of the nineteenth century, many, if not most, of those who studied nature in practice worked largely alone, and in a domestic rather than an institutional setting. They more often worked with members of their own families than with their peers. At a time when students of nature were forging their masculine professional identities, they were most likely to be collaborating with female relatives, who were skilled at drawing, and at classifying and preserving specimens.[16] The more formal collective activities, such as those promoted by the British Association for the Advancement of Science, which started in the 1830s, and the specialist, 'disciplinary' scientific societies, which began to be founded in the early nineteenth century, were important because they were new, or relatively so. Indeed it is arguable that provincial medical societies, starting in the 1770s, and medical periodicals, produced by groups of like-minded men from the mid-century on, played a central part in what is conventionally called 'professionalization', and that they were only able to do so because they were strikingly innovative.[17] They worked against the grain of most medical practice, which was solitary, and carried out in domestic settings. The importance of hospitals derives in part from their capacity to bring together medical men, whose other forms of practice were more individual. These features made the personal qualities of practitioners yet more important.

Institutions can be understood as having symbolic functions: they presented the public face of science/medicine as a collective enterprise. It is not contradictory that the late eighteenth and early nineteenth centuries are characterized both by the making of individuals into scientific heroes and by institutionalization; rather, these are complementary faces of the same coin. Heroes on their own could be construed as unstable, their idiosyncrasies untethered, while institutions without heroes were impersonal, lacked flair and could be felt to be dull. Even if it was to be decades before stable scientific and medical cultures were firmly established, the tacit goal of early nineteenth-century practitioners was to generate more security – psychic and social – for those who studied nature as a group. The persistence of the amateur is a notable feature of nineteenth-century British science, thus those who insisted that it should be a recognized occupation with collective rights were demanding something for which few indigenous models existed. Medicine, in a limited sense, did provide a model, since its practice could generate a regular source of income. Yet even doctors had little collective power in the early nineteenth century. Despite placing Frankenstein in a European setting, Shelley used themes familiar from the British scene, especially in so far as her hero pursues an individual quest inspired by a thirst for natural knowledge and by a sense of the history of science.

It is true that Mary Shelley makes Frankenstein's reclusiveness and inability to communicate with those close to him into a morbid state, but in doing so she took up a theme that had been common in the medical literature of the eighteenth century. After all, the condition of being a man of thought or reflection was one that, like other social conditions, possessed its own distinctive pathology.[18] To have a well-developed intellect could be seen as a mark of status, a way of differentiating mental refinement from cruder skills based on manual capacities, but it was also a precondition of a particular kind of pathology – introspection, melancholy, obsession. There is also a sexual issue here: masturbation was called the solitary vice and associated with selfish self-absorption; Frankenstein's transgressions rendered him less capable of forming normal adult relationships, especially with the woman destined to be his bride. Perhaps it is also significant that she was chosen for him, above all by his mother, and that she died before their relationship could be consumated. Tissot's famous admonitions concerning male masturbation, first published in the mid-eighteenth century, stressed that its reclusive nature required hunting out and exterminating, and that it disabled the indulger from living a full and productive adult life.[19]

There were many reasons why those who were devotees of science and/ or practitioners of medicine wanted to present themselves as men of reason, whose intellectual capabilities combined with deep humanity were their most striking feature, and as the modern equivalents of earlier philosophers, using as vehicles for this presentation styles and idioms that had authoritative connotations. This entailed a distancing from trade, from manual labour, from crude manners and from rudimentary educational attainments. At the same time, a thirst for knowledge, which produced an uncommon commitment to unveiling nature, was an important element of scientific/medical heroism. Natural knowledge was best produced by conspicuously disinterested behaviour, by a desire to generate knowledge for its own sake, for the sake of mankind and not for one's own personal advancement, for mere selfish gratification. Philanthropic activities were one vehicle through which these points could be made. The desire for knowledge came to occupy a different category from other kinds of desire, with which it might otherwise be confused. Two pairs of prints from the 1780s are relevant here; they both contrast the Benevolent Physician, who gives to his patients, with the Rapacious Quack, who robs them. The dominant issue was clearly money, but the broader implications of setting benevolence (the desire to do good) against rapaciousness (desire as greed for money, possessions and sexual domination) are unavoidable.[20] Just as there was a potentially patho-

logical aspect to solitary, contemplative work, so there was to the desire
to know nature, which could become a consuming passion, and, by that
token, something abnormal. In all these cases – history, seclusion, thirst
for knowledge – a careful balancing act was required in practice. Mary
Shelley picked this up, and showed the absence of balance. She thereby
pointed up the importance of balancing acts, not the unproblematically
'bad' qualities of scientists in general or of Frankenstein in particular.[21]

One of the most striking features of Frankenstein's personality is that
he feels driven to act on his new enthusiasm for natural knowledge, and
that his efforts meet with success. He is portrayed as, in a specific sense,
highly interventionist. Although no mention is made of it in the text, one
recent edition of the book associates his activities with surgery: 'she was
of course writing in the early 1800s when liver transplants and open heart
surgery were but considered fantasies in the minds of a few inventive
surgeons'.[22] In Mary Shelley's time, surgery consisted largely of bleeding,
the removal of limbs, the treatment of wounds, and dealing with ailments
such as bladder stone. Other operations were performed, but these
mostly consisted of *removing* growths and related procedures. Thus
surgery was active and manual, but not until the second half of the
nineteenth century did it entail much entry into body cavities. Surgery
was clearly not what Mary Shelley had in mind. Her emphasis was on
anatomy and physiology, on understanding life through the processes of
death. Opening organic beings for inspection, and then using them, or
parts of them, again, was Frankenstein's concern.

The fluid boundary between death and life – a dominant theme in the
bio-medical sciences of this time – was of such importance that
Frankenstein imagined that, in time, he might be able to 'renew life where
death had apparently devoted the body to corruption'.[23] The belief that
the boundary between life and death was reversible was widely held at
the time, indeed for most of the eighteenth century there had been
sustained interest in suspended animation, techniques for reviving the
drowned and the hanged, premature burial – indeed in any aspect of
medicine that held out the hope that death could be delayed, avoided,
held at bay.[24] Medical writers imagined doctors in a quasi-divine role,
shedding new light on nature's processes. For example, according to
David Ramsay, medical practitioner and early historian of the American
Revolution, experiments on animals have 'tended to enlighten physicians
in the god-like work of alieviating human misery'.[25] Ramsay was
eloquent about the medical benefits of treating the drowned: 'How many
must have been lost to their friends and the community, before mankind

were acquainted with the god-like art of restoring suspended animation?'²⁶ Ramsay often used metaphors of light, referring, for example, to
'a blaze of medical knowledge'.²⁷ 'From the midst of this darkness a
sudden light broke in upon me – a light so brilliant and wondrous, yet so
simple, that . . . I became dizzy with the immensity of the prospect which
it illustrated'; this is Frankenstein's description of his discovery of 'the
cause of generation and life'.²⁸ Mary Shelley has grasped perfectly the
fantasies of (at least some) medical practitioners of the time, which
involved imagining transcendent powers that were almost their own.

These fantasies comprised claims both to intellectual penetration and
to active skills. They were nurtured by a new breed of metropolitan
medical men, who were becoming successful in acquiring institutional
power and social prestige and were rather assertive about their achievements as medics. Examples of the phenomenon include John Abernethy,
Matthew Baillie, Sir Astley Paston Cooper and Samuel Foart Simmons,
all of whom were painted by Sir Thomas Lawrence, who also put the
likenesses of other medical and scientific heroes on canvas – Sir Joseph
Banks, Sir Humphry Davy, Edward Jenner and Thomas Young.²⁹ Also
members of this new breed were Sir Anthony Carlisle, professor of
anatomy at the Royal Academy, and Sir Charles Bell, author of one of the
Bridgewater treatises of the 1830s, who shared an interest in the
relationships between medicine and the fine arts.³⁰ Measuring power is
impossible, but the power of these men was probably more symbolic than
it was real; however, creating a *culture* of medical and scientific power
was one way of securing power itself. The portraits of such men are, in a
significant sense, romantic; they make their subjects assertive and
exciting but are not afraid to suggest the kinship between medicine and
death. At first sight, the inclusion of skulls and bones in a number of these
images is surprising, since they evoke a topic, death, which practitioners
generally found difficult to cope with. After all, doctors were widely seen
as the agents of death, and, in their anatomical role, as tormenters of the
dead.

The most unpleasant sides of Frankenstein's activities suggest an
inappropriate contact with and disturbance of dead bodies. There is no
evidence to indicate that the links between medicine and death became
any less troublesome in the years leading up to 1831 – the year the second
edition of *Frankenstein* appeared – and Ruth Richardson's work suggests
that, with the Anatomy Act of 1832, they became far more so, especially
at a popular level.³¹ How, then, are we to account for the fact that such
troubling associations surface in portraits of elite medical practitioners?

Robert Newton after Sir Thomas Lawrence, *Sir Humphry Davy*, 1830.
The Wellcome Institute Library, London.

H. Robinson after Sir Martin Shee, *Sir Anthony Carlisle*, 1838.
The Wellcome Institute Library, London.

Three possibilities present themselves, which are by no means mutually exclusive. The first is that these are the men who *legitimately* look death in the face, who know mortality in a way that *they* are claiming to be acceptable. They may be making such claims in the face of opposition, but they are making them none the less from a position where their rights were gradually being acknowledged by members of social groups whom they could accept as their peers, and by those who were still clearly their superiors. Second, being an old emblem, the skull could be used in this context to evoke long traditions of *memento mori* and of the contemplative life. Precisely because these were part of established traditions in high culture, they might be understood as alluding to the medical contact with death and with the human condition in its morbid states, in a manner that was softened, rendered elegant, by centuries of conventionalized use.[32] If skulls and bones had a certain formulaic quality, then the possibility that associations with death suggest a sharp, urgent critique of science and medicine would be lessened or undermined. The third possibility is that the presence of skulls may be understood in terms of a romantic portrayal of science and medicine at this time as domains of daring. There is absolutely no doubt that in building a set of self-images for those who unveiled nature, the vocabulary of romantic heroism and genius had huge importance.[33] Thus the frisson generated by the macabre side of medicine/death, added something to the image and self-image of those who studied such subjects.

The language of genius was also taken up by those in scientific circles more strictly defined, the pre-eminent example being Humphry Davy.[34] Certain biographical traits were commonly picked up in accounts of students of nature. Individual struggle was a frequent prelude to discovery, suggesting a sustained commitment to an overarching ideal. Uncommon talent was made manifest at a young age. Such men showed a predilection for long hours of work, for solitary study, with the implication that they sacrificed their own health in the process. They also possessed the ability to stick with ideas, even in the face of opposition, displaying bravery, tenaciousness, even a zeal, a passionate commitment. These themes were developed in the growing number of published biographical accounts in the early nineteenth century.[35] It was not even necessary for individuals to be at the top of their field or in the eye of a wide public for a romantic idiom to be applicable.[36] The traits I have just noted were present in Frankenstein's life and labours, but developed to such a degree that they became pathological. This was *always* a possibility for scientists and medical practitioners, and the extreme

Henry Meyer after Francis Simonau, *Sir Astley Paston Cooper*, 1819.
The Wellcome Institute Library, London.

I. Kennerly after H. Ashby, *John Haighton*, 1818.
The Wellcome Institute Library, London.

importance attached to reputation at this period suggests how fragile –
both in their internal lives and in their material circumstances – their
careers were. Perhaps 'careers' is not the best term, because it suggests a
far more structured course of life than was usually the case. Although by
the 1830s many doctors had institutional affiliations, these rarely offered
them any kind of security and most were 'honorary', while those about to
be designated 'scientists' had far fewer such niches available to them.
Often a scientific and/or medical life was pieced together, like Frankenstein's monster, made up of bits of lecturing, writing and practising
medicine, with the possibility of patronage from friends, relations or
sympathetic aristocrats.

   In these circumstances, it was attractive to create a certain aura around
scientific and medical activities that presented them not just as worth-
while in terms of contributing to the progress of knowledge and to
human well-being, but as thrilling. A good deal of mythologizing was
involved in terms already established as plausible at this particular
historical moment. None the less, this image/self-image was fragile, it was
delicately poised between social benefits deriving from knowledge well
used, and disasters derived from certain kinds of excess. Practitioners had
recourse to a range of devices to cultivate the former and keep at bay the
latter. Histories of their subjects did just this. These were quite explicitly
about fatherhood in both its good and bad forms. Hippocrates was the
father – the good progenitor – of medicine, Galen was the self-indulgent
obscurantist – the bad father – just as Frankenstein was.[37] Portraits of
practitioners, which would embody – literally – desired values, can be
viewed in a similar way. Other devices included the elaboration of intra-
professional etiquette, cultivation of patronage relations, and assertions
of moral and/or religious conformity.[38]

   My argument has been that, in the early nineteenth century, the
ambivalence surrounding a thirst for natural knowledge could not be laid
to rest. Perhaps it never has been – the afterlife of *Frankenstein*, the
history of science fiction as a genre, and the interest in films such as *Dead
Ringers* suggest as much. The resulting tensions and ambivalences had to
be actively negotiated. In the area of gender and sexuality there was a
need to create a secure masculine identity for practitioners of science and
medicine, which allowed that natural knowledge was exciting and to be
sought in the fashion of a quest, but which resisted any suggestion that it
was totally seductive. This would have led to a loss of self-control, or
generated auto-eroticism. It was important that the power flowing from
natural knowledge was purged of its magical and hubristic elements. In

other words, the cardinal tenet of the Enlightenment, that rational knowledge was a proper source of secular power, had to be further refined and clarified. The unveiling of nature, that profoundly instable term, was a source of valued insights, but it could also unleash that which was dangerous. This tension is much more apparent in languages like English, where gendered personifications stand out. And, as I have pointed out elsewhere, it is evident in the very idea of a veil, which simultaneously conceals and reveals and is thereby erotically charged.[39]

I am not claiming for *Frankenstein* some kind of 'documentary' status it does not possess. Rather, in its powerful evocation of the internal life of a student of nature, it tapped into a turbulent unconscious life that was experienced in a variety of ways by practitioners of the time. They tended to present this in its most stable form, Shelley in its least stable one. One of the monstrosities of the book is, of course, Frankenstein's psyche. We cannot understand the scientific/medical enterprises of the time without paying due attention to their internal psychic dimensions. Admittedly, such a claim is not unproblematic, since it raises questions about that which constitutes evidence of the psyche and about the manner in which it is to be interpreted. There are sources, however, in which these dimensions are so dramatically expressed that it seems perverse not to respond accordingly. For example, the theme of monstrosity was taken up quite explicitly in one place within medicine – man-midwifery. This is an important area because of the ways in which it has been invoked in writings on *Frankenstein*, as if Mary Shelley were mounting an explicit critique of men as midwives.[40] This was not, I believe, her concern, but the remarkable diatribe *Man-Midwifery Dissected* of 1793 is relevant to my argument because it indicates the depth of feeling aroused by the unstable identities of medical and scientific practitioners.[41]

Man-Midwifery Dissected contains a well-known frontispiece, that of a figure divided down the middle by a straight line; on one side is a male midwife with his drugs and obstetrical instruments, on the other is a female midwife, who requires few aids. Although the image is familiar, it is rarely analysed in any detail. It is all of a piece with the text, by a man, which decries man-midwifery as a French perversion, a threat to the nation's morals. In the caption beneath the image, the man-midwife is referred to as a monster lately discovered but not known in Buffon's time. Buffon's natural history, with which Mary Shelley was familiar, was not only a huge compendium of the natural world written by a prominent and powerful French savant, but a work widely read and appreciated for its literary elegance.[42] The monstrosity alluded to is of many kinds, but it is especially sexual. It rests partly on the idea that to join two utterly unlike things together – a man and a woman – is going against nature, and by that token, against morality. This example indicates the heightened language that already existed in the 1790s around the practice of medicine, and, by extension, science, a point that is reinforced by the equally vitriolic disputes about quackery.[43] Practitioners knew this, feared charges of improper conduct, and hence were already anxious about their identities on these grounds by the end of the eighteenth century, and the more they strove for respectability, the worse the fear, the higher the stakes became.

It is clear from her journals that Mary Shelley both read widely in what I have called natural knowledge, and that she was acquainted with a number of medical practitioners.[44] Percy Shelley was often preoccupied with his own health, and construed the resulting experiences as integral to his imaginative life.[45] In this sense the Shelleys drew on a cultural context in which science and medicine were not set apart, but were openly available to educated persons as intellectual and emotional resources. They were vehicles for general thought. It is mistaken, on a number of grounds, to see *Frankenstein* as a direct critique of science. Rather it is more helpful to interpret it as an exploration of intellectual energy, of practices that manipulated nature, and of the desire for mastery. Put this way it becomes clear that Mary Shelley was probably thinking about a number of different modes of knowledge – literary and philosophical as well as magical, scientific and medical, and possibly also about their diverse manifestations in different geographical and historical locations. Thus science was not unique, but like other activities in some respects, if not in others. Historians of science are likely to be intensely aware of its uniqueness – scholars often carry the baggage of the domain they study – and to wish to trace that uniqueness backwards. This accounts for the widespread tendency to see *Frankenstein* as a prophetic work, and to present twentieth-century science as the direct legacy that confirms its prophetic status.[46]

I have suggested another point of view, one in which Mary Shelley is a cultural commentator on a highly fluid situation, in which medical and scientific practitioners were striving to carve out niches for themselves, often against the grain of their actual situations. They wished for forms of social and cultural stability they could only fantasize about, while Mary Shelley imagined knowledge in its most unstable, transgressive form. This was possible, I have hinted, not so much because of the content of natural knowledge at the time, which is only lightly sketched in by her, as

Samuel William Fores, *A Man-Mid-Wife*, frontispiece to his *Man-Midwifery Dissected*
(published in London, 1793).

because she sensed something of the psychological complexities of a thirst for grand knowledge. Since the idioms she deployed were of her time, we can appreciate their immediacy in the context of late eighteenth- and early nineteenth-century anxieties about what unveilers of nature were like. Such people were potentially monstrous, in historically specific ways. At the same time, we, like Mary Shelley, also appreciate that the dangers of desiring knowledge are not limited to a particular historical moment, hence fears of monstrous forms of knowing can never be assuaged.

4
Frankenstein's Monster in Two Traditions

LOUIS JAMES

In the course of writing this essay I became aware that I was pursuing, and was being pursued by, a Monster of fearsome proportions and indistinct shape. If Mary Shelley's Monster has no name, paradoxically, in recent decades it has been given more identities than Melville's great white whale, and indeed, Frankenstein's Monster *has* been compared to Moby Dick.[1] A recent bibliography includes some 300 books and essays on *Frankenstein*,[2] but it is not comprehensive. Monstrous indeed.

Two works published in 1979 signalled the shift in critical theory surrounding Mary Shelley's novel: *The Madwoman in the Attic* by Sandra M. Gilbert and Susan Gubar, which brought the Monster into the area of Feminist studies; and George Levine and U.C. Knoepflmacher's collection of essays, *The Endurance of Frankenstein*. Both marked Anglo-American critical theory turning to examine the repressed presences beneath the surface conformity of Victorian fiction. This approach was further developed by Levine's *The Realistic Imagination* (1981), which presents *Frankenstein* as the fountain-head of what has been termed 'Victorian realism'. For Levine, the objective concern of the eighteenth-century novel drained it of a symbolic dimension, and, in reaction, novelists evoked the Monstrous to give form to inarticulate subjective fears and desires:

As reality becomes a kind of destructive and formless flood, we arrive at an art that focuses on individual consciousness, the only remaining source of meaning and action. . . . The mystery depends upon closely observed, but opaque, surfaces of ordinary things, which then transform, by metaphor, reiteration, or variation, into something else [the Monstrous].[3]

Levine traces a development from Mary Shelley's creation of Franken-stein's Monster, through Jane Austen, George Eliot, Trollope and Thackeray, to the fiction of D.H. Lawrence.

Interest in the Monstrous has developed in other areas of literary criticism. Marxist writers, such as Franco Moretti in *Signs Taken as*

Wonders (1983), have found in the Monster and the vampire potent images of social repression. Moretti sees the Monster as an image of the rebellious poor, 'whom the breakdown of feudal relations has forced into brigandage, poverty and death'.[4] On vampires he aptly cites Marx: 'Capital is dead labour which, vampire-like, lives only by sucking living labour, and lives the more, the more it sucks'.[5]

Poststructuralist studies of the Monster have been surveyed by Fred Botting in *Making Monstrous* (1991). Botting finds the Monster a perfect trope through which to express the inarticulate, the blind, *la différence* in literature. He compares the interaction of Frankenstein and the Monster in Mary Shelley's tale with the way Lacan, Derrida and Barbara Johnson interpret Dupin's search for the missing document in Poe's short story 'The Purloined Letter'. He notes that the Monster and Poe's unnoticed letter each 'function like a signifier, possessing its bearers as it blinds those who seek it out'.[6] Botting also relates the Monster to Barthes's concept of the multiplicity of creative writing, where everything is to be disentangled, nothing deciphered. He later points out that when Foucault describes the continuity of the author's presence in his literary creation, *écriture*, this has affinities with Frankenstein projecting his identity into the Monster. To modify a paragraph by Paul Sherwin:

If, for the orthodox Freudian, [the Monster] is a type of the unconscious, for the Jungian he is the shadow, for the Lacanian an *objet à*, for one Romantic a 'spectre', for another a Blakean 'emanation'; he has also been or can be read as Rousseau's natural man, a Wordsworthian child of nature, the isolated Romantic rebel, the misunderstood revolutionary impulse, Mary Shelley's abandoned baby self, her abandoned babe, a [Barthian] aberrant signifier, [Derrida's] *différence*, or as a hypostasis of godless presumption, the monstrosity of godless nature, analytical reasoning, or alienating labor.[7]

This summary does not, of course, exhaust the modern interpretations of *Frankenstein*. The Monster features in Gillian Beer's examination of the Darwinian debate on evolution, and she relates it to Caliban in Browning's long poem 'Caliban upon Setebos'.[8] Homi Bhabha and others have considered the Monster as a representation of the colonized Other. Mary Shelley's Monster has overlapped with other myths of creation and the Monstrous, notably, as will be explored below, with Pygmalion and Galatea, a fable that has obvious affinities with the Frankenstein story. As Burton R. Pollin notes,[9] Mary Shelley was alerted to Ovid's story through Mme de Genlis's dramatic sketch *Pygmalion et Galatée*, which Shelley read shortly before writing *Frankenstein*. In this Galatea is initiated into the evils of mankind through her reading of human injustice, in the same way that Mary Shelley's Monster learns of human injustice through the books in the De Laceys' cottage.

The popularity of the Pygmalion legend in the nineteenth century has been explored by J. Hillis Miller in *Versions of Pygmalion* (1990), and Marina Warner has considered its relevance for gender identity in *Monuments and Maidens: The Allegory of the Female Form* (1985). To some extent the Pygmalion and Galatea myth merges with the story of Frankenstein and his Monster, with Ovid's fable of ideal love turning into one of malign possession. In Robert Buchanan's early poem, 'Pygmalion: an Allegory of Art' (*c.* 1840), Galatea is indeed a Vampire figure:

> Then the Dawn
> stared in upon her: when I open'd eyes
> I saw the gradual Dawn encrimson her
> like blood that blush'd within her, – and behold
> she trembled – and I shrieked.[10]

It is important to note that up to this point we have considered Mary Shelley's story as primarily a *textual* creation. There is good reason for this: indeed, if any text was constructed to illustrate the relationship between *langue* and *parole*, or the nature of *écriture*, it is surely *Frankenstein*. It contains a narrative within a narrative; if we include the Monster's self-revelation when he tells his story to Frankenstein, the work contains three concentric discourses. The book is a palimpsest of subtexts, including the Bible, and works by Aeschylus, Milton, Coleridge and Shakespeare. Frankenstein approaches his quest to create life through reading Paracelsus, Cornelius Agrippa and Albertus Magnus. The Monster, too, creates a selfconscious identity by its precocious browsing through Volney's *Ruins of Empire*, Milton's *Paradise Lost* Plutarch's *Lives*, Goethe's *Sorrows of Werther*, and the eavesdropped histories of Felix and De Lacey. Addressing Frankenstein, the Monster cries: 'I should have been your Adam', and compares himself to Satan. The intertextual nature of the novel is signalled by its very subtitle: 'A Modern Prometheus'.

In its turn, *Frankenstein* was rapidly imbedded into subsequent texts. Mrs Gaskell, significantly confusing Frankenstein with his Monster, writes in *Mary Barton* (1848):

The actions of the uneducated seem to me typified in those of Frankenstein, that monster of many human qualities, ungifted with soul, a knowledge of the difference between good and evil.

The people rise up to life; they irritate us, they terrify us, and we become their enemies. Then, in the sorrowful moment of our triumphant power, their eyes gaze on us with a mute reproach. Why have we made them as they are; a powerful monster, yet without the means for peace and happiness?[11]

The structure of Mary Shelley's tale appealed immediately to an age anxiously searching for new identities in a changing society. The Monster became an image used by social commentators, cartoonists and satirists. In *Punch* magazine alone, there have been a succession of representations of the Monster, from Victorian images of the British working classes, the Irish labourer, and Tsar Nicholas I,[12] to a modern cartoon of Mrs Thatcher as Frankenstein creating a monstrous Conservative party for her unholy pleasures. It also entered the world of the novel. Dickens's *Great Expectations* (1860–61), for example, is a veritable Chinese box of Frankenstein motifs. Magwitch attemps to 'create' a gentleman out of Pip, a blacksmith's apprentice; Miss Havisham tries to fashion a heartless Monster out of the adopted Estella; Pip discovers that by being the focus for the convict's 'expectations', he created a new identity for Magwitch. The reference here to *Frankenstein* is explicit:

The imaginary student, pursued by the misshapen creature he had impiously made, was not more wretched than I, pursued by the creature which had made me . . .[13]

Monster-making is the common denominator in the interwoven subplots of *Great Expectations*. Estella slaps Pip as she utters 'You coarse little *Monster*' (my italics). In turn, when Pip goes to London as a newly fashioned 'gentleman' he turns Frankenstein himself:

For after I had made this monster out of the refuse of my washerwoman's family, and had clothed him with a blue coat, and the boots already mentioned, I had to find him a little to do and fret deal to eat; and with both of these horrible requisites he haunted my existence. This avenging phantom was ordered to be on duty at eight on Tuesday morning.[14]

If Mary Shelley's novel becomes imbedded in Victorian literature, it found another, and different, place in the non-literary culture. This 'popular' version of the Monster differs from its literary origins, and not only in its freedom from intertextual complexity. Where the Monster in the novel is usually invisible to anyone but Frankenstein, appearing only by moonlight, and erupting into a physical presence in isolated episodes of violence, the popular tradition foregrounds the Monster's size and physicality. Where Mary Shelley's Monster thinks, reads and reasons, the Monster of popular tradition is illiterate, and usually mute, expressing

John Tenniel, 'The Brummagem Frankenstein',
Punch, 8 September 1866.

Anon., 'Mrs Thatcher as Lady Frankenstein',
Punch, 28 November 1990.

intense but inarticulate feelings through mime. To understand this popular tradition, we must turn to the theatre. The trail leads us back to the fable of Pygmalion and Galatea, and in particular to Jean-Jacques Rousseau's 'scène lyrique', *Pygmalion*, written in 1762 and first performed in 1770. Mary Shelley, who was lodging in the Villa Diodati on the banks of Rousseau's Lake Geneva when *Frankenstein* was conceived, may well have known this piece, which by 1812 had become a well-known work in Rousseau's *œuvre*.

Rousseau refashioned the classical myth, and gave it its modern form. In Book x of Ovid's *Metamorphoses*, the depraved Propoetides deny Venus's divinity, and, in revenge, Venus turns their women into prostitutes with hearts of stone. They disgust Pygmalion, who in reaction to their crude lust creates and falls in love with an ivory statue. This is rewarded by Venus, who brings the effigy to life, and Pygmalion marries her, although, in Ovid's version, the statue remains nameless. Rousseau changes the story, leaving out the plot of Venus and the depraved women, removing the erotic tone, and focuses on the creative power of the artist's passion and imagination.

To dramatize the intensity of Pygmalion's emotion, Rousseau developed a form for which he coined the term 'le *mélodrame*'.[15] In his *Essai sur l'origine des langues* he argued that gesture and inarticulate sound are more elemental than speech, and in order to exploit this theory he wrote *Pygmalion* as monologue intercut with passages where music and mime transcend the words into a higher realm of experience.[16] The piece is an orchestration of the passions. Although the gods are invoked, all the interest is focused on Pygmalion. The effect is that of a profane Mass, with the inanimate transubstantiated into flesh and blood not by divine agency, but through the artist's emotion and creative imagination. Rousseau himself wrote *Pygmalion* in a period of exhausted depression, after creating the heroines of *Julie, ou La Nouvelle Héloïse* (1761), two fictional women that were more real to him than those in actual life. Perhaps for this reason, Pygmalion's last words in the play to Galatea are 'I have given you all my being, I only live in you'. In Ovid there is no such sense of loss. Rousseau sounds a dark note, which Mary Shelley may have remembered when she came to write her own myth of creation.

Although no performance of *Pygmalion* is recorded on the British stage, contemporary theatre in England had its own Monsters, and in 1823, when Mary Shelley's creation first appeared on the boards in Richard Brinsley Peake's *Presumption, or, The Fate of Frankenstein* at the English Opera House, the play inherited an already established

Frontispiece to Mary Shelley, *Frankenstein*
(revised edition, London, 1831).

tradition of theatrical prodigies. These Monsters were to bring together a curious grouping of theatrical types, including the statue, the Wild Man, the Clown; and, related to these, the stage sailor and the fairground 'freak'. Diverse as these Monsters may appear, they share a cluster of characteristics. They are ambivalent in identity, hovering between the human and the alien. They are physically powerful, and at the same time verbally inarticulate, sometimes mute. They respond ecstatically to music, and their emergence on the stage is directly related, as was *Pygmalion* itself, to the rise of melodrama.

Pygmalion bringing Galatea into life, and Frankenstein raising the Monster, both draw on the dramatic effect of the moving statue. This is related to the nature of theatre itself. The role of the Monster as the objectified Other has affinities with the place of masks in traditional theatre, and the puppet-like figures of the *commedia dell'arte*. Traditional melodrama relates simultaneously to intense subjective experience and to objective, highly stylized forms of appearance, speech and situation. Actual statues, from Hermione in Shakespeare's *The Winter's Tale*

(1610), to Mozart's vengeful effigy in *Don Giovanni* (1787), come to life on stage. Gothic melodrama also used moving statues for sensational effect, beginning with the vision of the Bleeding Nun in Monk Lewis's *The Castle Spectre* (1797) and continuing this practice well into the nineteenth century. Thus the anonymous *Lekinda! or, The Sleepless Woman* (1833) features three fiends who, for their crimes, are turned to stone, but are later reanimated on stage by the power of the wizard Zobaldi.[17] A decade later, the Royal City of London Theatre was offering *The Skeleton Hand: or, The Demon Statue* (1843), also anonymous, which included the following:

Scene by moonlight – Pedestal with statue. TERRIFIC INCANTATION! *Herman endows the statue with reason.*

The Statue falls in love with the heroine Lestelle, and commits a murder for which her sweetheart Wolfgang is accused. Wolfgang is saved from execution for the crime at the last moment, and the Statue appears from behind, mounting a peak of rock with Lestelle in its arms. Soldiers fire at it, the rock is blown up, and the Statue falls into a waterfall. Wolfgang rescues Lestelle, and a gigantic Skeleton Hand, the sign of retribution, appears above, in a GRAND TABLEAU.[18]

In its half-human, half-alien identity, the moving statue was allied to another Monster type, the 'Wild Man'. *Obi, or, Three-Finger'd Jack* (1801) is a serio-pantomime by John Fawcett, with music by Samuel Arnold, that played at London's Theatre Royal, Haymarket, later transferring to Covent Garden. Obi is a runaway Jamaican slave who uses sorcery against the slavers. Although monstrous in size and demonic in his vengeance, Obi evinces a bravery and dignified power that associates him with the Noble Savage, and, specifically, with the black rebel hero of Aphra Behn's *Oronooko: or, The Royal Slave* (c. 1678) which was successfully dramatized by Thomas Southern in 1695. The actor Richard John Smith had been given the soubriquet 'O' because of his celebrated playing of the title role in the first production of *Obi*. It is therefore significant that he should move from this to impersonate the Monster in H.M. Milner's *Frankenstein: or, The Man and the Monster* (1824), exploiting the same acting style, and again achieving great success.

Obi can be placed alongside two other popular early nineteenth-century plays that feature European 'Wild Men'. Thomas Dibdin's *Valentine and Orson* (Covent Garden, 1804) has origins in a medieval Flemish legend popular in English chapbooks of the seventeenth and

Frontispiece to H.M. Milner, *Frankenstein: or, the Man
and the Monster* (published in London, 1826).

eighteenth centuries, and it also has echoes of Shakespeare's *The Winter's
Tale*. It shows how the wronged Empress Belisanta of Greece is banished
following a false accusation, taking with her the infant twins. Orson and
Valentine. Orson is carried off by a she-bear, who suckles him; Valentine
is brought up as a knight at the court of Pepin, King of France. As a young
man Valentine is sent out to destroy a Monster, who is terrifying the
surrounding country. The 'Monster', though Valentine does not know it,
is his lost brother Orson. Valentine fights and subdues Orson, taking him
back to the court. Starting as a mocked, drunken beast, Orson is tamed.
He wears courtly clothes, gains manners and shows chivalric prowess,
although he remains dumb. As he has been brought up by a bear, he can
handle a magic shield that can only be used 'by a man not nursed by a
woman', and with this he defeats an evil giant that is threatening the
court. In the end Orson recovers his speech, and wins the hand of a lady.
Valentine and Orson is set in the romantic past. In C.I.M. Dibdin's *The
Wild Man* (Sadlers Wells, 1809) the Monster inhabits an exotic island
evocative of a pre-historic Eden:

Frontispiece to C.I.M. Dibdin, *The Wild Man*, 1809
(published in London, 1836).

When the scene opens, it is just previous to day-break; the Volcano is emitting
from its crater; the lava runs down its sides and is reflected in the water, and the
scene (supposed to be lighted by it) exhibits a lurid, igneous hue. Music. The
WILD MAN comes from the cave; seems delighted with the eruption of the
Volcano, and expresses his delight by outre antics and a kind of chattering; and
at length runs up the rock into the cave again.

As the morning breaks, the villain Rufus enters bearing a young boy, and
is about to stab the boy to death when he is frightened off by a wild boar.
The Wild Man emerges, and sees the child. He 'is quite delighted with it,
and taking it up in a careful, but awkward manner, he carries it into his
cave'. We learn that the child is Adolphus, the son of Prince Artuff, ruler
of the island. Muley, a Moor and the island's Vice-Regent, has arranged
that Rufus kill the boy in order that he himself might usurp the kingdom.
The play, whose complicated plot includes a curious intrusion from Don
Quixote and Sancha Panza, was largely a vehicle for the performance of
Joseph Grimaldi (1778–1837) as the Wild Man. The demands made on
Grimaldi, who exploited all his experience of acting pantomime and
dumb-show, were immense:

[It was] the most difficult part [Grimaldi] ever had to play – the multitude of passions requiring to be portrayed and the rapid succession in which it was necessary to present them before the spectators, involving such tremendous demands upon his nervous system that after the close of the first act he would stagger off to a small room behind the prompter's box and sob and cry aloud [so] that those about him were very often in doubt, up to the very moment of his being called, whether he would be able to go stage for the second act.[19]

The Wild Man's physical prowess was illustrated in the first act, in which he chases the wild boar that has terrified Rufus, returning with the Boar's leg, which he has torn off; yet, about to kill Artuff, he is easily restrained once 'the child beats him with his hand'. The Wild Man is also preternaturally affected by music. When Artuff plays his flute,

[the Wild Man] appears quite softened by the melody – which Artuff increases to 'moderato' – the eyes of the Wild Man brighten, and he expresses joy – Artuff increases to 'furioso': – this strain excites the Wild Man's feelings to passion and ferocity; and after running about furiously, tearing his hair, &c, he makes a spring at Artuff, but the child gets between them . . . Artuff plays 'affetuoso'; – this softens Wild Man, who cries; – Artuff increases to jig time – Wild Man dances with delight . . .[20]

The various exploits, which illustrate the Wild Man's immense strength and agility, culminate in the defeat of Muley and the restoration of Artuff and Adolphus to their rights to the island. In a water pageant (Sadlers Wells at this time featured a large water tank), the state barge passes across a lake, the Wild Man swimming before it. Muley seizes Adolphus and leaps into the water, but the Wild Man rescues the boy (yet again), and holds Muley under the water as a final spectacle opens up at the back of the stage.

To the Wild Man we can add to the genre of stage Monsters, curiously, the Clown. From 4 October to Christmas Eve 1806, the part of Orson in *Valentine and Orson* was played with enormous physical exertion by Joseph Grimaldi, who, as already has been noticed, was later to act the 'Wild Man'. Between these two performances he played the Clown in the 1806 Covent Garden pantomime *Harlequin and Mother Goose; or, The Golden Egg*, with such effect that he gave the role its Victorian soubriquet, 'Joey'. Grimaldi gave the Clown an identity that has largely continued through to today: a white-faced acrobat with elements of the grotesque; a comic figure undercut with pathos. Although Grimaldi played the Wild Man covered in skins, and the Clown in parti-coloured Harlequin dress, there was the same underlying persona, one simultaneously human and alienated.

Finally, two other figures lurk on the fringes of Monster iconography, the 'freak' and the stage sailor. The freak belongs to sideshows and exhibitions largely outside the theatre, although the 'Elephant Man' was to feature in both theatre and literature. A related if much later example of the Monster as freak can be seen in the film *King Kong* (RKO, 1933), where the great ape, a modern incantation of Dibdin's 'Wild Man' (Kong even inhabits a similar primeval forest) is captured through his sensitivity to beauty (Fay Wray as Anne Darrow), and is turned to violence by the New York society that exploits him. The 'freak' has obvious affinities with Frankenstein's Monster, separated from society by its monstrosity, and yearning for a humanity it can never share.

In contrast, the stage sailor is separated from his fellows by his very perfection. By mid-century the most famous stage Tar was the atheletic T.P. Cooke (1786–1864), a former sailor. Cooke's other starring role was as Frankenstein's Monster. The connection may appear tangential. But on the early nineteenth-century stage, the sailor, with his curious nautical speech and heightened physicality, united strength and goodness with an innocence that made him also an outsider and natural victim. In Cooke's most famous naval part, that of William in Douglas Jerrold's *Black-Ey'd Susan* (Surrey Theatre 1829), the hero saves his wife Susan from an attempted rape, impulsively striking down a drunken assailant who turns out to be William's captain. William only escapes execution by a last-minute intervention of Providence when it is discovered he had been discharged from naval service previous to the time of the assault. Melville was later to draw on the sailor's traditional dumb innocence for *Billy Budd* (1891).

Frankenstein's Monster on stage shared, therefore, an established iconography of Monsters, and dramatic versions varied in their allegiance to Mary Shelley's original. The playbill to *Presumption! or, The Fate of Frankenstein* (Covent Garden, 28 July 1823), takes both the scientific and Faustian elements in Mary Shelley's novel. The playbill declares that

The event on which this fiction is founded has been supposed, by Dr Darwin, and some of the physiological writers of Germany, as not of impossible occurrence. I shall not be supposed as according the remotest degree of serious faith in such an imagination; yet, in assuming it as the basis of a work of fancy, I have not considered myself as merely weaving a series of supernatural terrors . . . Exhibited in this story, is the fatal consequence of that presumption, which attempts to penetrate, beyond prescribed depths, into the mysteries of nature.[21]

A different version, however, was being offered across the Thames at the Coburg Theatre, a playhouse nicknamed the 'blood tub' for its allegiance to sensational melodrama (later it was to become the Old Vic). An early afterpiece was entitled *Frankenstein: or, The Demon of Switzerland*, staged on 18 August 1823: this claimed to be based on a still earlier version by H.M. Milner. The surviving text by Milner, *Frankenstein: or, The Man and the Monster*, was performed at the Coburg three years later (3 July 1826), and probably incorporates parts of the earlier versions. Whatever its tangled history, Milner's version was the vehicle for O. Smith's portrayal of the monster, and by the 1830s this was being taken as the standard stage version.

From the opening scene, the play significantly departs from Mary Shelley's original. Frankenstein is not an obsessive private scholar but a celebrated scientist being entertained by the Prince del Piombino, who has given him a room in a pavilion in which to execute his greatest experiment. The Prince is encouraged to do this by his attractive sister, Rosaura, who has romantic designs on Frankenstein. Frankenstein already has an illegitimate child by Emmeline, a country girl he seduced and abandoned. The moral implications of Frankenstein's neglect of his family responsibilities is developed in ways unthinkable in Mary Shelley's original.

The play opens, however, not with Frankenstein, but with Strutt and Lizetta. Strutt is Frankenstein's servant, a comic inversion of his master: 'My master's a great man, and I'm like the moon to the sun, I shine with a reflected brightness'. Where Frankenstein is obsessed with fame, Strutt is primarily concerned with food and drink, and, together with Lizetta, with more natural forms of creation:

Strutt [peering through the pavilion window]: Would you believe it, Lizetta, from all I can see, I really do think, at least it seems to me, that my master's making a man.
Lizetta: Making a man! – What, is he not alone?[22]

Later, Lizetta's father is to shout after Strutt and his eloping daughter: 'Go, both of you, and people the world with monsters, if you will'.[23]

Milner's Frankenstein brings the Monster to life and is repelled mainly by its ghostly appearance. Frankenstein cries 'Instead of the fresh colour of humanity, he wears the livid hue of the damp grave',[24] and his horror is followed by a piece of highly physical pantomime:

[The Monster] is surprised at the appearance of Frankenstein – advances towards him, and touches him; the later starts back in digust and horror, draws his sword and rushes on the Monster, who with the utmost care takes the sword from him, snaps it in two, and throws it down. Frankenstein then attempts to seize it by the throat, but by a very slight exertion of its powers, it throws him off to a considerable distance; in shame, confusion, and despair, Frankenstein rushes out of the Apartment, locking the doors after him. The Monster gazes about it in wonder, traverses the Apartment; hearing the sound of Frankenstein's footsteps without, wishes to follow him; finds the opposition of the door, with one blow strikes it from its hinges, and rushes out.[25]

Milner's Monster shows clear affinities with the Wild Man. He compassionately rescues Frankenstein's betrayed mistress, Emmeline, who has collapsed while wandering with her child in a storm. The Monster brings her to shelter, and is attempting to befriend her child when Emmeline's father, Ritzberg, fires at him and wounds him, driving him out. The Monster's shows innate gentleness and love of children, and sensitivity to music. Later, in a climactic scene, after he has been turned against mankind by the cruelty he has received, he again captures Emmeline and her child, bearing them to 'a tremendous range of craggy precipices, near the summit of Mount Etna'. After declaring, in mime, that all his friendly overtures to Frankenstein had been repelled with 'scorn and abhorrence', the Monster binds her to a rock and 'whirls [the child] aloft', preparing to dash it down on the rock:

At this moment a thought occurs to Emmeline – she pulls from under her dress a small flageolet, and begins to play an air – its effect on the Monster is instantaneous – he is at once astonished and delighted – he places the Child on the ground – his feelings become more powerfully affected by the music, and his attentions absorbed by it. At the air his feelings become more powerfully excited – he is moved to tears: afterwards, on the music assuming a lively character, he is worked up to a paroxysm of delight – and on it becoming mournful, is quite subdued, till he lays down exhausted at the feet of the rock to which Emmeline is attached.[26]

While Mary Shelley's version stresses the impotent isolation of the Monster, Milner's creation appeals much more openly to the audience's sympathy. He is pitted against Frankenstein, the heartless seducer of Emmeline, and the autocratic Prince del Piombino with his designing sister. In a dramatic climax the Monster enters the palace, and bare-handed routs the Prince's armed guards. Finally, the Monster ascends to take the throne itself:

[Frankenstein] seizes on the Monster – the Monster dashes Frankenstein to the earth, and by an exertion of his immense strength breaks through the opposing line – the Prince gives the word to fire – the Monster, snatching up the Officer holds him as a target before him – he receives the shots and falls dead – the Monster rushes up the steps of the throne and laughs exulting – a general picture is formed, on which the Drop falls.[27]

Although mortally wounded – by Strutt, not by Frankenstein – the Monster holds centre stage to the end, defying the Duke's troops and leaping into an erupting Mount Etna.

It is the 'popular' Monster rather than the literary tradition that has survived most potently into the present, particularly through its transposition to film. The first film version of *Frankenstein* was by Charles Ogle (Edison Studios, 1910), who presented him white faced and clown-like, as shown in the reproduced still from the film. This also apparent in Universal Studios' version of 1931, in which the Monster was mimed by an obscure actor Henry Pratt, who was to make his name as 'Boris Karloff'. Whale's film is probably the most important single retelling of Mary Shelley's story, shaping a visual image that has become firmly identified with the Monster in later films, in representations across the range of the mass-media, and in a major development of the Frankenstein legend there is no space to consider here – science fiction.

Whale's film differs radically from Mary Shelley's literary proto-type.[28] By the 1930s, the popular image of the scientist had changed: in a period of technological advance, the scientist could do no wrong, and the smartly groomed, prosperous Frankenstein, played by Colin Clive, with his society wife Elizabeth, embody hope in the future for a decade threatened by the Great Depression. In Whale's film the creation of the Monster takes place not within the privacy of Frankenstein's darkened study, but in a Gothic tower, (salvaged by Universal Studios from their recent hit, *Dracula*, of 1931), and surrounded by all the paraphernalia of quasi-magical science fiction. The act of creation is witnessed by a group that includes Victor, Dr Waldman, and even Elizabeth. Once the Monster has come to life, all are jubilant, and a delighted Frankenstein cries without apparent irony: 'Now I know what it feels like to be God!'[29]

Having removed the central point of Mary Shelley's story, Franken-stein's self-destructive obsession, the script-writers (Robert Florey and Garett Fort) had to find other explanations for what went wrong. To do this they went back to Milner's device of splitting Frankenstein into two and divided him between the successful scientist and a self-parodying *alter ego*, his servant. Florey's creation of Fritz is darker than Milner's Strutt, and the film presents him as a hunchbacked simpleton who is in every respect the mirror opposite of his suave master. It is Fritz who is chosen to steal a perfect brain from Dr Waldman's medical school, but he drops the chosen specimen and scuttles off with a jar labelled 'DISJUNCTIO CEREBRI–ABNORMAL BRAIN', the brain of a typical criminal. Frankenstein creates the Monster without reading this unusu-ally large notice, and it is only on bringing the Monster into the light that he becomes aware of a serious flaw in its nature.

Charles Ogle as the first film monster, in a still from the 1910 *Frankenstein*,
directed by Searle J. Dawley for Edison Studios.

In spite of his 'abnormal' brain, the Monster as portrayed by Karloff is
closer to the Wild Man and to Milner's Monster than to a typical
criminal. Karloff's Monster is drawn sympathetically to children. In one
scene it plays with a girl by the water, dropping her into the lake only
because it thinks she is a flower, and so will float with the other blossoms.
(Universal's sequel, *The Bride of Frankenstein* of 1935, follows the
earlier stage tradition further when it shows the Monster's love of music).
Karloff's face is heavily made up with white in the pantomime clown
tradition, although it invokes pathos without comedy. While Mary
Shelley's Monster speaks, the Monster of Florey and Fort remains as

dumb as it was on the nineteenth-century stage, expressing through mime an essentially sympathetic character.

In Whale's film of 1931 the Monster dies in a blazing mill. This change from the novel has attracted some attention. It has been suggested that Florey got the idea because he wrote the filmscript while lodging over the Van der Kamp Bakery in Los Angeles, whose trade mark was a windmill.[30] But why should a bakery trademark suggest a *burning* mill for the end of the Monster? The answer lies in the stage tradition. We have seen that fiery endings were a feature of stage melodramas. In Milner's version of *Frankenstein* the Monster dives into the erupting flames of Mount Etna. The climax of the burning mill entered stage history as early as 1812 with Isaac Pocock's *The Miller and his Men*, a play perpetuated into the twentieth century by the popularity of toy theatre versions that were enjoyed by, among others, Winston Churchill.[31] *The Miller and his Men* tells of another stage Monster, Grindoff, who by day is a respectable miller but by night, as the robber chief Wolf, leads bandits. His headquarters is in a mill overlooking the village, to which he is tracked at the climax to the play. The underground power magazine is fired, and Grindoff dies in the blaze.

The dramatic éclat of the burning mill was the basis of the play's success, and it offered a natural ending to a film that throughout, as Richard J. Anobile notes, owes more to the techniques of stage than to those of the cinema.[32] This ending not only takes over a popular melodramatic spectacle: as a closure the burning mill modifies the significance of the Frankenstein legend as a whole. In the novel Frankenstein dies in the cold, and although the Monster declares it will die on a funeral pyre amid the ice, we see only its sleigh disappearing into the eternal snow. The final focus in the novel is on Walton, a potential Ancient Mariner made wise by Frankenstein's story, who saves his own and his crew's lives by returning to home and friends. In the plays and the film the Monster remains defiant at the centre, destroyed but not defeated in an apocalypse of flame. Its death, if death it is, foregrounds the tragedy of the outcast and the rejected.

But if the film shows continuities with the nineteenth-century stage tradition, it also diverges from it. However sympathetic the portrayal of Karloff's Monster, according to Florey's script it is an outcast not because society is unjust, but because as a Monster it has been given the wrong brain. Although its drab clothes, in contrast with those of his wealthy creator, indicate a lower-class identity, the plot implies that the Monster's tragedy is caused by mental abnormality. The film ends not with the Monster, but with the servants tittering over the information that Frankenstein's injuries will not prevent him fathering a son by Elizabeth, who does not die but survives to provide Frankenstein with a happy bourgeois family.

Yet the myth cannot be deflected by a twist of the plot. Few who see the film feel that the Monster is simply the victim of a switched brain, nor in the popular imagination can the Monster be disposed of so easily. The film was made in 1931. Ahead lay the Great Depression, and beyond this World War II, Auschwitz, Hiroshima, Vietnam. The sequel, made in 1935, begins with the image of a monstrous hand rising from the debris of the mill, a hand groping upward, menacingly . . .

5

Impressionist Monsters:
H. G. Wells's 'The Island of Dr Moreau'

MICHAEL FRIED

In a little-known story by Rudyard Kipling, 'A Matter of Fact', published in his collection of 1893, *Many Inventions*, three newspaper men on a tramp-steamer from Capetown to Southampton undergo a horrific experience. One morning their little vessel, the *Rathmines*, is buffeted by a series of tidal waves generated by the eruption of an undersea volcano; then, in a blinding white fog, they hear what they take to be the steam-siren of another ship, frighteningly close to them; at the same time they become aware of an appalling smell, as of something from the bottom of the sea; and then there is this:

Some six or seven feet above the port bulwarks, framed in fog, and as utterly unsupported as the full moon, hung a Face. It was not human, and it certainly was not animal, for it did not belong to this earth as known to man. The mouth was open, revealing a ridiculously tiny tongue – as absurd as the tongue of an elephant; there were tense wrinkles of white skin at the angles of the drawn lips; white feelers like those of a barbel sprang from the lower jaw, and there was no sign of teeth within the mouth. But the horror of the face lay in the eyes, for those were sightless – white, in sockets as white as scraped bone, and blind. Yet for all this the face, wrinkled as the mask of a lion is drawn in Assyrian sculpture, was alive with rage and terror. One long white feeler touched our bulwarks. Then the face disappeared with the swiftness of a blind worm popping into its burrow, and the next thing that I remember is my own voice in my own ears, saying gravely to the mainmast, 'But the air-bladder ought to have been forced out of its mouth, you know.'[1]

A moment later the fog blows away and the men see the sea, 'gray with mud, rolling on every side of us and empty of all life'. There follows a long passage that I give in its entirety:

Then in one spot it bubbled and became like the pot of ointment that the Bible speaks of. From that wide-ranged trouble a Thing came up – a gray and red Thing with a neck – a Thing that bellowed and writhed in pain. Frithiof [the boatswain] drew in his breath and held it till the red letters of the ship's name, woven across his jersey, straggled and opened out as though they had been type badly set. Then he said with a little cluck in his throat, 'Ah, me! It is blind. *Hur illa!* That thing is blind', and a murmur of pity went through us all, for we could see that the thing on the water was blind and in pain. Something had gashed and cut the great sides cruelly and the blood was spurting out. The gray ooze of the undermost sea lay in the monstrous wrinkles of the back and poured away in sluices. The blind white head flung back and battered the wounds, and the body in its torment rose clear of the red and gray waves till we saw a pair of quivering shoulders streaked with weed and rough with shells, but as white in the clear spaces as the hairless, nameless, blind, toothless head. Afterwards came a dot on the horizon and the sound of a shrill scream, and it was as though a shuttle shot all across the sea in one breath, and a second head and neck tore through the levels, driving a whispering wall of water to right and left. The two Things met – the one untouched and the other in its death throe – male and female, we said, the female coming to the male. She circled round him bellowing, and laid her neck across the curve of his great turtle-back, and he disappeared under water for an instant, but flung up again, grunting in agony while the blood ran. Once the entire head and neck shot clear of the water and stiffened, and I heard Keller [one of the newspaper men] saying, as though he was watching a street accident, 'Give him air. For God's sake give him air!' Then the death struggle began, with crampings and twistings and jerkings of the white bulk to and fro, till our little steamer rolled again, and each gray wave coated her plates with the gray slime. The sun was clear, there was no wind, and we watched, the whole crew, stokers and all, in wonder and pity, but chiefly pity. The Thing was so helpless, and, save for his mate, so alone. No human eye should have beheld him; it was monstrous and indecent to exhibit him there in trade waters between atlas degrees of latitude. He had been spewed up, mangled and dying from his rest on the sea-floor, where he might have lived till the Judgment Day, and we saw the tides of his life go from him as an angry tide goes out across rocks in the teeth of a landward gale. The mate lay rocking on the water a little distance off, bellowing continually, and the smell of musk came down upon the ship making us cough.

At last the battle for life ended, in a batter of coloured seas. We saw the writhing neck fall like a flail, the carcase turn sideways, showing the glint of a white belly and the inset of a gigantic hind-leg or flapper. Then all sank, and the sea boiled over it, while the mate swam round and round, darting her blind head in every direction. . . . Then she made off to the westward, the sun shining on the white head and the wake behind it, till nothing was left to see but a little pin point of silver on the horizon. We stood our course again, and the *Rathmines* coated with the sea-sediment, from bow to stern, looked like a ship made gray with terror.[2]

I offer Kipling's creature from the bottom of the sea as the first of a number of impressionist monsters, but before proceeding to comment briefly on the passages I have just cited I had better say something about what I mean by literary impressionism in this context.

Very roughly, I am using the notion of literary impressionism to characterize the practice of ten or so authors working in the English language chiefly between 1890 and World War I at least some of whose texts are governed, wholly or in part, by a central problematic of *seeing* and *writing* (also of *impressing* in the sense of striking, stamping, imprinting). More precisely, what is at stake in a wide range of texts by those authors is one or another relationship to what, adapting Lacan and Derrida, I have called the materiality of writing, insofar as that materiality presented itself – and in a sense continues to present itself – as something that can be *seen*. So, for example, I have argued in 'Stephen Crane's Upturned Faces', the second chapter in my book *Realism, Writing, Disfiguration: On Thomas Eakins and Stephen Crane*,[3] that Crane's novels, stories and sketches can often be read as eliciting *and repressing* the materiality of writing, as in his characteristic practice of representing speech in dialect, where the words on the page appear at first glance unrecognizable, not intelligible units at all, then almost instant-aneously give rise to the powerful illusionistic effect of distinct lower-class or regional voices. (This is just one several devices – alliteration, onomatopoeia, pronominal ambiguity – I see as conducing to the same or a similar end.) So too in my essay 'Almayer's Face: On Impressionism in Conrad, Crane, and Norris',[4] I have tried to show that a wide range of major and minor texts by Joseph Conrad make new sense if interpreted as pursuing an imaginary project of *erasure*, understood both as the disfiguring of a prior representation – a kind of overwriting – and as the restoration of an original, even originary, blankness, the blankness of the as yet unwritten page.

In both cases I have related my readings to Conrad's famous credo in his Preface to *The Nigger of the Narcissus* (1897): 'My task which I am trying to achieve is, by the power of the written word, to make you hear, to make you feel – it is, before all, to make you *see*!', as though in Crane and Conrad, in different ways, what the reader is made to see are precisely those things that, *before all*, actually lay before the writer's eyes: the upward-facing sheet of paper itself, of a certain size, in the first place blank but soon covered (Conrad's term is 'blackened') with script, or rather the sheet of paper and the manual act of inscription together (this is particularly true of Crane). One recurrent figure for such a page is the *dis*figured, usually upward-turned face with staring but unseeing eyes that we encounter again and again in key texts throughout the impressionist corpus: think, for example, of Crane's laconic description of the first corpse Henry Fleming sees in *The Red Badge of Courage*,[5] or of Conrad's more sensational treatment of the dying helmsman pierced by a spear in the aftermath of the attack on the steamer in *Heart of*

Darkness. (Crane's brief tale, 'The Upturned Face', should also be cited; it lies at the centre not only of his *œuvre* but of impressionist writing generally.) I have further suggested that what distinguishes the body of work I call impressionist is both the perspicuousness and the necessity of that act of figuration, in that only if both writer and reader in a sense *lose sight* of the material page and (on the part of the writer) the act of inscription – only if these are not the main or explicit focus of their attention – can the novels, stories, sketches and works in other genres that I see as exemplifying an impressionist problematic successfully pursue their narrative and descriptive ends. This is also the force of the eliciting-followed-by-repression of the materiality of writing dynamic in Crane, as well as of the sheer verbal density of Conrad's prose even as it proliferates images of erasure and blankness: in both cases a certain relation to the scene and act of writing is simultaneously foregrounded and denied. That such a problematic has nevertheless finally become visible, hence analysable, owes almost everything to recent developments in theory and criticism. In addition to Lacan and Derrida, I will mention the close connection my work bears to that of Walter Benn Michaels.[6]

Along with Crane and Conrad, writers I think of as impressionist in the sense here defined, or who may be connected more or less closely with an impressionist problematic, include Kipling, Ford Madox Ford (for whom 'impressionism' was a watchword), W. H. Hudson (both in *Green Mansions* and in his nature writing), Frank Norris, R. B. Cunninghame Graham (whose sketch 'The Orchid-Hunter' rewrites Crane's 'The Upturned Face'), Erskine Childers (in *The Riddle of the Sands*), Jack London, and, not least important, the focus of this essay, H.G. Wells. Other writers who are not exactly impressionists in my sense of the term (Harold Frederic, Robert Louis Stevenson, Bram Stoker) nevertheless exhibit impressionist characteristics, or rather certain of their texts (*The Damnation of Theron Ware, The Master of Ballantrae, Dracula*) share some of the motifs and concerns that I associate – heuristically, not apodictically – with the impressionist problematic in its full-blown form. Two other major writers, Henry James and Edith Wharton, while not at all impressionists in my sense of the term, are never far away; and there is also a sense in which a recognition of the distinctness of literary impressionism as a historical problematic throws new light on the advent of English-language literary modernism around 1914 (or at least of a certain phase of literary modernism, taking the first issue of BLAST as a decisive event). For one thing, such an approach effectively demolishes the notion that modernism, by virtue of self-reference or the foregrounding of textuality or some equivalent notion, was more complex than what preceded it. But all this goes far beyond the scope of the present essay, which deals with a single text, H. G. Wells's *The Island of Dr Moreau* (1896).[7] And I want to prepare the ground for my engagement with Wells's unforgettable novel (or 'scientific romance'[8]) by making just a few points about the passages from Kipling's story I cited at the beginning.

First, a point so obvious it scarcely needs stating, the passages are another instance of the impressionist fascination with a horrific or otherwise disfigured face. Indeed our first glimpse of the monster is *only* of its face, an effect that is registered typographically by the use of a capital 'F' ('Some six or seven feet above the port bulwarks, framed in fog, and as utterly unsupported as the full moon, hung a Face'). The appearance of the Face is also registered – how shall we say: typographically? aurally? visually? all three? – by the alliteration that strikes the reader even before he or she reaches the final word.

Second, both the description of the face and the unfolding of the action thematize a certain disturbance of *seeing*. The monster itself is blind, with white eyes, 'in sockets as white as scraped bone' (a particularly unpleasant touch), but equally important is the narrator's sense that looking at it under these conditions (and there is of course no possibility of *not* looking at it, for the men on the steamer but also in a sense for the reader) involves violating a quasi-ethical norm or law. In Kipling's words: 'No human eye should have beheld him; it was monstrous and indecent to exhibit him there in trade waters between atlas degrees of latitude.' But who was doing the exhibiting if not the writer himself?

Third, a related point, no human eye should have beheld the monster because he belonged somewhere else – not exposed to view above the surface of the ocean but 'on the sea-floor, where he might have lived till the Judgment Day'. What's monstrous, in other words, is not just his appearance but also the fact that he has been displaced from his normal habitat far below the world of light and vision (hence his sightless eye-sockets) to another world, described as one of 'atlas degrees of latitude' – a phrase that economically evokes both the notion of surface as opposed to depth (of lateralness, so to speak) and the image of a specific printed book, an atlas, a collection of maps and charts that precisely image the surface of the earth.[9]

Fourth, the second passage contains a brief piece of description that will be decisive for my analysis. Let me quote two sentences again: 'From that wide-ringed trouble a Thing came up – a gray and red Thing with a neck – a Thing that bellowed and writhed in pain. Frithiof drew in his breath and held it till the red letters of the ship's name, woven across his jersey, straggled and opened out as though they had been type badly set.' Note in the first place the repetition of the word 'Thing' (with a capital 'T'), a word that plays a surprisingly prominent role in impressionist writing because it serves as a switchpoint between effects of animateness and ones of deathliness. That is, said of something alive, the word 'thing' implies a sort of deadness; said of something inanimate, it often suggests animateness; the quasi-interchangeability of those effects perfectly captures the peculiar status of writing as at once material and not merely material.[10] And note too the highly-charged verb 'writhed' ('a Thing that bellowed and writhed in pain'), which towards the end of the second passage will be followed by the gerund 'writhing' ('We saw the writhing neck fall like a flail') – another word that occurs often in impressionist texts where it hints at, where it comes close to spelling out, the almost identical word 'writing'. (As in Crane's astonishing sentence from his novella *The Monster*, describing jars of chemicals in the burning laboratory: 'For the most part, they were silent amid this rioting, but there was one which seemed to hold a scintillant and writing serpent.' The conjunction of 'rioting' and 'writhing', not to mention the image of a serpent, makes the connection all but inescapable. Or at least it does so in the context of all the other features of his prose I analyze in 'Stephen Crane's Upturned Faces.'[11]) But what I want to emphasize in the sentences I have just cited a second time is the apparently gratuitous detail of the letters of the ship's name on the boatswain's jersey straggling and opening out as he took and held a deep breath 'as though they had been type badly set'. Not only does this support the claim that a thematics of writing is at work in Kipling's story; it also combines with the notion that the monster has emerged from another dimension (also, it is implied, from an earlier epoch) to suggest that the ultimate source of the sense of monstrosity is a certain *reversion or regression* with respect to writing – from the printed page (as in an atlas, or a story in a journal or a book), itself not meant to be focused on as such, to the actual, material *process of printing*, as imaged by the letters of the ship's name moving apart, like a line of type breaking up, on the boatswain's jersey. It's as if Kipling's story thematizes an inherent instability in the printed text, or rather a certain fear or dread of such an instability – as if one concomitant of the impressionist focus on (though also scotomizing of) the materiality of writing was an uneasy sense of the several *states* of materiality a given text passes through in the journey from the written to the printed page. With this tentative conclusion, we are at last in a position to turn to *The Island of Dr Moreau*.

A brief plot summary will be useful here. The novel purports to be the manuscript of a first-person account by one Edward Prendick of his adventures following a shipwreck in which he was presumed to have been lost. After drifting for a time in a dinghy Prendick was picked up in a state of collapse by a schooner *en route* to an island where he was forced to disembark. In effect the island was ruled by an older man, the Dr Moreau of the book's title, who with the assistance of a younger man, Montgomery (who had been on the schooner and who had nursed Prendick following his rescue), conducted grisly experiments on animals with the purpose of making them into humans, or at least into 'humanised animals – triumphs of vivisection' (p. 45). (The parallel between Wells's story and Mary Shelley's *Frankenstein* has always been recognized.[12]) All this emerges only gradually and excruciatingly: *The Island of Dr Moreau* must be one of the most unpleasant books to read in world literature (a feature of the text worth taking seriously); the truth does not become plain until roughly half-way through the narrative, in a chapter entitled 'Dr Moreau Explains', in which Moreau gives an account of his aims and methods. I shall have more to say about that account further on, but here what I want to stress is Moreau's acknowledgement of his great failure: the ineradicable tendency of his humanized animals eventually to revert to mere animals again, despite the surgery that has altered their physical forms and the more mysterious process, apparently akin to hypnosis, by which a version of the moral law has been instilled in them. 'I *have* been doing better', Moreau says to Prendick. 'But somehow the things drift back again: the stubborn beast-flesh grows day by day back again' (p. 50). And a page or so further on:

'These creatures of mine seemed strange and uncanny to you so soon as you began to observe them; but to me, just after I make them, they seem to be indisputably human beings. It's afterwards, as I observe them, that the persuasion fades. First one animal trait, then another, creeps to the surface and stares out at me. But I will conquer yet! Each time I dip a living creature into the bath of burning pain I say, "This time I will burn out all the animal; this time I will make a rational creature of my own!" '

But in fact 'they revert. As soon as my hand is taken from them the beast begins to creep back, begins to assert itself again' (p. 51).

The remainder of the narrative bears this out. For one of the 'Beast

Folk', as Prendick calls them (he also refers to them as 'monsters'), the Leopard-Man, violates the injunction against eating flesh (he kills and devours a rabbit) and in effect goes wild; confronted by Moreau in front of the other Beast Folk, at first he is cowed but then attacks Moreau and runs off; finally he is cornered and although Moreau wishes to take him alive, Prendick, responding to the Leopard-Man's terror at the prospect of being returned to suffer 'the horrible tortures of the enclosure' (p. 62), shoots it between the eyes. Some time later a puma on which Moreau had been working breaks loose from the laboratory, attacks Prendick in passing (breaking his arm), and eventually kills Moreau and is killed by him. By this time other animals have regressed to the point of becoming dangerous; more violence follows and Montgomery too is killed. Prendick attempts to convince the Beast Folk that although Moreau has died he is really alive in a world above them, that he watches all their actions, and that he will come again (to this extent Wells's novel is a satire on Christianity, as has also been recognized), but the process of reversion cannot be halted. Eventually Prendick is forced to kill a carnivorous Hyena-Swine that has lost all fear and restraint, and realizes that if he remains on the island his own death is just a matter of time. Providentially a small boat arrives at the island (its occupants are dead) and Prendick embarks on it and after a few days is rescued. The manuscript is near its end, and the closing pages recall those of *Gulliver's Travels*: Prendick describes how, once returned to civilization, 'I could not persuade myself that the men and women I met were not also another Beast People, animals half wrought into the outward image of human souls, and that they would presently begin to revert, to show first this bestial mark and then that' (p. 86). As he also says: 'I see faces keen and bright; others dull or dangerous; others unsteady, insincere – none that have the calm authority of a reasonable soul. I feel as though the animal was surging up through them; that presently the degradation of the Islanders will be played over again on a larger scale' (p. 86). A period in London is especially disturbing: 'I could not get away from men: their voices came through windows; locked doors were flimsy safeguards. I would go out into the streets to fight with my delusion, and prowling women would mew after me; furtive, craving men glance jealously at me; weary, pale workers go coughing by me with tired eyes and eager paces, like wounded deer dripping blood . . .' (p. 87). Even in libraries, 'the intent faces over the books seemed but patient creatures waiting for prey', though worst of all it seems 'were the blank, expressionless faces of people in trains and omnibuses; they seemed no more my fellow-creatures than dead bodies would be, so that I did not dare to travel unless I was assured of being alone' (p. 87). Prendick accordingly leaves London to live near 'the broad free downland', where he spends his days

> surrounded by wise books – bright windows in this life of ours lit by the shining souls of men. . . . My days I devote to reading and to experiments in chemistry, and I spend many of the clear nights in the study of astronomy. There is – though I do not know how there is or why there is – a sense of infinite peace and protection in the glittering hosts of heaven. There it must be, I think, in the vast and eternal laws of matter, and not in the daily cares and sins and troubles of men, that whatever is more than animal within us must find its solace and its hope. I *hope*, or I could not live.
>   And so, in hope and solitude, my story ends (p. 87).

My interest in *The Island of Dr Moreau* is quite specific: I am fascinated by the implications of its story of inescapable reversion for the problematic of seeing and writing I associate with impressionism generally. But in order to make this good I now must bring out aspects of Wells's text I deliberately ignored or minimized in sketching its broad outlines.

First, the theme of monstrosity is largely conveyed, especially before Prendick fully understands the meaning of his observations, by descriptions of half-human, half-bestial *faces*. This may seem natural enough, but in light of the larger thematic of faciality in impressionist texts it is anything but innocent. So, for example, chapter III, 'The Strange Face', involves a careful description of the face of a disturbing figure, an oddly misshapen man (Prendick assumes) who accompanies Montgomery as a kind of servant or assistant. 'In some indefinable way the black face thus flashed upon me [when the figure turns around] shocked me profoundly', the narrator writes. 'It was a singularly deformed one. The facial part projected, forming something dimly suggestive of a muzzle, and the huge half-open mouth showed as big white teeth as I had ever seen in a human mouth. His eyes were bloodshot at the edges, with scarcely a rim of white round the hazel pupils. There was a curious glow of excitement in his face' (p. 8). Prendick is 'astonished beyond measure at the grotesque ugliness of this black-faced creatue'. He continues: 'I had never beheld such a repulsive and extraordinary face before, and yet – if the contradiction is credible – I experienced at the same time an odd feeling that in some way I *had* already encountered exactly the features and gestures that now amazed me' (p. 8). Later, being towed to the shore of Moreau's island by Montgomery and a crew of Beast-men in a launch, Prendick is struck by their faces as well. 'I saw only their faces', he writes, 'yet there was something in their faces – I knew not what – that gave me a queer spasm of disgust. I looked steadily at them, and the impression did not pass, though I failed to see what had occasioned it' (p. 17). Not long after, Prendick sees several Beast Folk talking together and suddenly realizes what had given rise to

two inconsistent and conflicting impressions of utter strangeness and yet of the strangest familiarity. . . . Each of these creatures, despite its human form, its rag of clothing, and the rough humanity of its bodily form, had woven into it – into its movements, into the expression of its countenance, into its whole presence – some now irresistible suggestion of a hog, a swinish taint, the unmistakable mark of the beast (p. 27).

(The last phrase will turn up again further on.[13])

The narrator's or say the story's apparent obsession with faces is also expressed in the fact that on the three occasions when Prendick finds it necessary to kill one of the Beast Folk he does so by shooting it in the face (pp. 62, 69, 84), 'between the eyes', as if the act of killing were less important than that of obliterating the face itself. And in fact this would seem to be the implication of his account of the second of those killings: 'I fired', he writes, 'and the Thing still came on; fired again, point-blank, into its ugly face. I saw its features vanish in a flash: its face was driven in' (p. 69). Think in this connection of the destruction of Henry Johnson's face by burning chemicals in Crane's *The Monster*, or of the deliberate obliteration of the drowned Malay's face in Conrad's *Almayer's Folly*, just two of many such scenes in impressionist literature.[14] (In another early story by Kipling, which just happens to be called 'The Mark of the Beast', a leper known as the Silver Man has no face at all.[15]) A somewhat different note is struck after Moreau himself is killed and brought back to his compound; although it is night, a bright moon casts shadows 'of inky blackness' at the narrator's feet. 'Then I shut the door', the narrator writes,

locked it, and went into the enclosure where Moreau lay beside his latest victims – the staghounds and the llama and some other wretched brutes – with his massive face calm even after his terrible death, and with the hard eyes open, staring at the dead white moon above. I sat down upon the edge of the sink, and with my eyes upon that ghastly pile of silvery light and ominous shadows began to turn over my plans (p. 72).

Again, there are countless upturned faces with unseeing eyes in other impressionist texts (this essay will close with one), though what is perhaps distinctive here is the hint in the final phrase of something material being leafed through, literally turned over, within the narrator's mind. Montgomery's death, too, gives rise to a similar description. 'I bent down to his face', we read,

put my hand through the rent in his blouse. He was dead; and even as he died a line of white heat, the limb of the sun, rose eastward beyond the projection of the bay, splashing its radiance across the sky and turning the dark sea into a weltering tumult of dazzling light. It fell like a glory upon his death-shrunken face (p. 74).

In Crane, as I have argued in 'Stephen Crane's Upturned Faces', the word 'line' inevitably carries connotations of a line of writing (as in the first sentence in the passage from *The Red Badge of Courage* cited in n.5); I don't say that that is the case here, though the curiously excited description of a limb-like spread of light across the sky and then the transfer of that light both to the previously dark sea and to the dead Montgomery's upturned face suggest a process of something like stamping or printing that belongs to the larger technology of literary production, a point to which I shall return. Finally, the next chapter, 'Alone with the Beast Folk', begins: 'I faced these people, facing my fate in them, single-handed now – literally single-handed, for I had a broken arm' (p. 74). Here too a single sentence resonates with others in impressionist texts – think for example of Marlow's account in *Lord Jim* of Jim facing a courtroom of faces demanding facts that themselves assume the character of a face – but what I want to emphasize is the foregrounding of writtenness (the alliteration recalls the sentence from Kipling cited much earlier) with the insistence on a certain literalness, a combination I take as raising the possibility that single-handedness in this context *also* refers to the activity of writing as practiced by a man wielding a pen.

Second, the theme of reversion or regression is of course a well-known naturalist motif (a number of the texts I think of as impressionist have long been considered classics of naturalism), as for example in Norris's exemplary *Vandover and the Brute*. But what is distinctive about the treatment of reversion in *The Island of Dr Moreau* is its close association with a problematic of language, writing, and – crucially in my view – printing. Key passages in this regard occur early and late in the book. Shortly after Prendick arrives on the island he learns that the older bearded man who in effect controls it is named Moreau. For a while the name awakens no associations but suddenly a phrase enters his head:

'The Moreau Hollows' – was it? 'The Moreau –' Ah! It sent my memory back ten years. 'The Moreau Horrors!' The phrase drifted loose in my mind for a moment, then I saw it in red lettering on a little buff-coloured pamphlet, to read which made one shiver and creep. Then I remembered distinctly all about it. That long-forgotten pamphlet came back with startling vividness to my mind' (p. 21).

The second passage occurs much further on. Following the deaths of Moreau and Montgomery the narrator has been living among the Beast Folk when he becomes aware of various changes in their behaviour whose significance is unmistakable. 'It was about May when I first distinctly perceived a growing difference in their speech and carriage, a growing coarseness of articulation, a growing disinclination to talk', he writes.

My Ape-Man's jabber multiplied in volume, but grew less and less comprehensible, more and more simian. Some of the others seemed altogether slipping their hold upon speech, though they still understood what I said to them at that time. (Can you imagine language, once clear-cut and exact, softening and guttering, losing shape and import, becoming mere lumps of sound again?). . . . They were reverting, and reverting very rapidly (p. 81).

I associate these passages with one another on the grounds that the second is figuratively the radical undoing of the first. In the first the name 'Moreau' triggers the startlingly vivid memory not simply of an earlier scandal but specifically of a buff-coloured pamphlet with printed red lettering spelling out 'The Moreau Horrors' on its cover. And in the second, human speech in the course of reverting to its animal equivalent is characterized not just as palpably material but more precisely as analogous to *printer's type* that is in the process of melting back (note the word 'guttering', meaning burning with a low flame) into unformed matter, that is, into molten lead: an operation that recent type-casting machines, most famously Ottmar Mergenthaler's Linotype machine, had made part of the modern process of printing.[16]

   Or consider certain moments in the extended conversation between Moreau and Prendick that takes up the whole of chapter XIV. Moreau explains that he wanted to use vivisection to give animals the refined larynx that would enable them (in his words) 'to frame delicately different sound-symbols by which thought could be sustained' (p. 47), on the grounds that this above all marks the great divide between man and monkey (and more broadly man and beast). The narrator then asks 'why he had taken the human form as a model'. Adding: 'There seemed to me then, and there still seems to me now, a strange wickedness for [i.e., in] that choice'. The passage continues:

[Moreau] confessed that he had chosen that form by chance. 'I might just as well have worked to form sheep into llamas and llamas into sheep. I suppose there is something in the human form that appeals to the artistic turn more powerfully than any animal shape can. But I've not confined myself to man-making. Once or twice – ' He was silent, for a minute perhaps. 'These years! How they have slipped by! And here I have wasted a day saving your life, and an now wasting an hour explaining myself!' (p. 47)

It's hard not to feel that Moreau's explanation of the grounds for his choice of the human form (and face) is less than adequate, and harder still not to wish to know more about the experiments with *other* forms.

The wish is soon gratified. Several pages further on Moreau returns, seemingly reluctantly, to the topic.

'The fact is, after I had made a number of human creatures I made a Thing.' He hesitated.
'Yes?' said I.
'It was killed.'
'I don't understand,' said I; 'do you mean to say – '
'It killed the Kanaka [one of six natives of the South Sea islands Moreau originally brought to the island] – yes. It killed several other things that it caught. We chased it for a couple of days. It only got loose by accident – I never meant it to get away. It wasn't finished. It was purely an experiment. It was a limbless thing, with a horrible face, that writhed along the ground in a serpentine fashion. It was immensely strong, and in infuriating pain. It lurked in the woods for some days, until we hunted it; and then it wriggled into the northern part of the island, and we divided the party to close in upon it. Montgomery insisted upon coming with me. The man had a rifle; and when his body was found, one of the barrels was curved into the shape of an *S* and very nearly bitten through. Montgomery shot the thing. After that I stuck to the ideal of humanity – except for little things.' (p. 50)

If we ask on what this particular creature was modelled, the answer would seem to be: on handwriting as distinct from the printed page. That is the implication of Moreau's description of its writhing, serpentine, ground-hugging movements and also, equally important, of the seemingly gratuitous fact that the gun barrel of the man the creature killed 'was curved into the shape of an *S*' – the letter 'S' in this context representing cursiveness as such, or say the very essence of written script. (Again, Crane is a basic term of reference; see for example his sketch 'The Snake', which I discuss in my chapter on his work.[17]) The point is underscored in the next chapter by the narrator's reference to the same creature as 'the writhing Footless Thing' (p. 53), a designation that perhaps carries the added suggestion of the writing of *prose*.[18]

The contrast between the writhing Footless Thing that was never meant to be allowed to get away and the other, humanized creatures that could be trusted on their own would then be readable as figuring the difference between a handwritten and a printed page – the idea being, apparently, that the latter is evolutionarily more advanced or at least more stable (i.e., 'finished') than the former. And if we now put this together both with Moreau's philosophically traditional claim that the possession of articulate speech – more broadly, of language – marks *the* distinction between humans and animals and with the imagery of type in terms of which he implicitly metaphorizes language in its 'clear-cut and exact', i.e., its fully human, manifestation, humanness (or at least humanlikeness) and printing emerge as figures for one another. And this is to say that the process of reversion in *The Island of Dr Moreau* is ultimately to be read in terms not only of the degeneration of the humanoid Beast Folk back to mere brutes[19] but also of the movement from the printed page back towards brute matter: not just towards the lead type itself (which so long as the type remains clear-cut and exact is no reversion at all) but *further* back towards the 'mere lumps' of stuff into which, in the advanced machines that were in the process of revolutionizing publishing, the type was melted down after use – and, even more to the point, out of which it was originally formed. Reread in this light, the straggling and opening out of the letters of the ship's name on the boatswain's jersey in Kipling's 'A Matter of Fact' – 'as if they were type badly set' – figures a less extreme reversion of the printed page back towards its material origins. (And of course the very notion of setting type belongs to an earlier phase of the technology of printing.) But even that partial analogy is helpful here, in the first place because it enlarges the frame of reference to include another major author and in the second because it does so in a way that comes close to being explicit. I will only add that reversion from the printed page *to the written one* is another form that impressionist reversion takes: for example, in R. B. Cunninghame Graham's sketch 'Progress', which begins 'A friend in Mexico sent me the other day a little book' and proceeds to retell the violent story of that book in terms that figuratively reduce the latter to so much manuscript.[20] And in Kipling's story 'Wireless', which appears in many anthologies (but what do its admirers think that it means?), what is dramatized as the trance-like identification of a tubercular apothecary's assistant, Mr Shaynor, with the poet Keats (whom he has never read) and then his regression back to the actual process of composition of some of Keats's greatest lines.[21] (Shaynor is also in love with a girl named Fanny *Brand*, a play on the name 'Brawne' that not incidentally thematizes something like writing or impressing.)

Finally, there is the difficult question of the relations between materialism and pain in Wells's story. The topic emerges explicitly when Prendick
challenges Moreau to justify the extreme pain the latter systematically
inflicts on the animals he is working on. 'The only thing that could excuse
vivisection to me', Prendick goes on to say, 'would be some application – '. Moreau cuts him off:

'Precisely', said he. 'But, you see, I am differently constituted. We are on
different platforms. You are a materialist.'
'I am *not* a materialist,' I began hotly.
'In my view – in my view. For it is just this question of pain that parts us. So
long as visible or audible pain turns you sick; so long as your own pains drive
you; so long as pain underlies your propositions about sin – so long, I tell you,
you are an animal, thinking a little less obscurely what an animal feels.' (p. 47)

The argument becomes more complex when Moreau goes on to argue
that the sole function of pain among men is as 'our intrinsic medical
adviser to warn us and stimulate us' (p. 48), and that with the progress of
evolution men will increasingly 'see after their own welfare', which is to
say that pain will sooner or later be made needless and 'ground out of
existence' (p. 48).[22] Moreau even claims to be a religious man in the sense
of understanding 'the ways of this world's Maker' and he assures
Prendick that 'This store which men and women set on pleasure and pain
. . . is the mark of the beast upon them – the mark of the beast from
which they came!' (p. 48).
    In one sense, of course, the notion that mankind should transcend
considerations of pain (and pleasure) recurs frequently in the history of
ethics. But there is a fundamental difference between a Stoic, Kantian, or
Christian attitude of ideal indifference towards pain and Moreau's
deliberate *inflicting* of extreme physical pain on his animals in the
interests of humanizing them. Which is to say that it never becomes clear
what, in Moreau's sense of things, the *alternative* to materialism is, unless
it is simply the 'intellectual passion' of the scientific investigator (p. 48),
which enables him to ignore the sufferings of the animals under his knife.
(But doesn't this rather embody materialist doctrine in its purest form?)
By the same token, although Prendick is appalled by the pain involved in
Moreau's procedures and obviously doesn't accept Moreau's character-
ization of him as a materialist, he also fails to give an account of his
position that would distinguish it fundamentally from Moreau's: he
never gives his own views a name, and he is willing to accept vivisection if
it is for a useful end.
    Another way of framing the question would be to ask whether the pain

to which the animals are subjected in the course of Moreau's experiments is vital to their humanization. The general tenor of Moreau's remarks implies that it is, and his statement 'Each time I dip a living creature into the bath of burning pain, I say, "This time I will burn out all the animal; this time I will make a rational creature of my own" ' (p. 51) seems to say so explicitly, but he also speaks of the need for his experimental subjects to forget their sufferings in order to emerge as rational beings (p. 48), which suggests that the hypnosis-like process (pp. 47, 52) by which Moreau implants the Law in them is somehow intrinsically connected to the infliction *and the forgetting* of pain. Yet the Law itself includes the formulae '*His* is the House of Pain. *His* is the Hand that makes. *His* is the Hand that wounds. *His* is the Hand that heals' (p. 38), which seems to rebut that suggestion. In view of Wells's penchant for exact scientific explanations elsewhere in his *œuvre*, the apparent contradictions and general failure of specificity on these points must be considered significant.

In other words, pain plays a crucial and, I think we can say, inadequately theorized role not just in Moreau's practice but in the narrative generally. Indeed when we reflect that it would have been possible for the animals on which Moreau worked to have been anaesthetized, the authorial decision *not* to anaesthetize them, coupled with the inconclusiveness of the exchange between Prendick and Moreau, itself may come to seem just the smallest bit monstrous. My point, however, is that Wells in *The Island of Dr Moreau* appears uncertain as to the ultimate status of pain, not just with respect to the philosophical issue of materialism but specifically as regards the impressionist problematic of writing and printing I have been developing (more on this in a moment).

A similar uncertainty turns up in the story's closing pages, where Prendick, returned to civilization, becomes convinced that the faces around him will all sooner or later show signs of reversion. Among the faces he singles out with distaste, it will be remembered, are the intent faces of people reading, which he compares with 'patient creatures waiting for prey' (p. 87). Yet he goes on to surround himself with what he characterizes as 'wise books, bright windows, in this life of ours lit by the shining souls of men', and reports that he spends his days in reading and doing chemistry and his nights in the study of astronomy (the avoidance of biology is significant). And he concludes by saying that 'it must be, I think, in the vast and eternal laws of matter, and not in the daily cares and sins and troubles of men, that whatever is more than animal within us must find its solace and its hope' (p. 87). So a certain materialism is apparently vindicated after all, and moreover is equated with a notion of the 'more than animal', as if to conclude that the distinction between animal and human is not equivalent to one between materialism and something 'higher' but rather to different modes of or stances towards materialism (as figured for example by the difference between vivisection and astronomy).

Put in terms of an impressionist problematic, *The Island of Dr Moreau* thematizes what might be described as a sense of the ontological instability of the printed text, whose material nature enables it to be seen and read but at the same is precisely that which it has in common with mere or brute matter, from which nevertheless it is crucially distinguished – but by what? One is tempted to say by its relation to language, but the reversion of language to mere lumps of sound towards the end of the narrative implicitly thematizes language in terms of print and printing, not the other way round. By the act of printing then? But the same passage, and the overarching theme of reversion to the brutely material, extend the notion of ontological instability to type itself, which is to say to the material origins of the printed text. The insufficiently theorized status of pain in the story perhaps represents the wholly untheorized, and for Wells no doubt untheorizable, remainder or difference that distinguishes both writing and printing from their material bases (see n. 19).

My larger claim is that something of this same uneasy metaphysical conscience with respect to the materiality of writing and printing haunts Wells's prolific *œuvre*. For example:

In *The First Men on the Moon* (1901) the moon-dwellers, or Selenites, are able to dispense with writing owing to the superior capacity of their outsized brains, in which however thoughts may be seen almost visibly to inscribe themselves (one 'material' practice taking the place of another).[23]

In 'When the Sleeper Wakes' (1899), *Tono-Bungay* (1909), and other texts, a thematics of flying may be read as expressing a desire for a liberated writing that would somehow transcend the physical constraints of ordinary surface-bound writing.[24] But the narrator of *Tono-Bungay* crashes his flying-machine, disfiguring his face in the process, and a few pages later writes: 'I think the reader would be amused if he could see the paper on my desk as I write all this, the mangled and disfigured pages, the experimental arrangements of notes, the sheets of suggestions balanced in constellations, the blottesque intellectual battlegrounds over which I have been fighting.'[25] (The Selenites, by the way, are astonished to learn that human beings have restricted themselves to living merely on the surface of their world.)

Most obviously, perhaps, in the masterpiece that immediately followed *The Island of Dr Moreau*, I mean *The Invisible Man* (1897), the moral of which I take to be that the protagonist's feat of making himself invisible by becoming perfectly transparent not only doesn't liberate him from the constraints of materiality but in fact makes him especially vulnerable to them. This in turn may be read as a commentary on the texts of the impressionist nature writer W. H. Hudson, an *anti*-Moreau figure if there ever was one (Hudson was the foremost birder of his day and led campaigns against the abuse of animals) and an author whose prose was admired by Ford Madox Ford, Conrad and others precisely for its self-effacingness *as* prose, which is to say for its virtual 'transparency' as a medium of communication of thought and perception (although it seems surprising now that Hudson was widely considered the greatest stylist of his time).[26] In other words, Wells's most famous novel may be taken as a critique of Hudsonian 'transparency' as a stylistic ideal, or at least as suggesting that such an ideal in no way escaped the material conditions of all writing.[27] The climactic scene comes when the Invisible Man has been hunted down and killed; as the townspeople who had surrounded him watch in horror and amazement, his body, in death, gradually becomes visible again before their eyes:

When at last the crowd made way for Kemp [the Invisible Man's betrayer and principal tracker] to stand erect, there lay, naked and pitiful on the ground, the bruised and broken body of a young man about thirty. His hair and beard were white, – not grey with age, but white with whiteness of albinism, and his eyes were like garnets. His hands were clenched, his eyes wide open, and his expression was one of anger and dismay.

'Cover his face!' said a man. 'For Gawd's sake, cover that face!' and three little children, pushing forward through the crowd, were suddenly twisted round and sent packing off again.

Someone brought a sheet from the Jolly Cricketers, and having covered him, they carried him into that house.[28]

6

James Whale's 'Frankenstein': The Horror Film and the Symbolic Biology of the Cinematic Monster

MICHAEL GRANT

The value of the horror film was first recognized in and by the horror film itself. It was the sophistication of certain films of the Sixties, such as *Peeping Tom* (1960), *Psycho* (1960) and *The Birds* (1963), a sophistication about the film medium and the viewer's relation to it, that for critic and film-maker alike provoked a new interest in films of this type. Hitchcock's films in particular were to prove influential both for those critics such as Raymond Bellour, Roger Dadoun and Robin Wood who contributed extensively to a reassessment of the horror film and for the horror cinema itself, as it developed during the 1970s and 1980s. *Psycho* is the underlying influence and point of reference for films as varied as *Sisters* (1972), *Halloween* (1978), *Dressed to Kill* (1980) and *Psycho II* (1983), as well as for slasher films more generally. *The Birds* also influenced later work, especially by way of George A. Romero's *Night of the Living Dead* (1968), which, together with Roman Polanski's *Rosemary's Baby* (also 1968), is often taken to inaugurate much that is characteristic of the last twenty years of horror cinema. For example, the theme (central to *Night of the Living Dead*) of invasion leading to social and human breakdown, a theme deriving not only from *The Birds* but also from Don Siegel's 1956 *Invasion of the Body Snatchers*, was taken up and developed in *The Texas Chainsaw Massacre* (1973), *It's Alive* (1973), *Carrie* (1976), and *The Hills Have Eyes* (1977). Furthermore, as Gregory Waller has argued, *Night of the Living Dead* presents, along with a new level of explicit bodily horror, an uncompromising critique of American institutions and values:

It depicts the failure of the nuclear family, the private home, the teenager couple, and the resourceful individual hero; and it reveals the flaws inherent in the media, local and federal government agencies, and the entire mechanism of civil defense.[1]

Romero's film, produced in Pittsburgh for $114,000, encouraged other directors to produce similarly independent and critical work away from the mainstream, directors as various as Brian De Palma, Larry Cohen, David Cronenberg and Abel Ferrara. As a result, a number of films from this period, including Carpenter's *The Thing* (1982), a radical reworking of Howard Hawks's film *The Thing* of 1951, and Cronenberg's *Scanners* (1983), go beyond the critique of values and institutions to a more far-reaching subversion of human identity and psychic wholeness.

One such film is Romero's *Martin* (1976), a genuinely innovative work that plays on and challenges many of the conventions of the vampire film and of standard Hollywood narrative motivation. Martin may be either a disturbed teenager, with distinctly psychopathic tendencies, or an 84-year-old vampire. As he protests to his ageing cousin, 'There's no magic anymore', an opinion which the old man, who is convinced he has proof, in the shape of family documents and old photographs, that Martin is truly a vampire 'from the old country', vigorously rejects. The narrative never resolves this conflict, leaving the film's motivation suspended, in the manner of the fantastic, between natural and supernatural explanation. Romero's use of this indeterminacy is to be seen in his handling of the death sequences, one of which occurs at the opening of the film. As Martin boards a train for Pittsburgh, he notices a young woman, to whom he is clearly attracted. After an elapse, during which the train hurtles on into the gathering darkness, Martin leaves his seat, enters the toilet and prepares a hypodermic syringe. He then moves down the corridor, and picks the lock to his victim's sleeping compartment. As he enters we have a subjective shot in strongly contrasting black and white of a young woman (not the woman he has seen on the train) dressed in a revealing nightgown of the last century and opening her arms to him from the bed of a room that seems part of an ancient castle.

Though the scene is reminiscent of a cinematic Dracula's approach to Mina or Lucy, Romero never establishes whether these subjective shots, a device that occurs three times later in the film, are fantasies or memories. In the opening sequence, what follows the subjective shot is a violent physical struggle that lasts until the sleeping drug Martin has forcibly injected into his victim takes effect. 'With both parties naked, Martin now enacts a strangely tender simulation of love-making, kissing and stroking the woman's inert body, until, at last, in direct analogy to orgasm, he spills her blood across his own chest just before drinking it. The act of vampirism is no longer a metaphor for sex; it *is* sex'.[2] There is no possibility, given the film's organization, of establishing whether

Martin is truly a vampire. Despite our access to his 'subjectivity', we are excluded from his self-understanding and we have no basis for deciding whether the action of his cousin, Cuda, in finally staking him, is justified. Martin is an indeterminate figure who, by virtue of his indeterminacy, is a monster, and is at the same time, as the film makes clear, a being created in his indeterminacy by purely cinematic means.

Carrie (1976) similarly identifies Carrie's existence as a monster with the cinematic means used to establish that monstrosity. The film is part of the cycle begun by *Rosemary's Baby*, and continued in *The Exorcist* (1972) and *The Omen* (1976), in which a child becomes the agent of forces destructive to the established order of things. De Palma presents Carrie in a way that makes her and the destruction she brings about inseparable from devices such as highly elaborate and extravagant camera movements, split screen, colour shifts, insistent music and reverse motion. By the end, Carrie's domination of the film's world is complete, and even the nightmares of her closest friend, Sue, are under her sway, despite the fact that Carrie herself is dead.

It is this highly self-conscious and self-reflexive work of the 1970s and 1980s that illuminates retrospectively much of what is of greatest aesthetic interest in horror films produced during the studio period of the 1930s and 1940s. *Cat People*, produced in 1942 by Val Lewton for RKO, and directed by Jacques Tourneur, is a work whose complexity of effect depends on subtle shifts in motivation and narrative explanation. The scene in the swimming-pool, during which Irena threatens her rival, Alice, produces its effects by suggestion. We never see Irena during Alice's panic in the water, the threat that she poses being evoked through the play of sound and light. This scene, together with the sequence in which Alice is seemingly pursued by Irena down a dark street only intermittently lamplit, effectively identifies the horrific figure with the cinematic devices whereby she is represented. In the latter sequence, the camera tracks along a trail left by someone in high-heeled shoes, and as it does so the traces gradually dissolve into paw-marks, the camera continuing on to disclose the carcasses of mutilated sheep. There is then a cut to Alice, whose increased agitation is shown in the rhythm of her footsteps, a rhythm echoed by a deep and regular breathing and the rustle of parting undergrowth. At the very moment when Alice and the audience expect an unmistakably feline hiss to initiate a fatal attack, a bus pulls into the frame from the right, and as it does so the sound of the cat blurs into the pneumatic discharge of the opening doors.

Moving further back in time, J. L. Schefer has considered the aesthetic significance of a more radical intervention of the cinematic apparatus in his account of Carl-Theodor Dreyer's *Vampyr* (1931).[3] Schefer begins by noting a paradoxical inscription of time in cinema, as when the wheels of a chariot, say, appear to stand still, even though the chariot itself is hurtling forward. The spokes of the wheel appear to stop and then to oscillate backwards and forwards. In this way a visual differentiation between movement and speed is effected and the one becomes detached from the other. This stroboscopic effect is caused by the operation of the cinematic apparatus itself, the operation by means of which the film image is laid down and made visible – the film stock, the film speed, the intermittent movement of the camera and the projector.

For Schefer, it is an intrusion at the level of the apparatus that characterizes the concluding sequences of *Vampyr*, since it is in these scenes that the operation of the apparatus induces in us a paradoxical double awareness, of death in life and life in death. The movement of the mill-wheel, as it throws flour down onto the figure of the vampire's assistant, the doctor, trapped in a cage below the millstones, exemplifies the stroboscopic oscillations that manifest the movement whereby dead images are endowed with life, a life in and of death. Dreyer's film projects the paradoxical nature of its own existence into a sequence that turns back onto the viewer the abolition of what is there to be seen. As the pulsating whiteness of the flour envelops the image and the doctor disappears into it, we see effected the erasure of the narrated world, and in that very erasure we are brought to abstract from it the death that has hitherto sustained it. The end of *Vampyr* can be taken as a commentary on the final sequence of Friedrich Murnau's *Nosferatu* (1921): the vampire, pierced and destroyed by the beam of light which obliterates him from the screen, disappears into that which has made him visible.

It is perhaps with James Whale's *Frankenstein* (1931) that the horror cinema finds its most truly representative work. The film concerns itself with the process of creation and the consequences of it, a process that involves not only Frankenstein's creation of the monster but also the articulation whereby the film itself comes into being. The film works to identify the events that are narrated and the narration of those events with each other. The resulting duration is one in which the thrust of the film's narrative derives from a differentiation between creator and created that is increasingly difficult to sustain as the monster comes to embody for his creator, Henry Frankenstein, the impossibility of what he has brought into existence. The film concludes as the two are drawn back

– as one – into the inevitable consummation of the originating fire. The relation between the film's narrative structure and the paradox of the monster's existence is effected by style, in particular by Whale's use of the moving camera. For example, at the end of the sequence in which the monster inadvertently drowns Maria we see in the uncut version the creature, moaning pitifully, stagger towards the camera as it tracks back with him, his hands reaching out before him into the emptiness off screen left, a movement that repeats his beckoning gesture to Maria as they played together beside the lake, throwing flowers into the water and watching them float. This is the set-up for the subsequent sequence, in which Maria's father carries her drowned and bedraggled body through the crowded and festive streets of the village in which Henry's forthcoming nuptials are being celebrated. As the father walks forward, in a prolonged, virtuoso take, the streets fall silent, and the difference between this shot and the earlier one becomes apparent. Where the monster's arms were empty, the father's are full, and where the monster moaned in bewilderment and confusion, the father is silent, walking stiffly forward as the camera keeps up with him. The subtlety of the film at this point lies in its treatment of childhood, innocence and the metamorphoses of life and death. It is no longer possible to see film as no more than the medium into which concepts are translated; it has become, in Whale's handling of it, the medium in which they are created and formed. In the final sequences of the film (to which I shall return) Frankenstein and his creature confront one another inside the burning windmill, and again on an upper balcony overlooking the horrified crowd of villagers below. The movements of the mill's gears and of the burning sails as they rotate against the darkened sky intimate those movements of the apparatus (of the shutter and the Maltese cross) that for Schefer inform the last reel of *Vampyr*. Just as the hesitations induced by the apparatus differentiate between movement and speed, so in the imaginative organization of *Frankenstein* death detaches itself from life, and as it does so the film is projected forward – and backward – into a self-defining figuration that has no object to sustain it that is other than itself. On this view, the horror film – at least in certain of its most significant manifestations – exemplifies a concept of art in which representation itself is compromised. The dominant conventions, of reference and imitation, are rendered suspect, so that structures of temporality and spatial depiction are no longer wholly trustworthy. The orders of representation in which they would make sense are disrupted from within, and, partially at least, discredited.[4] These are procedures to be found in Percy Shelley, Poe and Hoffmann, as well as in the writings of Le Fanu and Stevenson. They induce an art addressed to its own creation:

> Only by the form, the pattern
> Can words or music reach
> The stillness, as a Chinese jar still
> Moves perpetually in its stillness.

It is crucial to the effect of impossibility created by *Dead Ringers* (1991) that the failure of the Mantle twins to separate themselves from one another should become internal to the formal ordering of the narrative. The patterns of repetition across the film, particularly as the twins' mutual destruction gathers pace, project the action forward towards an end that – as the film brings us to recognize – was there at the beginning. The lives of the characters are gathered into a formal configuration that creates them even as they take precedence over it. What is presented to us is not something that we imagine to have taken place in a world elsewhere, a world of possibilities realized only in a fiction which derives its aesthetic potency from its verisimilitude. What Cronenberg confronts us with is 'a manifested actuality in a world of lived experience,'[5] the experience of cinema. The horror of *Dead Ringers* lies not in the threat posed to normality by a monster or by the Other (as Robin Wood has argued). The power of the film is inseparable from its creation of a movement through time that is not based on logic or discourse, and that as a result will not yield itself to an approach that sees it as a cryptic allegory or as a fragmented treatise calling for a more complete exposition. The special effects are used to warn us that meaning of that sort is simply not there. What Cronenberg makes clear is that understanding the film requires something of us that we will discover only in the film itself. And what we discover may not be sayable apart from cinematic events so shaped by the film as to make us live them in their elapsing.[6]

Psychoanalysis has been the underpinning of a major part of academic film study in Britain and the USA in recent decades. The development of a theory of cinematic subjectivity based on the work of Lacan constituted a central plank of the programme of *Screen* from the early 1970s until the journal's change of ownership in the late 1980s. Similar intellectual commitments have been evident over the same period in American journals such as *Camera Obscura*, *Wide Angle*, *Film Comment* and *October*. This kind of analysis has, of course, been inseparable from the consideration of issues of ideology and sexual difference. It is hardly

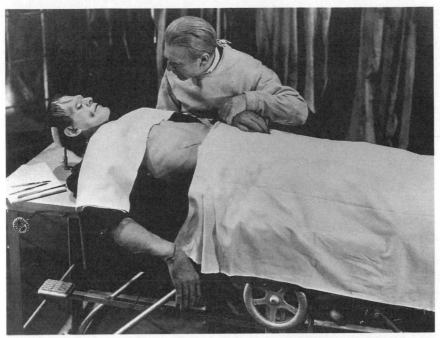

'The monster and Dr Waldman', production still from the 1931 film
Frankenstein directed by James Whale.

'It's alive!', production still from James Whale's *Frankenstein*.

'The monster and Maria', production still from James Whale's *Frankenstein*.

surprising, then, given this kind of intellectual milieu, that writers on the horror film should similarly have been drawn to Freud and Lacan. Robin Wood's early studies of the genre attempt to explain the effect of the horror film in terms of the return of the repressed. Mark Nash took up questions of enunciation and the Lacanian subject in relation to Dreyer's *Vampyr*, while, more recently, Barbara Creed's discussion of *Alien* and the 'monstrous-feminine' draws extensively on Kristeva's notion of abjection.

Psychoanalytic readings of Whale's Frankenstein have been particularly concerned to address the relation between Henry and his creation, the monster. T. R. Ellis has summarized the arguments of a number of recent critics.[7] For instance, Margaret Tarrant, drawing on Freud, is persuaded that the monster embodies Henry's 'repressed sexual desires, the impulses of the id'. The monster personifies the sexual drive that estranges him from Elizabeth. Walter Evans similarly sees the monster as an embodiment of Frankenstein's sexuality, and goes on to argue that, if Henry is to enter into a normal sexual relationship with Elizabeth, he must give up his 'dangerous private experiments', that is, masturbation.

Harvey Greenberg considers the real purpose of Frankenstein's investigations to be 'the resolution of his sexual ignorance and angst'. Like Evans, Greenberg takes Henry's research, embarked on out of fear of a sexual relationship with Elizabeth, to be a form of masturbation. For Greenberg, the 'appeal of the monster movie may, at least in part, be traced to our fascination with the child-like innocence of these fearsome creatures'.

One of the most distinguished articles of recent years to draw on psychoanalysis in order to address the question of monstrous and imaginary beings in the cinema, including Dracula and Frankenstein's creature, has been Noël Carroll's 'Nightmare and the Horror Film: The Symbolic Biology of Fantastic Beings', first published in 1981 (and reworked in *The Philosophy of Horror*, 1990).[8] For Carroll, psychoanalysis is not a hermeneutic method that can be applied unproblematically to any kind of film or work of art. The appropriateness of psychoanalysis to the study of horror cinema derives from the fact that within our culture the horror film is 'explicitly acknowledged as a vehicle for expressing psychoanalytically significant themes such as repressed sexuality, oral sadism, necrophilia, etc.'. For Carroll, it is simply the case that within our current social tradition psychoanalysis is the common idiom of the horror film and 'thus the privileged tool for discussing the genre'.[9] However, this seems confused. While it is true that, as Carroll puts it, many horror films seem little more than 'bowdlerized, pop psychoanalysis, so enmeshed is Freudian psychology with the genre',[10] it does not follow from this that psychoanalysis, of the Freudian variety or any other, is uniquely equipped to explain the psychological effects of a given horror film. The fact that psychoanalysis provides a privileged set of themes for the horror film does not thereby justify the conclusion that psychoanalysis will explain the psychological effects of the films themselves. None the less, it is precisely this that Carroll proposes. He argues that horror novels have been tied to dream and nightmare since the inception of the modern tradition. The assertion, common to many of the most notable of these works, such as *Frankenstein* and *Dracula*, or *Dr Jekyll and Mr Hyde*, that they originated in dream or nightmare, is part of a culturally established framework for presenting and understanding the horror genre. For Carroll, 'this makes the resort to psychoanalysis unavoidable'.[11]

Carroll turns for his conceptual apparatus to Ernest Jones's *On the Nightmare*. Central to Jones's treatment of nightmare imagery is conflict. Carroll draws out the significance of this by insisting on the simultaneously attractive and repulsive nature of the products of the dreamwork, a conflict that arises inasmuch as the dream functions to express both a wish and its inhibition. The wish that engenders a nightmare is incestuous. Carroll cites Jones:

The reason why the object seen in a Nightmare is frightful or hideous is simply that the representation of the underlying wish is not permitted in its naked form so that the dream is a compromise of the wish on the one hand and on the other of the intense fear belonging to the inhibition.[12]

It is this conflict between attraction and repulsion that is central to Carroll's understanding of the horror film. Carroll, however, is by no means happy with what he sees as Jones's overemphasis on the degree to which incestuous conflicts shape the nightmare. He cites John Mack to support his view that Jones's approach is too narrowly Freudian. According to Mack, nightmares are the expression of the earliest and most archaic of impulses and conflicts, those involving 'destructive aggression, castration, separation and abandonment, devouring and being devoured, and fear regarding loss of identity and fusion with the mother'.[13] Carroll concludes from this that the effect of the horror film is to be identified with the effect of the horrific or fantastic beings they represent, and that it is the meaning or 'symbolic biology' of these fantastic beings to be the incarnation of the archaic, conflicting impulses of nightmare: 'The fantastic beings of horror films can be seen as symbolic formations that organize conflicting themes into figures that are simultaneously attractive and repulsive.'[14]

There are at least three problems with this. First, Carroll appears to think that the 'meaning' of the fantastic beings is inherent in or internal to their conflictual organization. In other words, it is the inner structure of the creatures that stipulates how they are to be understood and responded to. However, no such singular and unitary effect can be ascribed to them. We react to them in different ways, and no one response can be associated unequivocally with any one such figure. Second, Carroll's argument presupposes the notion of horror that he wishes to give an explanation of: his account of nightmare assumes that nightmares are horrific in the way horror films are. However, Carroll gives no grounds other than those derived from aesthetic convention for taking the conditions engendering nightmare to be the conditions that are productive of the horrific effect in horror cinema. The third problem is related to this. Carroll, in effect, is running two categories into one. He is offering to give a close description of the formal and aesthetic characteristics of horror film imagery – 'the symbolic meaning and structure' of such figures as vampires and Frankenstein's monster – which is at the same time a causal account of the psychological effect of the horror film, the conflict between attraction and repulsion that he sees as the fundamental experience produced by such films.

The points at issue can be clarified by reference to a remark of Wittgenstein's on J. G. Frazer's *The Golden Bough*:

> The religious actions or the religious life of the priest-king are no different in kind from any genuinely religious action today, say, a confession of sins. This also can be 'explained' (made clear) and cannot be explained.[15]

As P.M.S. Hacker has argued, it is not that Wittgenstein thinks one could adequately describe the Catholic confessional without mentioning the beliefs involved.[16] However, it is by no means '*obvious* that Catholic dogmas about the Apostolic succession, priestly ordination and the power to absolve from sin *explain* the practice'.[17] For Wittgenstein, as Hacker makes clear:

> In elucidating a rite it is not only historical, legendary, and mythic beliefs that enter the description, but also mystical and magical beliefs. They belong to the rite. But ritual actions do not stand to such non-empirical beliefs as an instrumental action stands to a belief in a causal nexus. One cannot elucidate the Catholic Mass without elaborating the participants' belief that they are mystically partaking of the body and blood of Christ.[18]

In a causal nexus, the elements involved are each identified independently of the other, and the participants have no privileged role in their identification. However, a ritual 'is no more intelligible independently of the belief that informs it than the belief is of the ritual'.[19] Belief and ritual are related internally to each other. The belief *belongs* to the practice. As Hacker puts it: 'Once the connection of belief and ritual action has been spelt out in a description, the participants' reasons for acting as they do – the only reasons which can render the action intelligible – have been given. And *there is no further explanation*.'[20] To try to get behind or below the ritual act is misguided; what has to be understood is the act itself. Ritual is not performed as a means to an end: it 'aims at some satisfaction and achieves it. Or rather, it does not *aim* at anything; we act in this way and then feel satisfied.'[21] The essence of a ritual is that precisely *these* actions be performed. A particular sequence of actions is uniquely appropriate: no other will do. If the right actions are not performed, or are performed in the wrong spirit, of mockery or indifference, say, the act may be one of desecration or sacrilege. In ritual, what is expressed cannot be distinguished from the means of expression.

These reflections on ritual and ceremony bear directly on the role aesthetic judgement plays in our lives, particularly inasmuch as our judgement engages with works of artistic and imaginative power. The significance of such a work (a work, that is, such as Whale created in *Frankenstein*) lies in its direct impact on the individual members of its audience. Our response to an important work of art is inseparable from the experience we have of it in its *uniqueness*. To give one's reaction to a work of this order reflects that experience in which its beauty and significance suddenly impress themselves on us. Such a response is not an act or event external to what is responded to: in genuine imaginative participation, there is no action at a distance. Wittgenstein distinguishes between two ways in which we may use the word 'understand':

We speak of understanding a sentence in the sense in which it can be replaced by another which says the same; but also in the sense in which it cannot be replaced by any other. (Any more than a musical theme can be replaced by another.)[22]

In the first case, the thought in the sentence is common to different sentences; in the second it is 'something that is expressed only by these words in these positions. (Understanding a poem.)'.[23] The first sense of 'understand' is that in which we can get someone to understand a sentence by explaining its meaning, and this we can do by giving another sentence that 'says the same'. But this is not so with the other sense, where something different holds:

But in the second case how can one explain the expression, transmit one's understanding? Ask yourself: How does one *lead* anyone to the understanding of a poem or a musical theme?[24]

For Stanley Cavell, writing of lines such as Wallace Stevens's 'As a calm darkens among water-lights' from 'Sunday Morning', and Hart Crane's 'The mind is brushed by sparrow wings' from 'For the Marriage of Faustus and Helen', it is precisely understanding of this second kind that modern poetry demands of its reader:

Paraphrasing the lines, or explaining their meaning, or telling, or putting the thought another way – all these things are out of the question. One may be able to say nothing except that a feeling has been voiced by a kindred spirit and that if someone does not get it he is not in one's world, or not of one's flesh.[25]

In these lines, language constitutes the very element in which meaning lives: the thought expressed is expressed by *these* words in *these* positions. To respond to the artist's creation requires of the spectator a reciprocal act of creativity, in which feeling, interpretation and judgement each have their part to play. This, then, is to oppose the psychoanalytic assumption – of Freud, Jones, and Carroll himself – that the life of art and the imagination can be clarified and understood by way of the principle of cause and effect. Carroll argues that the monstrous figure has the effect it does because it has the same unconscious origin as the nightmare. However, this argument fails to engage with what Carroll calls 'symbolic meaning'. The principle of unconscious cause and conscious effect cannot discriminate one type of fantastic being from another. The same law (of archaic conflict) is to determine the meaning not only of Frankenstein's monster but also of figures as varied as the vampire, the werewolf and the double. It is this position that Wittgenstein's remarks give grounds for refusing. They lend support to the view that the significance of any such fantastic figure derives not from its originating cause (whether psychic or historical) but from its specific artistic realization. The crucial question to pose in this context is not 'What is the underlying cause of the cinematic monster's effect?' but 'What is the meaning for me of this monster in this film?' If Carroll's explanations fulfil a positive function, it is in relation to this encounter.

Carroll sees Frankenstein's monster as a composite figure, created by what he calls 'fusion', that is, a process whereby conflicting themes are yoked together into a single, unified figure. (It is worth noting that critics variously designate the monster by 'he' or 'it'.) On the one hand, Whale's film associates the monster with images of loathsomeness. The creature is incapable of speech, a being made out of waste, dead things, in 'Frankenstein's workshop of filthy creation'. His creation is presented as ghastly, the result of a confusion between the excremental and the reproductive. 'The monster is reviled as heinous and as unwholesome filth, [and] rejected by his creator – his father.'[26] On the other hand, these same images of loathsomeness are fused with opposing qualities. The monster, in the film, is virtually omnipotent and indestructible. Dr Waldman's attempts to subdue the creature prove fruitless, and, as he is about to begin his dissection, it strangles him. The monster is, on this view, both helpless and powerful, worthless and godlike. This paradoxical conception of the creature – an inversion, perhaps, of the Christian paradox of the Incarnation – points to what underpins the figure's aesthetic power. The monster's initial loathsomeness triggers his rejection by his creator, causing him 'to explode in omnipotent rage over [his] alienation'.[27] It is this rejection and consequent alienation that together spur the creature on to 'rampaging vengeance', in which he combines 'fury and strength in infantile orgies of rage and destruction'.[28] The monster's alienation is thus central to the film, which foregrounds it in a number of ways: the killing of Maria, the contrast between the monster's wandering over the countryside and the wedding preparations, and the opposition between Frankenstein's preoccupation with the monster and his concern with producing an heir to the family name and estates. In other words, for Carroll, the conflictual nature of the monster – aesthetically clarified in terms of a structure derived from an analysis of the nightmare – embodies and engenders what is fundamental to the film's imaginative logic.

The paradoxical nature of the monster is made particularly evident in the creation scene. Many critics, including R.H.W. Dillard and Ellis, have noted Whale's organization of *Frankenstein* into an overall contrast between light and darkness, and the relation of this contrast to an imagery of fire. This pattern of contrasts and similarities is manifest in Whale's presentation of the monster's creation. In the creation sequences, set in Frankenstein's laboratory, fire is represented as a life-giving force. Out of the darkness of the storm comes the creative energy of lightning, which Dillard sees as 'the most active and meaningful fusion of light and fire',[29] an energy that gives life to a creature of darkness. As Frankenstein exultantly points out, his creature has never lived. It is composed of pieces of bodies that Frankenstein has himself brought together: 'The brain of a dead man waiting to live again in a body I made with my own hands. With my own hands.' The monster is thus a creature of death, of darkness and the night, as the opening sequence of the film, set in a graveyard from which Frankenstein and Fritz steal a newly buried corpse, makes clear. The creature is called out of the darkness of the grave by fire ('the great ray'), and it is fire that, at the end of the film, will return him to the darkness from whence he came. As Ellis points out, the monster's fear of fire is tied, first, to his own violent origins and, second, to the Promethean overtones of the film. The monster seems to remember the shock of his birth and the role of fire in that birth, a memory manifest in his fearful response to Fritz tormenting him with a burning torch, as well as in his pitiful and demented screams as the flames finally engulf him on the windmill. The second aspect of the monster's fear arises from the fact that Henry is, as the subtitle of the novel states, a modern Prometheus. He is, however, a false Prometheus. Prometheus, the Titan of Greek mythology who created man, stole fire from heaven to ensure the survival of the being he had created. Henry also calls on fire to endow his creation with life, but 'the great ray' is natural, not divine. The monster is created by a man subordinate to nature, not a being who was more than a man and more than nature. The creature's extreme fear of fire can be seen, then, as deriving from his origin in the non-divine, the human. Whale uses the suffering and confusion induced by the monster's conflictual nature, and endured by him throughout the film, as an expression of the paradox inherent in his creation. If Frankenstein has created a new Adam, then, in Ellis's words, 'this "Adam" will never inhabit a garden of Eden, but a world of pain and fear'.[30]

The monster can, therefore, be seen as an embodiment of the flawed creativity that has produced him. Henry's creativity is that of a crazed, false god. At the moment at which the monster's hand first moves, indicating that he has come to life, Henry screams repeatedly – 'It's alive! It's alive!' However, there is dialogue in this scene that was censored before the release of the print as we now have it. In the fuller version

Henry's God-like aspirations are explicitly noted. As he screams, 'It's alive! It's alive!' Victor rushes to him and says, 'Henry, in the name of God!' Henry replies, 'Oh, God – Now I know what it feels like to *be* God.'[31]

The flawed creativity of Frankenstein is embodied in that which he creates, and it is for this reason that his creation returns to destroy him (in an echo of the Christian paradoxes surrounding the Crucifixion, in which the Creator is put to death by His creation). Despite the tacked-on ending, it is clear that, as Dillard has said, 'the last real scene in the film was at the burning windmill, the last real shot a descent away from that windmill'.[32] This view is also borne out by Colin Clive, who had left for England before the last scene of the released version was filmed. In an interview just prior to his departure, he remarked: 'I think *Frankenstein* has an intensely dramatic quality that continues throughout the play and culminates when I am killed by the Monster I created.'[33] Not only does the film put religious connotations drawn from the Crucifixion into play, but, as Ellis has pointed out, it also echoes and reverses the Resurrection. The opening scene in the cemetery presents Frankenstein and Fritz as 'Resurrection men', grave-robbers, in a setting that makes extensive use of images of the Cross, a statue of the crucified Christ and a statue of Death. It is against this background of death that Whale cuts to a close-up of Henry holding onto the casket he and Fritz have raised out from the earth: 'He's just resting', he says, 'waiting for a new life to come.'[34] The story of Henry Frankenstein is represented in terms of connotations that effect a reversal of Christ's passion. The story begins with a pseudo-Resurrection (the graveyard scene leading to the creation of the monster) and ends with a false Crucifixion (the burning arms of the windmill suspended in a fiery cross in a final image after the monster has died in the fire and Henry's body has been borne away by the villagers). The union of creator and creature in death – a perverted passion – is evident here. The complexity of this final image – of the mill as a fiery cross – is further reinforced by suggestions it draws in from the earlier sequences portraying the hunt for the monster. The baying dogs tugging at their leads, the torches, and the swirling movements of the crowd of villagers, are all suggestive of American lynch-mobs and the Ku Klux Klan. Henry leads one of the search parties, hunting down his own creation, for whose existence and whose crimes he is himself responsible. Henry is both hunter and hunted, creator and destroyer, finally unable to escape the being he has brought into existence.

The origin of Henry's creative persona lies in a certain Romantic vision of the poet, a vision shared, of course, by Percy Shelley. It is in relation to this sense of the poet and the creative imagination of which Henry is the embodiment that the aesthetic power of the film, including its horrific effects, can most satisfactorily be elucidated. So far as the novel is concerned, it is clear that Percy Shelley's work proved a significant influence on Mary Shelley's conception of Victor Frankenstein. As Maurice Hindle has argued in his introduction to the recent edition of *Frankenstein*, Percy Shelley's poem 'Alastor' provides many of the distinctive features of Victor's persona. And in this respect, the film remains true to the novel. The poet's address to Nature is pertinent not only to Victor Frankenstein but also to Whale's protagonist, Henry:

> I have watched
> Thy shadow, and the darkness of thy steps,
> And my heart ever gazes on the depth
> Of thy deep mysteries. I have made my bed
> In charnels and on coffins, where black death
> Keeps record of the trophies won from thee,
> Hoping to still these obstinate questionings
> Of thee and thine, by forcing some lone ghost
> Thy messenger, to render up the tale
> Of what we are. (ll. 20–29)

As Hindle says, 'we can be sure that a good part of Frankenstein's ambitious persona has its origin here'.[35] The relation between 'Alastor' and Whale's film can, however, be taken further.

The aesthetic presuppositions of Shelley's poetry are complex. Writing of nineteenth-century poets (and particularly of Shelley) in relation to

'In the mill', production still from James Whale's *Frankenstein*.

'In the mill', production still from James Whale's *Frankenstein*.

poets of the preceding neoclassical period in England, Earl Wasserman
has argued that

> an additional formulative act was required of the poet, for he must simulta-
> neously employ the syntactical features of poetry to shape an order that has no
> assumed prototype outside the creative act, and with this internally contained
> order create the poem. Within itself the modern poem must both formulate its
> own cosmic syntax and shape the autonomous poetic reality that the cosmic
> syntax permits: 'nature', which once was prior to the poem and available for
> imitation, now shares with the poem a common origin in the poet's creativity.[36]

For Shelley, a poem could no longer be seen as a reflection or imitation of
an order existing autonomously outside itself. 'The creation of a poem is
also the creation of the cosmic wholeness that gives meaning to the poem,
and each poet must independently make his own world-picture, his own
language within language'.[37] The paradoxical consequences of this are
suggested by Percy Shelley in his 'Essay on Life': 'Each [life or being] is at
once the centre and the circumference, the point to which all things are
referred, and the line in which all things are contained.'[38] It is this
theological paradox that finds expression in 'Alastor', as the lines on the
wandering poet's death make clear:

> . . . the pulse yet lingered in his heart.
> It paused – it fluttered. But when heaven remained
> Utterly black, the murky shades involved
> An image, silent, cold, and motionless,
> As their own voiceless earth and vacant air.

Even as a vapour fed with golden beams
That ministered on sunlight, ere the west
Eclipses it, was now that wondrous frame –
No sense, no motion, no divinity –
A fragile lute, on whose harmonious strings
The breath of heaven did wander – a bright stream
Once fed with many-voicèd waves – a dream
Of youth, which night and time have quenched for ever,
Still, dark, and dry, and unremembered now. (ll. 658–71)

The syntax breaks up into a series of units that effect the inextricable interpenetration of the poet and a nature of which he is the creator and in death the creature. That to which Alastor's powers of imagination have given shape and meaning becomes on his death the force that sustains him in all the complexity and ambivalence of poetic being. He is at once 'An image, silent, cold, and motionless', 'A fragile lute', 'a bright stream', and 'a dream / Of youth, which night and time have quenched for ever, / Still, dark, and dry, and unremembered now'. The poet lives in death: he is paradoxically begotten of the poetic text, of which he is the 'image' and with which he is at one.

In the film, as Ellis has suggested,[39] a similar paradoxical unity between Henry and his creature is expressed in two memorable scenes. The first occurs on the mountain, when Henry faces the monster. The relation of unity is shown in a four-shot sequence: a medium shot of Henry is followed by a medium shot of the monster, after which a close-up of Henry is followed by a close-up of the monster. The shots are of the same duration and the faces of the two characters wear the same expression. The shots are also lit similarly, and taken from similar angles. The second sequence is in the windmill. Again, shot/reverse shot scene construction is used to present Henry and the monster as they stare at each other through the turning gears of the windmill. The framing of the two shots through the spokes of the turning wheel is similar, and again the characters wear similar expressions. The sequence stands out in terms of its composition, shot duration and graphic matching: what it draws attention to is the unity in death of Henry and his creation. Henry Frankenstein is thus not simply an embodiment of the mad scientist. He is (like Alastor) the incarnation of a perversity without which the Romantic conception of the poet would not be the conception that it is. The symbolic biology of the monster, of Noël Carroll's nightmare creature, is expressive of a creativity that is turned against itself as the very condition of its existence: it is a creativity poisoned at its source. In his account of

William Blake, Georges Bataille has argued that poetry cannot at the same time express the 'sacred' or 'myth' and 'sovereignty' (the poet's individuality):

Blake's mythology generally introduced the problem of poetry. When poetry expresses the myths which tradition proposes to it, it is not autonomous: it does not contain sovereignty within itself. It humbly illustrates the legend whose form and meaning can exist without it. It is the autonomous work of a visionary, it defines furtive apparitions which do not have the power to convince and only have a real significance for the poet. Thus autonomous poetry, even if it only appears to be the creation of a myth, is a mere absence of myth.[40]

The difficulty confronting Bataille, and which he takes to be fundamental to Blake's writing, is also one that informs not only the writing of 'Alastor' but also the filmic and imaginative organization of Whale's *Frankenstein*.

My overall argument has been towards endorsing the view that an account such as Carroll gives of *Frankenstein* and other works of the horror cinema would in the end explain nothing if they did not help us gain a perspicuous overview of the films in question. In attempting to draw out the Romantic implications of *Frankenstein* I have tried to suggest something of the specific organization of the work, and to delineate the areas in which its aesthetic strengths are most profitably to be looked for. At the same time, if we are to account for the imaginative effect of the film, then it becomes necessary (in Wittgenstein's words) to 'appeal to a tendency in ourselves.'[41] At this point, I refer to a remark of Hacker's, in order to suggest how it is that the explanations of horror films given by Carroll and other critics whose approach is similarly psychoanalytical are open to the same kinds of consideration as those to which Wittgenstein subjected Frazer's account of ritual. In effect, what holds for Frazer's explanations holds also for Carroll's account of the monstrous figure. Of Frazer's explanations, Hacker has had this to say:

An arrangement of Frazer's data . . . will only be explanatory, i.e. elucidatory, to the extent that the rituals can be seen as symbolic, ritualized, expressive behaviour which articulates, in the framework of magical, mystical, religious belief – primal impulses and responses to the human condition.[42]

Commenting on Frazer's hypotheses concerning the Beltane (or May Day) Fire Festivals of eighteenth-century Scotland, the crucial issues for Wittgenstein are, as Frank Cioffi has argued, 'how we stand to such practices and how are *our* feelings about them to be accounted for'.[43] Hacker has amplified Cioffi's position in the following terms:

[Wittgenstein's] interest is in why *we* find the eighteenth-century, seemingly innocuous, Scottish Beltane Fire Festivals, for example, 'terrible and sinister', and in what that tells us about ourselves. His concern is not with 'How did these sinister practices originate?' nor with 'What do they mean?' but with 'What do they mean *to us*?'[44]

We might, of course, argue, as Frazer did, that it is the idea or hypothesis that these rituals have their origin in human sacrifice that makes them so disturbing. As Wittgenstein puts it:

Why should it not really be (partly, anyway) just the *idea* that makes the impression on me? Aren't ideas frightening? Can I not feel horror from the thought that the cake with the knobs once served to select by lot the victim to be sacrificed? Hasn't the *thought* something terrible? – Yes, but that which I see in those stories is something they acquire, after all, from the evidence, including such evidence as does not seem directly connected with them – from the thought of man and his past, from the strangeness of what I see in myself and in others, what I have seen and have heard.'[45]

To feel the imperative necessity of human sacrifice – to feel the overwhelming requirement to appease the gods by the offering of human blood – is something we no longer think to experience; but Wittgenstein's response to Frazer's account of it is to suggest that such forms of behaviour may be closer to us than we care to acknowledge.

In *Frankenstein*, the creativity of its protagonist, Henry, is inseparable from a violation of the holy, the sacred, the sacrosanct. This evocation of the Romantic vision of creativity is part of the film's originality and also part of what contributes to its effect. The ways in which we respond to the film cannot, therefore, be described only in terms of what the film pictures or presents on screen, the monster and his creation, for example. We must also take up the question of what the film represents, of its significance, a question that involves, among other things, the inverted and blasphemous majesty of Frankenstein's hubris (his 'presumption'), his violation of the distinction between life and death, and his perversion of the natural order. However, it is, in the end, only possible to understand the film's significance and effect against the background of a shared sense of wonder, a shared sense of awe. For as Wittgenstein put it, there is a common wonder of mankind at the living world around us, at

the rain, the thunderstorm, the phases of the moon, the changing seasons, the way in which animals are similar to and different from one another and in relation to man, the phenomena of death, birth, and sexual life, in short, everything we observe around us year in year out.[46]

As Hacker makes clear, 'a culture which lacked a sense of wonder, that was not impressed by lightning and thunder, dawn and dusk, love and hatred, etc., etc., would find the symbolic rites and beliefs of magic wholly unintelligible, and would perhaps think to account for them, as Frazer did, simply in terms of erroneous proto-scientific beliefs'.[47] It is only against the background of a sense of wonder shared in this way that we can hope to make critical sense of the expressive and symbolic forms of the films of the horror cinema and to elucidate the uniqueness of any such film's imaginative life.

This is a conclusion which Schefer's reading of cinema would also seem to support. Inasmuch as it is possible to speak of *Frankenstein* as a work addressed to its own creation – an idiom that is evidently appropriate with respect to *Vampyr* – then we may also speak of the film engaging us in the way Hacker suggests. It is only by taking for granted a sense of wonder at tempest, lightning and other tremendous natural events, all so potently evoked in the film, that the failure of Frankenstein's sovereignty (to use Bataille's term) can be given its due expressive weight in the film's aesthetic order. There is, in other words, a paradox at the heart of *Frankenstein*. As the film opens itself up to the imaginative space, the clearing, in which its aesthetic presuppositions are made manifest, and the film's project is realized, so, in that same moment, the creative sovereignty of Frankenstein, the film's central and energizing presence, is defeated. The film may therefore be said to enact the problem or difficulty inseparable from the nature of the claim to autonomy made by Romantic poetry. As I argued earlier, the film is so organized as to draw attention to itself and so to the temporal order that it creates and is sustained by. The film asserts itself – it foregrounds its textuality, the imaginative logic of its folding and unfolding – but it does so only at the expense of the creative act that has given rise to it and which it is the project of its narrative to explore. Whale's film, like much of the writing of Percy Shelley, is able to achieve its autonomy, but the process whereby that achievement is accomplished is also the process whereby that autonomy is inevitably denied to it. The achievement and the negation of the achievement are, at least in this context, inseparable from each other. The film itself exemplifies the features its own narrative attributes to Henry Franken-stein.

It is part of the inadequacy of the psychoanalytic reading of the horror cinema that it fails to illuminate this sense of filmic autonomy and uniqueness. Like semiotic theory in general, it aims to produce a general theory of the laws of all representation, or the laws of all meaning. The effect of this is to incorporate films such as *Frankenstein*, *Vampyr* or *Nosfertatu* within systems of grandiose and all-encompassing interpretation that not only reduce the films in question to little more than exemplars of the theory being proposed but also infect the theoretical project itself with confusion and self-defeating circularity.

7
Artificial Life and the Myth of Frankenstein

JASIA REICHARDT

> Every workman knows that even machines, without
> consciousness or feeling, must be humoured.[1]

At the end of March in 1987, in an interview in *The Times*, Robert Runcie, then Archbishop of Canterbury, gave vent to his feelings about the general loss of what he called 'moral energy'. Among the things he was appalled by was the way we treat 'the biological and zoological threads which join us to the animal creation . . . this way of dealing with genetic material as if it were disposable waste, makes for a sick society'. He put his finger on something that had been uncomfortably squeezed into the back of our minds for decades. Generation of life was becoming a matter of increasingly urgent concern. The creation of new life was no longer the province of those who create fantasies in books or on the screen, and of scientists who patiently discover new truths about the world. The field had expanded, and it seemed that anyone sufficiently interested and motivated could have a go at making a new collage of old and/or new parts. Proto-life inveigled itself into the public arena.

Today, we approach the creation of life from several different, if not separate, directions: those of biology and engineering, or more precisely biotechnology and electronics, or even more precisely genetics and neural networks. We also approach it from the other end, that of media technology, with which we have resuscitated the dead and reinvented the living.

No new life can be made without a thought for the story of Frankenstein because, like stories from the Bible, it has passed into general and universal mythology. Of all the stories about man's desire to create new life, it is the most emotive and tragic. Unlike the classic Faustian legend in which the natural forces once unleashed are beyond human control, the fates of Victor Frankenstein and his creation – an assemblage of human carcasses – are not without promise. It is not a

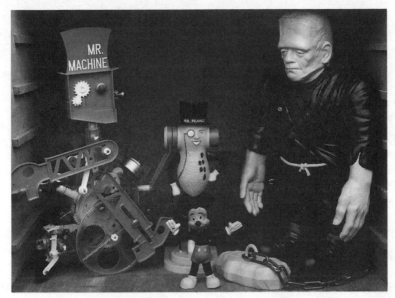

Into everyday mythology: 'Frankenstein', with Mickey Mouse and Mr Machine, in the toy cupboard of the Krazy Kat Arkive in the Archive of Art & Design at the Victoria & Albert Museum, London.

story about alchemy and magic but about science, or more precisely, about natural philosophy, chemistry and galvanism. Although the task Victor undertakes is impossible in scientific terms, the fact that he calls on science to realize his dream gives it a rational association. The tragedy is to be found in the contradiction between the protagonist's rationally planned adventure and his irrational behaviour. To us, Victor's inability to tolerate extreme ugliness may seem an insignificant human inadequacy, and yet it is the key to everything that follows. It is not so surprising that he made a hideous creature he could not control, as it is that he should immediately disown it because it was loathsome to look at. Some people believe that Victor turned away from his creation because he was stunned by the enormity of his transgression. I prefer to believe that he was disgusted by the result of his inadequate workmanship.

What we must remember is that Victor is seventeen when he enters Ingolstadt University. He is nineteen (i.e., the same age as the pregnant Mary Shelley at the time she wrote the story) when he discovers 'the cause of generation of life' and starts work on what he himself describes as the 'new species' that will bless him as its creator. The actual making of the monster took about eighteen months, and so he is about 21 years old on the 'dreary night of November, that [he] beholds the accomplishment of his toils'. By the standards of today, Victor may seem somewhat young to have been assuming the responsibility for making 'new species', but from Mary Shelley's perspective he would have seemed wholly adult, a mature man.

The professor whose ideas about chemistry fired Victor's imagination, announced in a lecture:

The ancient teachers of this science promised impossibilities and performed nothing. The modern masters promise very little; they know that metals cannot be transmuted, and that the elixir of life is a chimera. But these philosophers, whose hands seem only made to dabble in dirt, and their eyes to pore over the microscope or crucible, have indeed performed miracles. They penetrate into the recesses of nature, and show how she works in her hiding-places. They ascend into the heavens: they have discovered how the blood circulates, and the nature of the air we breathe. They have acquired new and almost unlimited powers; they can command the thunders of heaven, mimic the earthquake, and even mock the invisible world with its own shadows.

No greater incentive was needed to fire the imagination of a young man. Consequences must take second place in the mind of the experimenter. They are too distant to be extrapolated and taken into account, and how otherwise should science progress? In that sense nothing has changed, neither in science fiction nor, dare I say it, in science.

Every reader of science fiction knows that respect, appreciation and due acknowledgement are the basic requirements of man/machine interaction, whether the machine is made of metal, plastic or, like androids, of proto-human parts. Myriad stories are based on the contravention of these essential tenets, just as detective fiction is based on the contravention of law. Without things going wrong, without travesty of an implicit contract, there would be no story. Of the prevailing preoccupations in science fiction, it is ethics or a sense of responsibility between the maker and his creations that stand out as the principal hurdle. The problems that beset man's relationship with his creations are increasingly recognized as a subject of central importance. There is no surer sign of this trend than the number of books about Mary Shelley published in the past fifteen years.

The tragic story of Victor Frankenstein's nameless creation, *who for better or worse has become known by the name of his maker*,[2] touches on several topical preoccupations. These involve monsters and the travesty of what we assume to be natural laws; our attitude to automata and robots; and, finally, what it means to create life artificially.

THE MONSTER

Only a human being or a humanoid can be a true monster. No monstrous cupboard, chair, plant or teapot could engender real fear, horror and fascination all at once. The essential condition for a monster is that the human characteristics it possesses must not be changed too far. When departure from the norm is complete, as in a caricature that has forfeited recognizability, the result will evoke fear and disgust. Transforming a person into a monster is achieved by the exaggeration of one or two features. A line-drawing of a person's face is compared to an ideal face that represents the norm. Deviations from the norm are then exaggerated. With a slight degree of change, the drawing becomes a caricature. As the exaggeration proceeds the likeness is lost, and the result becomes a hideous travesty of the, still recognizable, individual. This result is unpleasant, but not frightening. It is, after all, only a two-dimensional image, a drawing, and it could never be as horrific as is 'Frankenstein' himself. The difference between a computer image and 'Frankenstein', as described by Mary Shelley, is that the first is a mechanical extrapolation from the original and the second a fantasy painted in our imagination with whatever fertile material has already been accumulated in the mind. There is nothing more powerful and, in computerspeak, more configurable. The only work of art that resembles Mary Shelley's monster in spirit and form is Dali's *Premonition of Civil War* of 1936.

The monster is able to tap emotions of fear, disgust or alienation primarily through its subversion, or inversion, of expectations. We react violently when what appears natural proves not to be, and to some extent vice versa. Subverted certainty is a cue for fear. Twenty years ago, at the Tokyo Institute of Technology, Professor Masahiro Mori made a study of the response of human beings to artificial dummies and machines. He pointed out that there is a considerable degree of unpleasantness in shaking a normal-looking hand but feeling instead the squeeze of foam rubber or wax. He made a graph of unpleasant feelings provoked by encounters with the unexpected. At the positive extreme is total familiarity, and at the other extreme is strangeness. The example he gives of 100 per cent familiarity is a normal, healthy human. The same normal healthy human in a condition of total stillness is already at the beginning of what Mori calls the 'uncanny valley', the valley in which what we know as the norm begins to be subtly subverted, and where fear increases as we sink lower. At the entrance to the uncanny valley we find the Bunraku Puppet (a near life-size puppet manipulated on the stage by unseen operators).

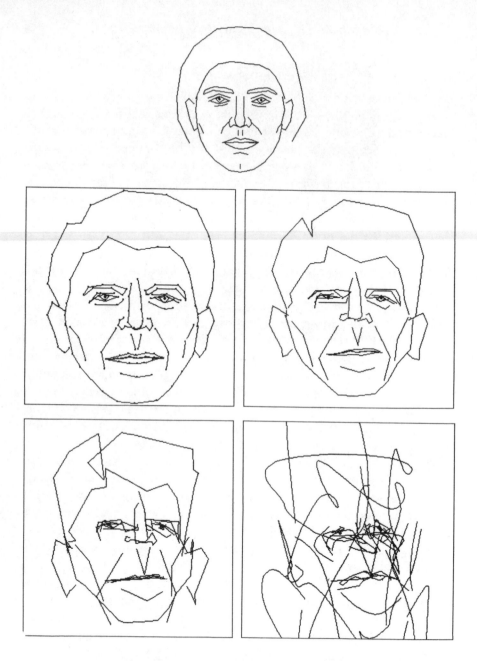

Computer graphics: Ronald Reagan treated by 'FACEBENDER';
from *Scientific American*, October 1986.

*In 1986 Susan E. Brennan developed a caricature program, 'FACEBENDER', as part of
her master's thesis at MIT. Ronald Reagan's face is first of all compared with
a standard and androgynous face and then presented in four stages until
it becomes unrecognizable.*

Salvador Dalí, *Soft Construction with Boiled Beans (Premonition of the Civil War)*,
c. 1936, oil on canvas. Philadelphia Museum of Art
(Louise & Walter Arensberg collection).

An artificial electric hand that looks like a real hand is halfway down. At the utmost depth of the valley is a total contravention of normality – a moving, dead man. The effect of the 'moving, dead man' and 'Franken-stein' seem to me to belong to the same category. The difference is that 'Frankenstein' appears to arouse not only fear but violence.

In Shelley's novel few people encounter 'Frankenstein' face to face. The first is an old man, sitting in a hut preparing his breakfast. On seeing the monster he gives a loud shriek and flees. As 'Frankenstein' is seen walking into a cottage, children scream and a woman faints. When 'Frankenstein' encounters Victor's brother, William, whom he wants to befriend, the child fearfully calls 'Frankenstein' a 'hideous monster, ugly wretch', afraid that he will be eaten. Victor himself describes 'Frankenstein' as a horrid apparition, gigantic monster, and calls him variously 'fiend', 'demon' and 'devil'. While hiding for months in a timber hovel outside a village, 'Frankenstein' develops a longing for the friendship and pro-tection of a family that lives in a neighbouring cottage. Yet, it is not difficult to imagine the reactions of Felix, Safie and Agatha, the three young people whose protection he seeks. 'Who can describe their horror and consternation on beholding me?' confesses 'Frankenstein' subse-quently. We learn that Agatha faints and Safie rushes out of the cottage,

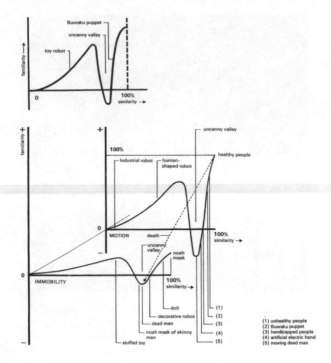

Masahiro Mori's graph displaying the 'uncanny valley'.
This represents a whole range of feelings of strangeness
when our expectations are subverted.

while Felix, 'Frankenstein' relates, 'with supernatural force tore me from his father, to whose knees I clung: in a transport of fury, he dashed me to the ground and struck me violently with a stick'.

We are given a very precise description of 'Frankenstein'. Apart from having a powerful and gigantic frame – he is eight feet tall no less – that could move at superhuman speed, he was not remarkable at a distance. It is the monster's face 'of loathsome and appalling hideousness' that was his misfortune. Watery, dull yellow eyes, wrinkled yellow skin scarcely covering the muscles and arteries beneath, straight black lips, all this combined with beautiful lustrous black hair and pearly white teeth. This is no monster from films by James Whale as played by Boris Karloff. Mary Shelley's description is far more extreme. Her monster's appearance combined with a 'heart fashioned to be susceptible of love and sympathy' is an equation for tragedy.

Denied a mate, 'Frankenstein' was right to have imagined that he might find human companionship among children. Children like to be

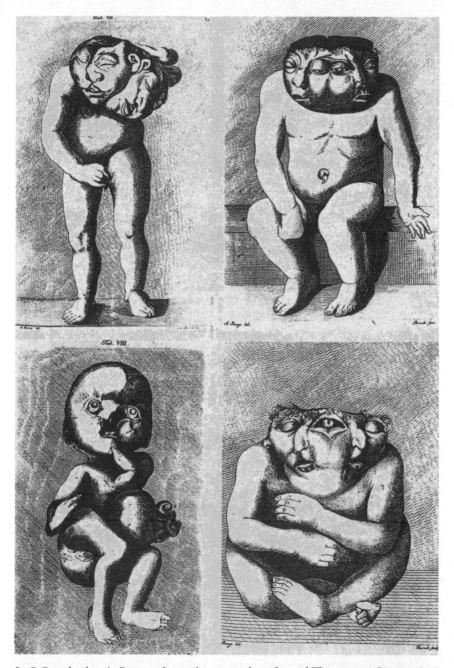

L. C. Berndt after A. Range, plates of monsters from Samuel Thomas von Sömmerring's
Abbildungen und Beschreibungen einiger Missgeburten . . ., Mainz, 1791.

A giant and a dwarf, from Johann Kaspar Lavater's
Essays on Physiognomy (London, *c.* 1775–78).

frightened, although, in some respects, they do not frighten so easily as do
adults. Although observation of young babies leads us to believe that a
pretty face elicits a smile more readily than an ugly one, this predis-
position changes in the course of childhood. A contemporary youngster,
brought up on a diet of science fiction and horror comics, might be proud
to befriend something as ugly and as large as 'Frankenstein'. On
confronting real-life travesties of normality, adults may experience
curiosity, fascination and, later, unease. Horror is seldom felt, if only
because the giants, dwarfs and midgets that one could have met at the
turn of the century, were seen at fairs and in exhibitions, rather than in
the forest at night. They were presented for entertainment and edifica-
tion: the greater the departure from the norm, the greater the entrance
charge to see them. The term 'monster' was gradually replaced by 'freak',
and in turn by 'prodigy'. With a few exceptions, freak-shows came to an
end during the 1930s. Mary Shelley's monster belongs to a period when
the world of popular amusement thrived on departures from the norm
that were not only more common, but also more cruelly exploited.

    At the beginning of this century the Barnum and Bailey circus travelled
the world with the 'Greatest Show on Earth', which consisted of a large
exhibition of 'Human Phenomena' and 'Nature's Bizarre Creations'.

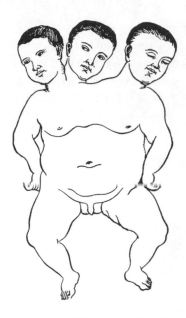

A three-headed monster, based on
a drawing by Luigi Galvani.

Joseph Clark, from Henry Morley's
Memoirs of Bartholmew Fair
(London, 1859).

*The late 17th-century double-jointed
posture master, Joseph Clark, who
imitated many kinds of deformity and was
so accomplished in this deceit that
doctors pronounced him incurable.*

Among the exhibits were a girl with the skin of a leopard, Siamese twins, bearded ladies (advertised as the consequences of unhappy love), giants and dwarfs, a man covered in hair top to toe, a three-legged man, a gorilla woman, and the only real and beautiful half-lady in the world, Violetta, celebrated in poems and songs, who was poised on a circular stand. These were today's disabled, victims of aberrant nature, with occasional help from unscrupulous showmen. The last of these entertainments was closed as recently as 1984, after public outcry against a New York freak-show manager who was exhibiting 'Otis the Frogman'.

Human aberrations ceased to be exhibits because it was deemed to be amoral and inhumane. The practice of creating monsters moved elsewhere and the word 'monster' has fallen out of use, perhaps so that experiments may continue unimpeded.

ONE KIND OF NEW LIFE

Genetic engineering is no longer new although it is always news. While fiction writers have toyed with the idea for decades, in the real world we have had transgenic animals for ten years. New animals have become an industry, making products that can be patented. A professor of law[3] called 'creating life in the laboratory . . . just scare words'. A journalist called it 'A Molecular Auschwitz'.[4]

Andrzej Czeczot, *High Yield Cow*, a drawing
from his book *Gumno* (Warsaw, 1979).

Three incidents early in 1994 demonstrate surrealist aspects of making new life that are worthy of Mary Shelley's fiction.

1. A new class of genes ('that control a master switch in DNA molecules that tells cells whether they are to become skin, bone or muscle') have been given the name Hedgehogs, after the computer game character Sonic the Hedgehog.[5]

2. Early in February 1994, the USA and Britain 'withdrew applications for patents on thousands of fragments of human DNA' after two years of protests from researchers working on the Human Genome Project, who objected to patenting anything human. Until the application was withdrawn, few were aware that it had been made in the first place.[6]

3. Under the heading 'Frankenchips', it was mentioned in *Time* magazine that it is now possible to grow individual nerve cells from rats onto computer chips that will lead to the development of biochips.[7]

We know that everything *can* be altered by science, and either has been

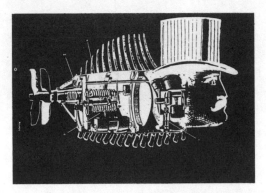

Jan Lenica, design for a poster for a Polish showing
of Karel Zeman's 1958 film *Diabolical Invention*.

or is being altered by science. This provokes many different reactions. As
Igor Aleksander said, how you approach the problem of artificial
intelligence, or neural networks, or consciousness in the computer, is and
will be a question of belief. While the ethical debate goes on, biotechnology, whose cloning techniques date back to 1967, provides a general
source of anxiety. We have seen photographs of new pigs with wrinkled
skin and sheep-goats. We have also seen collages of fish with the bodies of
chickens, giant fish spilling out of lakes, and new hybrids that are half
tomato and half cat. It does not matter that these are just pictures, that
they may not have been made yet, because many believe that they will be
made. To the scientists this may be the fantasy of anxiety. Even so, they
know that they cannot predict whether transgenic crops will not become

An engraving of the fabulous horse
of Civray, Vienne, France.

so liberated as to run wild. They cannot predict that genes that escape into the environment will not, by some chance, promote the vigorous development of weeds.

As Victor's professor said, scientists 'penetrate into the recesses of nature, and show how she works in her hiding-places . . .'. In Victor's wake we continue the experiment.

ANOTHER KIND OF NEW LIFE

During the 1960s, when machines were still supposed to be innocent of education, of responsibilities, and of feelings, Andy Warhol said that he would rather be a machine. 'Wouldn't you?' he asked. He thought that it would be easier to face the world as a piece of metal. Pushing this notion further, he had a robot made in his likeness and used to sent it to dinner parties which he did not feel like attending himself. He mused about how much better it would be if everyone were alike, and generally tried to invent new ways to abdicate the responsibility of being human. Behind the banality of his utterances were some inspired truths that would have been dismissed out of hand had they been voiced by anyone else. By making himself marginal, Warhol was free to express new ideas. We know from his diaries that he befriended television sets and married his tape recorder. He also said: 'If I had a good computer I could catch up with my thoughts over the weekend if I ever got behind myself. A computer would be a very qualified boss.[8] Andy Warhol loved plastic, any kind of artificial material, everything hygienically man-made that would not burden him with sentimental or emotional involvement. He died before neural networks came on the scene and before machines were thought of as a form of life.

While genetic engineering deals with the alteration of existing material, artificial life is the creation of autonomous evolving systems. In the past, machines and living things were totally separate but this is no longer the case. Artificial life crosses the boundaries of organisms with their flesh and blood, with their proteins, enzymes and strands of DNA. Life in its man-made variety exists in the computer, in neural networks, in cyberspace and in various combinations. Nobody can be sure that approximations and incomplete experiments should be elevated to the status of 'life' as it is known. Is it just a matter of how we use words? In 1950 A.M. Turing observed that as language changes, our concepts change with it. In his famous article 'Computing Machinery and Intelligence',[9] Turing posed a question and provided an answer. 'Can machines think?' he asked:

I believe [this question] to be too meaningless to deserve discussion. Nevertheless I believe that at the end of the century the use of words and general educated opinion will have altered so much that one will be able to speak of machines thinking without expecting to be contradicted. I believe further that no useful purpose is served by concealing these beliefs.[10]

One of Turing's examples of a thinking machine was a chess-playing computer, a learning machine that improves its game. He could not have imagined that, thanks to new computer speeds, today's chess programs have a wide enough range of possibilities to respond to situations for learning itself to be no longer at a premium. As for thinking, during the past 50 years two other terms have come to the fore: 'artificial life' and 'consciousness'.

In discussions of technological progress, anthropomorphism is far more useful than one might at first imagine. Without Mary Shelley's emotive language, without her monster's humanity, his tragedy would elude us. If 'Frankenstein' had been a whistling wheelbarrow clamouring for its maker's attention, Victor's dismissive attitude towards it would have been pardonable. The fact that the monster's language was as elegant as Victor's, that he was acquainted with Milton's *Paradise Lost*, Plutarch's *Lives* and Goethe's *Sorrows of Werther*, sets him apart from any other human-made creations. He was one of us.

Using terminology applicable to humans in discussing machines may engender an attitude of unnecessary identification. And yet, how otherwise should we deal with words like 'thinking' or 'consciousness'. These words must be tested against experience, and whose if not ours? Of course, there are bound to be misunderstandings. Norbet Wiener reminds us of how emotive the problem of language can be. Two hundred years ago, anyone claiming that machines might one day reproduce themselves would have been vulnerable to the wrath of the Inquisition.

The new manifestations of life are tenuous and limited, hardly deserving the name of 'life' and yet some people, like Chris Langton of the Santa Fe Institute, New Mexico, think that they represent a significant beginning. *Life Game* devised by the mathematician John Conway in the early 1960s, is a prototype of 'life' from which many physicists, mathematicians and engineers have made variants. They all spring from the basic deterministic cellular automaton conceived by John von Neumann in 1940: a logical, self-operating, self-replicating machine. It is a machine, as Norbert Wiener explained, that generates a message that generates another machine.[11] In its simple version, *Life Game* can be played with counters on a checkerboard that might easily extend into

several rooms. It is not really a game, because once set up there is little
further to do. Players make the initial step of introducing a population of
counters or cells, setting up a set of rules or a program. They then either
watch the computer screen, or mechanically assist in Life's realization by
moving the counters by hand. The outcome is determined by a set of rules
applied to an initial configuration of counters, which is variable. In the
original game the rules specify: (1) a counter with two or three
neighbours survives; (2) a counter crowded by more than three neighbours dies; (3) a counter with only one or no neighbours dies of

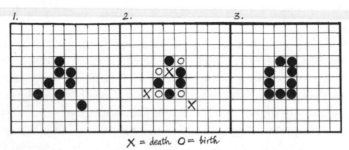

X = death O = birth

John Conway's 1960s *Life Game*; the ● = 'living' pieces.

loneliness; (4) an empty square with 3 neighbouring counters gives birth
to a counter. As populations of cells appear and disappear, the evolving
configurations of counters range from simple figures to vast and
enormously complex structures, which demand the capacity of a powerful computer to sustain their growth. Conway thought of *Life Game* as a
self-reproducing animal, a weak form of living. Others, like Ed Fredkin,
believed that cellular automata is what the world is made of, and not only
that digital codes can mimic life, but that if a computer cannot do it,
nature cannot either.

Unlike organisms, artificial life can function almost anywhere. Once
the level of complexity increases, self-reproduction with more elaborate
offspring can begin. It is these artificial organisms that are seen as
potential inhabitants of those planets that for us are inhabitable.

Chris Langton, a leading researcher into the creation of artificial
systems, believes that games like the *Life Game* can develop behaviour
that was not originally anticipated in the program. Two separate sets of
elements with two different programs can enter into an unpredictable
state of collaboration. Such unexpected events add to the excitement of
studying artificial life with cellular automata. Langton believes that in

some sense the program is a manifestation of life: he has spoken of his reluctance to turn off the computer when running a program of self-replicating loops, and of the sensation of another presence in the room; he is not the only one to regard artificial life in these terms. The field is still both so new and so malleable that it can be looked at from widely divergent points of view. As Igor Aleksander says, 'it is a matter of belief'. For him, man-made systems can be remade. His own neural network MAGNUS (Multiple-Automaton General Neural Unit System), highly sophisticated though it is, is still just a program. It only needs five wires for it to be downloaded into another computer. Nothing will happen if it is switched off. It is the creations of spontaneous evolution, us human beings, that need protection, says Aleksander. With a computer program, it is the programmer who performs the work of evolution.

MAGNUS is a box with mental images. MAGNUS 'lives' in a virtual environment that simulates the real world as closely as possible. The environment exerts its own demands, and this is what provides stimulus, or motivation, without which there would be no activity. Within it, MAGNUS memorizes, assembles, recalls and manipulates images and information. Its response is a subjective representation of inputs from the simulated world. In due course MAGNUS will enable a robot to look around a real environment, to memorize it and to make use of the accumulated knowledge.

There are five attributes that Aleksander puts forward as necessary for consciousness in a neural net: learning, language, planning, attention and inner perception. Intuitive interpretation of experience has not entered his equation yet, because nobody knows how to calculate, let alone define, intuition. Is it possible to have intuition without a body?

Gerald Edelman has developed the idea from a different direction by first giving his machine a body. He too talks about 'life', but uses inverted commas and distinguishes 'life' from consciousness. Edelman's concept of mind/brain is that the brain is a system that adapts to the body's activities, editing and reinforcing good results (physical or emotional) by creating stronger relevant neural connections. Thus the relevant synapses are strengthened, and an individual goal that is reached once can be achieved more easily the following time.

His robot, NOMAD (Neurally Organized Multiply Adaptive Device), 'lives' at the Neurosciences Institute in La Jolla, California, and is, according to Edelman, 'the first nonliving thing capable of "learning" in the biological sense of the word'. NOMAD's brain lives in another room, and communication takes place by television and radio. It sits on a

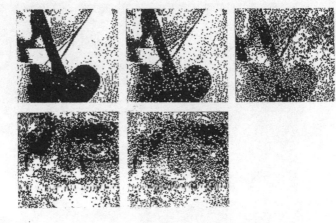

Computer printout of mental images of a neural network, or, what MAGNUS (Multiple-Automaton General Neural Unit System) sees. Dept. of Electrical & Electronic Engineering, Imperial College, London.

MAGNUS is a complex program, a neural net that is capable of memorizing and recalling an image. It has a movable window through which it can explore a picture — in this instance that of Einstein's face. The operator gives an identification to some features of the picture with letters: E for the eye and P for the pipe. Once the picture is removed, MAGNUS's 'mental state' is tested. First of all the image reproduced is just 'noise', but when the operator provides MAGNUS with the letter E, the 'mental state' recalls the eye in three stages. (No pictures are stored in this system: each black dot is the firing of one of 16,384 neurons.)

When MAGNUS is presented with the letter P, it not only finds the pipe, but recalls the trajectory of the earlier exploration, thus showing that it 'knows' the relative positions of the eye and the pipe.

When MAGNUS is requested to produce an image corresponding to an unfamiliar letter (here an 'S'), the result is a visual jumble.

The NOMAD (Neurally Organized Multiply Adaptive Device)
at the Neuro-Sciences Institute, La Jolla, California.

platform with wheels and can propel itself around its environment.
Instead of a program, the hardware is endowed with a preference, or
motivation, or what Edelman calls value. The objective of NOMAD's
predecessor, DARWIN III, was a scale of values related to light and
lighted objects. NOMAD, however, seeks electrical stimulation, and its
'snout' picks out magnetic blocks of different colours and sizes. Edelman
believes that on the basis of perceptual machines like NOMAD, there is no
reason why one of their kind should not develop into a conscious
artefact. He concedes that this may take some time.

'Why does science take so long?' Andy Warhol asked Edelman at a
party. When Edelman explained how exact everything in science had to
be, Warhol sympathized. 'Isn't that terrible?' he said. Warhol was in a
hurry to join the ranks of machine artefacts. In this, he would still be an
exception today.

While NOMAD appears to behave spontaneously, and is able to adjust
to changes in its environment, it is still at the stage of a primary school.
Which is maybe just as well. The uniqueness of human identity is at risk.
Any progress towards the autonomy of machines makes sensitive
demands on our tolerance. Can we get used to such an idea? Marvin
Minsky has talked, off and on for years, about the possibility of
downloading the contents of our brains into a machine. Who will this
machine belong to?

ONE MORE KIND OF NEW LIFE — A COLLAGE OF EXISTING PARTS

While thinking machines are still being educated and live in the safe precincts of universities, everyday life has its own significant stake in the future and in the creation of new life. The idea of animating the dead has not been abandoned. When Victor made his monster, the raw materials were provided by corpses. He had no thoughts of bringing the dead back to life, only that of making something new. Today we have an unprecedented choice of making something new, or nearly new, or a new version of something old. The difference between something that exists in the present time and something that exists as a record of history is becoming eroded. The means of erosion include video, photographs and sound recordings. You can record your own duet with Caruso, you can partner Nureyev on the stage and climb Everest with Hillary and Tensing. If it is becoming difficult to separate history from a theme park, it is because anything that can be digitized can be re-rendered in any size and in any version. Everyone can add to this inexhaustible evolution of mutations and hybrids — a new sort of zoo. The theme park could become a generating ground for new inventions because this is where media technology will be concentrated. Eventually, it will be the depository of its own history — a digital life in epitome.

Whether or not the creation of new life in any form is a desirable thing is unanswerable. When it comes to artificial life, there is one rather special advantage. There can be no ownership or copyright of a group of digital details any more than there can be ownership of a cluster of molecules. In this sense, various versions of artificial life are the only egalitarian products ever invented.

Morphed photographs, combinations of cartoon animation with human actors, computer animation using real people, are parts of both the art world and the entertainment industry. The two overlap. In the early experimental stages of these techniques, it is the artists that invent ways of putting images together. By the time the technology has become sophisticated enough, commercial interests take over.

The February 1994 issue of *Scientific American* carried a feature on digital forgery. The cover showed a reversed image of Marilyn Monroe as she appeared in 1955 in *The Seven Year Itch*, but here holding on to the arm of Abraham Lincoln whose formal portrait was taken 92 years before. Marilyn Monroe, all pale with skirt flying, knickers exposed and a huge grin, is contrasted with Lincoln, upright and dressed in black,

A hybrid, drawing of 1967 by Roland Topor from his
Stories and Drawings, London, 1968.

Still from Peter Gabriel's 1993 video, *Steam*, directed by Stephen R. Johnson,
reproduced in *Vida Artificial/Artificial Life*, Barcelona, 1993.

looking impatiently up at the ceiling as if he had had enough of all her frivolous nonsense.

In the future, the 92 years that separate the two protagonists of the cover picture will shrink to hours and minutes. Gradually they will become contemporaries. Lincoln might be thought of as the American president who was her lover and the picture will acquire a new veracity.

We can animate Marilyn Monroe on the screen and associate her with whoever we wish, regardless of fact. In due course, her essential features may find their way into a *Life Game*. It might be her smile, her voice, her gesture. In this new form, she would become an aggregate of zeros and ones, a bit of digital code in a stocklist of artificial life available to anyone with a computer. At this point 'consciousness' and 'life' will once more be redefined, and this redefining will happen increasingly often. Our twentieth-century reality of Monroe will gradually disappear. The one she herself was involved in will be the first to go. Future generations will know her from films that she never made, that will have been spliced together, enhanced with new songs, new leading men and new stories. She will disappear into the collective consciousness as an icon. Mythology will acquire new currency.

This unexpected possibility of immortality in a computer could fill a nineteen-year-old student with the same wonder, passion and excitement that Victor Frankenstein felt when his professor talked about the scientists' 'almost unlimited powers, ability to command the thunders of heaven, mimic the earthquake, and even mock the invisible world with its own shadows.' These are fiery, irresistible, prophetic words, even today.

In September 1949 John von Neumann, the inventor of the atom bomb, wrote to Norbert Wiener, who invented cybernetics: 'reproductive potentialities of the machines of the future' should be kept out of the press.[12] It is now far too late to keep artificial life out of anything, or to put a brake on the thousands of experiments in progress. Even so, students playing with anything remotely resembling life, whether cells or silicon, should be advised to heed Gore Vidal's caution: 'there is need for empathy with others not like yourself'.[13]

8

Narrating the Monster:
From Mary Shelley to Bram Stoker

ROBERT OLORENSHAW

There are evident reasons for bringing together *Frankenstein* and *Dracula*. First, Polidori's *The Vampyre* (a source of inspiration for Bram Stoker) and *Frankenstein* were conceived that same wet night in June 1816 at the Villa Diodati when Lord Byron suggested to his guests that they each write a horror tale. Second, cinematographic interpretations of both works have largely supplanted in the popular imagination the original works of fiction. 'Frankenstein' has become Boris Karloff and his parodies, just as Dracula seems to have his rightful home more in the Hammer studios than in nineteenth-century fiction.

The most cursory examination of the novels, though, brings out differences that are equally evident. In Mary Shelley's novel the monster is an ideal human being longing for the integration and recognition that are denied him on account of his appearance. Count Dracula looks like a human being, but is in reality a monster wishing to integrate society only to feed on its members. In *Frankenstein* there is no possibility of contagion between the monster and his victims, whereas in *Dracula* a victim can become a monster. Dracula is not only a name with an ancient history, the Count's sense of identity is inseparable from the historic actions he had accomplished against the infidels in 'Turkeyland'. Frankenstein's nameless monster can only gain a vicarious access to society and history.

FRANKENSTEIN: SCIENCE ENTERS LITERATURE

Moving from *Frankenstein* to *Dracula* is also to travel from the Romantic milieu of the early nineteenth century to late Victorian England, yet, for many, *Frankenstein* appears to be the more modern work since it firmly places science, our science, or rather our images of it, at the centre of its concerns. This would imply that the novel presents important differences with the genre, the Gothic tale, with which it is usually identified. What are these differences? In his *Introduction à la littérature fantastique*, Tzvetan Todorov maintains that a defining feature of this kind of literature is 'the hesitation experienced by a being who only knows natural laws faced with an event that is in appearance supernatural'.[1] However, not only is the creature in *Frankenstein*, even when first observed by Walton, never presented to the reader as a supernatural being, but also no character in *Frankenstein* 'hesitates' in Todorov's sense, that is, no-one grapples with the question as to what order of reality, sublunar or supernatural, he or she is confronted with. In other words there is no *enigma* in Mary Shelley's novel around which the tale's chain of events is organized. Roland Barthes's hermeneutic code, whose function is to 'articulate a question, its answer and the various accidents that can prepare the question or delay its answer',[2] and which is singularly strong in the Gothic tale, is singularly weak in *Frankenstein*. Significantly in this respect, the creature is the impossible presence and necessary absence in the novel's trials and judicial enquiries, events whose successful resolution is central to so many works of fiction in which the hermeneutic code is dominant.

Thus the question of the nature and identity not only of the monster but also of the work of fiction itself is problematical. This aspect of *Frankenstein* did not escape Percy Shelley. In the 1818 preface he wrote:

The event on which this fiction is founded, has been supposed by Dr Darwin, and some of the physiological writers of Germany as not of impossible occurrence. I shall not be supposed as according the remotest degree of serious faith to such an imagination; yet [. . .] I have not considered myself as merely weaving a series of supernatural terrors. The event on which the interest of the story depends is exempt from the disadvantages of a mere tale of spectres or enchantment.[3]

By explicitly acknowledging the break with the tradition of the Gothic tale, with its enigmas and supernatural presences, and by grounding *Frankenstein* in the influence of physiology, Percy (who provided the 'author's preface') is stating that a new genre has emerged, but one that *has no name*. This absence of a name will only cease many years after Mary Shelley's death, with the recognition of science fiction as a distinct genre.

The break with the Gothic tale is also apparent in the treatment of key images, especially those associated with thunderstorms. Thunder and lightning, as markers of significant transitions and plot developments, had by Mary Shelley's time become, and were to remain, frequent features of the Gothic novel and its descendants. A typical use of the thunderstorm in tales of this sort can be found in the opening pages of *Dracula*, when Jonathan Harker and his travelling companions see before them the Borgo Pass: 'There were dark, rolling clouds overhead, and in the air the heavy, oppressive sense of thunder. It seemed as though the mountain range had separated two atmospheres, and that now we had got into the thunderous one. I was now myself looking for the conveyance which was to take me to the Count.'⁴

In *Dracula* the thunderstorm is part of the décor but no more than that, symbolically representing a division between two worlds and prefiguring Jonathan Harker's 'hesitation' as 'experienced by a being who only knows natural laws faced with an event that is in appearance supernatural'. The thunderstorm in Dracula, then does not determine plot or character, nor does it, as far as I am aware, the plot or character of any gothic tale. This is not the case in *Frankenstein*. When a boy of fifteen, Victor witnesses

a most terrible and violent thunderstorm. It advanced from behind the mountains of Jura, and the thunder burst at once with frightful loudness from various
quarters of the heavens. I remained, while the storm lasted, watching its progress
with curiosity and delight. As I stood at the door, on a sudden I beheld a stream of
fire issue from an old and beautiful oak [. . .] and so soon as the dazzling light
vanished, the oak had disappeared, and nothing remained but a blasted stump.
When we visited it the next morning, we found the tree shattered in a singular
manner. It was not splintered by the shock, but entirely reduced to thin ribbons
of wood. I never beheld anything so utterly destroyed. [. . .] On this occasion a
man of great research in natural philosophy was with us, and, excited by this
catastrophe, he entered on the explanation of a theory which he had formed on
the subject of electricity and galvanism, which was at once new and astonishing
to me. All that he said threw greatly into the shade Cornelius Agrippa, Albertus
Magnus and Paracelsus, the lords of my imagination.⁵

Seen metaphorically, lightning here fulfils its classic role as marker of transitions. In *Frankenstein* these transitions take the form of trans-gressions. Lightning is the point of junction of the powerfully charged antonyms of ignorance and knowledge, creation and destruction, heaven and earth, being and non-being. Lightning, though, also acts as a narrative trigger, setting into motion a series of events that will eventually lead to the discovery of the principle of life. While at Ingolstadt, Victor Frankenstein exhausts himself

examining and analysing all the minutiae of causation, as exemplified in the
change from life to death, and death to life, until from the midst of this darkness a
sudden light broke in upon me – a light so brilliant and wondrous, yet so simple,
that I became dizzy with the immensity of the prospect which it illustrated. After
days and nights of incredible labour and fatigue, I succeeded in discovering the
cause of generation and life; nay, more, I became myself capable of bestowing
animation upon lifeless matter.⁶

The lightning that enters Frankenstein's soul (later he will say to Walton 'I am a blasted tree, the bolt has entered my soul') is a lightning that has become interiorized and thus *invisible*, as is the animating spark that gives life to the monster.

Mary Shelley, then, took an image that had already become common currency, if not a cliché, and revitalized it, first, by extracting from it its non-literary 'truth' as guaranteed by the science of her age and, second, by placing that truth at the heart of her narrative. But this process of 'deliterization' raises the same question as the issue of genre, since it is inseparable from the discovery of something – the principle of life – which will not (and cannot) be represented or described in the novel.

It would be useful here to ask why science made such a sudden entry into literature in the Romantic period, given that since the Renaissance, and especially during the Enlightenment, the prestige and influence of scientific endeavours in every domain had continued to grow. The answer is that science, or rather its objects, including the objects of the life sciences, shifted radically towards the end of the eighteenth century. The consequences of these changes can be read in *Frankenstein*.

Scientists redefined the criteria of what constituted an adequate analysis of the organism, displacing the physiology established by the British empiricists, and especially by John Locke, in the seventeenth century. In his essay 'Anatomie', written in 1668, Locke maintained that the body is an infinitely visible and hence describable entity ('Though we cut into these organs inside, we see but the outside of things and make a new superficies for ourselves to stare at'), but that it will ever refuse to disclose to the analyst 'the tools and contrivances by which nature works'. It is for this reason that Locke argued against 'searching into the bowels of dead and living creatures' since 'All that Anatomie can doe is only to show us the gross and sensible parts of the body [. . .]. Soe that he that knows but the natural shape, size, situation and colour of any part is as well learned [. . .] as he that can describe all the minute and sensible parts of it.'[7] There is, therefore, no need to disect and analyse organs *ad infinitum* (Locke even considered 'the assistance of glasses' to be unnecessary), since what is accessible to knowledge and what can be named coincided with what can be perceived by the naked eye.

Identical presuppositions dominated, or rather constituted, natural history for much of the eighteenth century. According to Michel Foucault,

Natural history is the space opened up in representation by an analysis which anticipates the possibility of naming [. . .] it is the possibility of seeing what will be able to be said. Its object is given by surfaces and lines and not by functions or invisible tissues. Plants and animals are viewed less in terms of their organic unity than in terms of the visible cross-sections of their organs.[8]

Towards the end of the eighteenth century new taxonomic principles were forged that were determined not so much by visible surfaces but by the inner dynamics of living beings. 'Beginning with Cuvier, the non-perceptible elements of life forms presuppose the exterior possibility of a classification [. . .]. Arising from the depths of life and from what is most remote from the eye (there emerged) the possibility of classifying.'[9] A zoologist like Cuvier takes as his object of study not visible elements but functions such as reproduction, feeding, respiration and locomotion. The classifications that are thereby established are subordinated to these functions, requiring the effort to search 'into the bowels of dead and living creatures' and to bring to the surface vital elements that had remained hidden from the 'superficial' gaze of scientists of the preceding generation.

It is interesting to note that a similar role was accorded the invisible by the new science of geology. For James Hutton, whose *Theory of the Earth* was published in 1795, a store of extreme heat at the earth's core causes the transformation and elevation of the earth's surface, a surface that only much later is subject to the visible effects of erosion and deposition. It is also significant that geological configurations and life forms are now considered to be the manifestation of immanent forces: divine power is no longer accepted as the prime mover or explanatory principle of the world and its inhabitants.

Frankenstein, too, is a scientist for whom the conquest of knowledge is not so much a question of extension as it is of depth. On hearing Professor Waldman's panegyric on the unlimited powers of the modern scientist ('They penetrate into the recesses of nature, and show how she works in her hiding-places. They have acquired new and almost unlimited powers and can command the thunder or heavens'), the young Victor exclaims, 'I will pioneer a new way, explore unknown powers, and unfold to the world the deepest mysteries of creation'.[10] While on the path to the solution of these mysteries, Frankenstein also dislodges the divinity, but in a far more radical way than Cuvier or Hutton. Frankenstein's materials are the parts of human corpses taken most often from graveyards, that is, stolen from God: 'A churchyard was to me merely the receptacle of bodies deprived of life.'[11] Death and resurrection no longer have as their shared locus the divine mystery, but are subject to the sovereign mind and will of the individual-in-the-world. Frankenstein steals God's lightning: 'Life and death appeared to me ideal bounds, which I should first break through, and pour a torrent of light into our dark world.'[12]

In philosophical terms, we can say that the principle of life, the 'deepest mysteries of creation' are akin to a Kantian Idea, i.e., a 'necessary concept of reason but to which no object might be given within experience'.[13] For Kant, man is a radically finite being and it is this finiteness that determines our knowledge of the world. The figure of the Absolute is relativized and brought down to the level of an Idea of reason whose objective reality must for ever remain indemonstrable. Victor Frankenstein has challenged Kant, has broken through the boundaries of the Idea and has made immanent and manipulable the Absolute itself.

With this eruption of immanent forces and the corresponding eviction of a transcendental divinity, it is not surprising that Romantics like Percy Shelley were not only attentive to scientific advances but also elaborated poetic theories that paralleled developments in the sciences. Mind, Spirit, the Soul are likewise immanent and hidden forces. For the imaginative being, according to Shelley, 'the efficiency, the essence, the vitality of actions derive [their] colour from what is nowise contributed to from any external source',[14] and it is only from within this immanence, through the controlled creation of the poetic work, that knowledge and expression of the universal Spirit may occur.

For Mary Shelley though, as indeed for her mother, creation does not occur *ex nihilo*. In her brief discussion of art in *A Vindication of the Rights of Woman*, Mary Wollstonecraft wrote:

I do not forget the popular opinion that the Grecian statues were not modelled after nature. I mean, not according to the proportions of a particular man; *but that beautiful limbs and features were selected from various bodies to form an harmonious whole* (my emphasis)[. . .]. It was not however the mechanical selection of limbs and features but the ebullition of an heated fancy that burst forth, and the fine senses and enlarged understanding of the artist selected the solid matter, which he drew into this glowing focus [. . .]. For only insipid lifeless beauty is produced by a servile copy of even beautiful nature.[15]

The perfect work of art is the product of the judicious combination of imitation (here based on a selection from various bodies) and subjectivity, the 'heated fancy' of the artist. Victor Frankenstein also selects the finest features for his creature ('His limbs were in proportion, and I had selected his features as beautiful'), but his creature is so hideous that it cannot be *seen*: 'Unable to endure the aspect of the being I had created, I rushed out of the room'.[16] The beauty has been transformed into hideousness because Frankenstein's raw materials have been infused with the principle of life. It is precisely this principle that cannot be represented in art, science or philosophy. The 'unseeability' of the monster is a consequence of the impossibility of representing what he represents, 'the deepest mysteries of creation'. It also signifies, as we shall see, that in an important sense the monster cannot be narrated.

Concerning her own conception of the creative process, Mary Shelley wrote in her introduction to the edition of 1831 of *Frankenstein*: 'Invention, it must be humbly admitted, does not create out of a void, but out of chaos; the materials must in the first place be afforded: it can give form to dark, shapeless substances, but cannot bring into being the substance itself.'[17] There is an undeniable parallel between Mary Shelley's conception of the creative process and this process as carried out by Victor Frankenstein, who, likewise, does not create from out of a void but from out of the 'chaos' of corpses before 'bringing into being the substance itself'. But if there is convergence of theory and practice between Mary Shelley and Frankenstein, we shall see that it is also possible to say that she, in turn, by creating the scientist and the monster, by infusing the spark of life into a novel, let loose a murderous being, *a homicidal text* that kills those nearest to it. To support this claim a closer look at the monster created in the novel is necessary.

A Creature of the Enlightenment: The conditions of creation of the monster are 'post-empiricist', but the creature himself learns, thinks and acts as a pure product of the empiricist, Lockean Enlightenment. The knowledge he possesses originates exclusively from the sense experiences received from the outside world. These experiences teach him to separate the diverse phenomena that impinge on his sensibilities (heat and cold, light and dark, etc.), to speak a language, to learn the difference between what is agreeable and what disagreeable and hence to formulate judgements. The first judgements that the creature pronounces are aesthetic ones: 'I found that the sparrow uttered none but harsh notes, whilst those of the blackbird and thrush were sweet and enticing'.[18] These judgements are also applied to himself, and on exactly the same epistemological basis:

How was I terrified when I viewed myself in a transparent pool! At first I started back, unable to believe that it was indeed I who was reflected in the mirror; and when I became fully convinced that I was in reality the monster that I am, I was filled with the bitterest sensations of despondence and mortification.[19]

The creature, and those he encounters, cannot escape from a purely specular, 'empirical' relationship to his body. As essence, the creature has emerged from unspeakable depths, but as being he is nothing but surface.

Sense experience also determines ethics. The first moral act performed by the creature occurs when, spying the De Laceys from his hideout, he observes they are hungry. Since the creature has himself experienced hunger he can understand the suffering it causes in others and acts accordingly. He resolves to stop stealing food from the De Laceys and to eat only berries, nuts and roots. Similarly, it is because the creature has understood the difference between heat and cold that he replenishes his 'family's' wood-pile each night. Later, he will feel 'the greatest ardour for virtue rise within me, and abhorrence for vice, as far as I understood the signification of those terms, relative as they were, as I applied them, to pleasure and pain alone'.[20]

Here, the creature clearly illustrates Godwinian ideas concerning man's natural goodness. In the *Enquiry Concerning Political Justice*, Mary Shelley's father wrote that 'Mind without benevolence is a barren and cold existence. It is in seeking the good of others, in embracing a great and expansive sphere of action, in forgetting our own individual interests, that we find our true element.'[21] The 'benevolence and generosity' of the De Laceys aroused in the creature an ardent desire 'to become an actor in the busy scene where so many admirable qualities were called forth and displayed'.[22] The fact that the creature's entry onto this busy scene is met with horror and violent rejection encourages us to examine the admirable qualities in question.

The 'conte héroique' of the De Laceys: The sub-narrative concerning the tribulations of the De Laceys forms a classic *conte héroique* – an adventure story, popular in the eighteenth century, whose characters embody heroic ideals (or their opposite) – that is worth summarizing. A Turkish merchant, unjustly condemned to death, is rescued from a Paris gaol by a morally outraged young aristocrat, Felix De Lacey, who falls in love with the merchant's daughter, Safie. Safie, equally enamoured with Felix, wishes to live in 'a country where women were allowed to take a rank in society,'[23] and is thus eager not to assume the traditional role of a Muslim wife. Safie and Felix, with Safie's father, flee to Italy, but when the French authorities learn of Felix's part in the Turk's escape they decide to throw the blind, old De Lacey and his daughter, Agatha, into prison. Felix hastily returns to Paris, where he is forced to share the fate of his father and sister. Five months later, the De Laceys, stripped of their wealth and position are forced into exile. Meanwhile, the Turk, although he owes his life to Felix, is determined that his daughter shall not marry a Christian, especially a destitute one, and he tries to engineer a final separation between Safie and her beloved. The merchant is foiled in his attempts and Safie manages to become reunited with Felix in the cottage where the creature, living in his adjoining hovel, has become acquainted with the family.

So far, this exotic tale displays a text-book morphology, containing such easily discernible functions as Abduction, Flight, Entrapment, Separation and Reconciliation, and where the overcoming of obstacles (another classic function of the folk-tale) is not only an individual achievement but also a victory for the Enlightenment over despotism and the state. As Godwin wrote: 'We should not forget that government is an evil, an usurpation upon the private judgement and individual conscience of mankind; [. . .] it behoves us, as the friends of reason and the human species, to admit as little of it as possible.'[24] Once safely installed in their cottage, free from the tyranny of the state and devoid of fortune and rank, the De Laceys may revert (or progress) to a state of nature and compose the microcosm of an ideal society where harmony and benevolence reign unopposed.

Patriarchal despotism has also been banished from their household but, as with the question of Mary Wollstonecraft's aesthetics, there is simultaneous acceptance and rejection by Mary Shelley of her mother's positions. In her *Vindication* Mary Wollstonecraft, attacking Rousseau for wanting to 'cramp a woman's mind', cites the following passage from *Emile*. (It is, in addition, and of all the lengthy quotations from *Emile*, the only passage that appears in italics in the 1792 edition):

Every daughter ought to be of the same religion as her mother, and every wife to be of the same religion as her husband: for though such religion should be false, that docility which induces the mother and daughter to submit to the order of nature takes away, in the sight of God, the criminality of their error.[25]

Acceptance/rejection is first apparent within the De Lacey *conte héroique* since Safie (the allusion to Rousseau's Sophie is almost certainly intentional) frees herself from paternal despotism precisely *because* she adopts 'the same religion as her mother (and) as her husband'. Second, is not Mary Shelley at the time of writing *Frankenstein* a very young woman who is also expected to adopt and submit to the 'religion' of her mother and of her husband? That she will not can be read in the brutal ending of the De Lacey idyll.

The termination, or rather the complete destruction of the De Lacey sub-plot – the day after the monster's irruption into the cottage Felix exclaims 'The life of my father is in the greatest danger. . . . My wife and sister will never recover from their horror'[26] – is inseparable from a turning-point in the monster's own life, which occurs when the blind De Lacey asks the creature to state his identity. If an adequate answer were to be given to this question ('Great God! Who are you?'), then not only recognition of the creature but also his transition from one order of being to another would be made possible. But, as we know, this is not to be so.

I use the word transition, but transition to what exactly? One critic, Peter Brook, opts for a broadly Lacanian interpretation, maintaining that the creature cannot effect the transition from the 'mirror stage', from a purely specular relationship either with himself or with others, into the symbolic order of language:

The imaginary order is that of the specular, of the mirror stage and is based on deception, on the subject's relation to itself as other. The symbolic order is that of language [. . .] the cultural system into which individual subjects are inserted. In any specular relationship the Monster will always be the 'filthy mass': only in the symbolic order may he realize his desire for recognition.[27]

Peter Brook, quite logically, holds that for the creature 'language [is] the symbolic order that must compensate for Nature'. However, we should remember that in *Frankenstein* we are confronted with a fictional character, a monster eight feet tall composed of *membra disjecta*, not with a typical Lacanian subject! With this distinction in mind we must qualify Brook's analysis and make it clear as to precisely what order of language we are dealing with. The creature cannot cross over from an order determined by the specular to an order determined by language, that is, the creature cannot be recognized, identified or circulate as a proper name in the discourse of the Other because the creature is unnarratable. The monster is a monster not on account of his exclusion from the symbolic order of language *per se* but on account of his inability to enter and be accommodated within the syntagmatic order of narration.

The creature's 'desire to become an actor in the busy scene where so many admirable qualities were called forth and displayed' is none other than the desire to become a character in somebody else's tale. The three works of literature that the creature devours – *Paradise Lost*, Plutarch's *Lives* and *The Sorrows of Werther* – certainly acquaint him with a moral cosmogony, the nature of political action and the lineaments of an *éducation sentimentale*, but more important, the creature learns from these works what it is to be an identifiable and acknowledged actor within a causal narrative chain, and consequently that he is excluded from any such order: 'I was dependent on none, related to none'. The monster wishes to traverse simultaneously the threshold of the De

Lacey's abode and of 'narratability', but since the monster represents the unrepresentable this threshold can never be crossed by him.

The creature's complete isolation is subordinate to his 'unnarratability'. He cannot become a character, 'an actor on the scene' of the *conte héroique* because, once perceived by the characters of such a tale, he tears asunder the genre's rules of verisimilitude. What formalist function could he possibly fulfil in the life stories of Felix and Safie? Of what ideal could he be the vehicle? The creature's function is to be the operator of a narrative anacoluthon, the destroyer of a dual code of verisimilitude and of motivation. By causing him to irrupt into the De Lacey abode Mary Shelley annihilates the ideals of the preceding revolutionary period, of her own mother, father and husband, and, at the same stroke, destroys a species of literature through which those ideals found an expression.

But, it could be argued, we *do* have *Frankenstein*. The monster *is* described and narrated. Nevertheless, the conditions in which this narration occurs strengthen rather than weaken the case for 'unnarratability'. The story of Frankenstein and the monster is told by Walton in letters written to an absent sister while his expedition is in grave danger close to the North Pole. Certainly, Walton is an overreacher whose ambitions parallel those of Victor Frankenstein, but it should also be remembered that Walton's sister cannot receive the tale of Frankenstein and the monster *while it is being written* – indeed, she may never receive it. The eventual 'unreadability', or *invisibility* of the text is thus embedded into the representation of its composition. *Frankenstein* is a novel that puts itself in danger, and only at the end, when Walton abandons his 'mad' expedition and heads southwards, will the 'safety' of the text be ensured.

The murderer: The monster's realization that he will never be able to become integrated into human society, or rather into its narrations, even if the latter contain the most irreproachable and desirable of characters, leads directly to the desire for vengeance. First the monster will reduce the De Lacey's cottage to ashes, symbolically destroying any material trace of their tale. Then he will strangle all his victims. Since the monster declares he has the strength to dismember people with ease, we are entitled to ask why he invariably chooses the first mode of elimination. By strangling his victims, the monster attacks their voice. Incapable of being narrated, he extinguishes the faculty of speech. Incapable of crossing the threshold of the discourse of Others, the monster is condemned to absolute isolation, but he will, from his side of the threshold, be able to wreak his revenge on the very principles that preside over his solitude.

The autobiographical dimension: To say that a character in a novel 'is' its author even if the autobiographical connection is deliberate and evident, implies that there can be an equivalence between two incommensurable entities. The individual inhabits a perpetual present and his life has neither structure nor finality. A fictional character is, on the other hand, from the first sentence in which he appears, the object of a destiny.

At the most it is possible to describe articulations between life and fiction. One such point of contact can be established, as we have seen, between the author's conception of creation and the creative process as enacted by Victor Frankenstein. Now, we know that the monster and his creator are inseparably linked in life and death and that the former follows the latter like his shadow. If, then, there is a point of contact between Mary Shelley and Victor Frankenstein, between author and a Prometheus *plasticator*, we could also expect to find a connection between author and monster.

The most important 'coincidence' uniting Mary Shelley and the monster is to be found in the absence of a proper (*propter*) name. Mary Shelley had no Christian or family name that was her own. She was Mary Wollstone-croft Godwin Shelley, that is to say, her name was composed of the disparate parts of other identities, just as her monster was composed of the disjointed sections of other bodies. The 'nominal' fragmentation of Mary Shelley did not incite her to adopt a pseudonym but to write using her 'own', that is, other people's names. The very fact of becoming a novelist not only entailed self-affirmation but also acquiescence to a particularly onerous parental heritage. As she pointed out in the preface to *Franken-stein*: 'It is not singular that, as the daughter of two persons of distinguished literary celebrity, I should very early in life have thought of writing'.[28] However, it is the affirmation that will prevail over any acquiescence as Mary Shelley simultaneously created a literary genre and two categories of character new to fiction, both of whom possessed a demoniacal will and strength. In a sentence Mary Shelley, in order to infuse a spark of life into her own unnarratable 'dark shapeless substances', created a monstrous text that murdered her mother, her father and her husband. Little wonder that she called *Frankenstein* 'my hideous progeny'.

DRACULA: THE UN-DEAD NOVEL

In Bram Stoker's work science has strictly limited powers in comparison with religion, or rather with religious symbols. In fact, no greater

contrast could be found than that between Victor Frankenstein and
Abraham Van Helsing. One is a man whose scientific knowledge is not
only the most developed of its time but is also put to practical effect,
while the other is 'a philosopher and a metaphysician and one of the most
advanced scientists of his day',[29] but whose 'science' is never put to any
use (we are simply told that Van Helsing had made the study of the brain
his speciality). Indeed, faced with the vampire, Van Helsing openly
acknowledges the shortcomings of science: 'It is the fault of our science
that it wants to explain all; and if it explain not, then it says there is
nothing to explain.'[30]

Vampires, or similar creatures, had haunted European culture for
centuries before making their entry into fiction in the nineteenth century.
For the Enlightenment it was a question of yet another superstition kept
alive by a Church that had recognized the existence of vampires in the
fifteenth century. In his *Dictionnaire philosophique* Voltaire exclaimed:
'What! It is in our eighteenth century that there have been vampires! It is
after the reign of Locke, of Shaftesbury and Diderot that people believe in
vampires.' After stating that vampires had become the talk of the town
earlier in the century, Voltaire concluded that

the result of all this is that a large part of Europe was infested with vampires for
five or six years and now there are no more, that we had *convulsionnaires*
[fanatical Jansenists who fell prey to convulsions] for twenty years and now we
have no more, that we had the possessed for 1,700 years and that there are no
more and that we had Jesuits in Spain, Portugal and France and now there are no
more.[31]

Voltaire rejects, and in accordance with his deist principles, any corporeal manifestation of the divinity. It is the claimed presence of another
being within the human body (possession) that has to be discarded, and
this rejection means that for the following century, and true to the
Enlightenment critique, such possession will become the province of two
distinct regimes, namely psychiatry and fiction, with the latter remaining
the one culturally sanctioned outlet (at least in Britain) in which vampires
could be resurrected and believed in, albeit in a special way. *Dracula*
graphically discloses what such a resurrection entails. We could say that
the novel itself is an Un-Dead work, moving in an intermediate state
between a realist novel that is attentive to the social *hic et nunc* as well as
to aspects of modernity, and the world of ancient superstition and folk
beliefs, pronounced dead, but which contaminates the 'living' characters
of a late Victorian work. Bram Stoker is like Count Dracula, crossing
spatio-temporal boundaries and infecting, 'Transylvanianizing', a realist

genre with dangerous foreign elements that are the 'life-blood' of the fiction but which also have to be fought against and destroyed.

The clearest illustration of what the introduction of these elements entails for the society depicted by *Dracula* can be read in the transformation of Lucy Westerna from coquette to vampire. At the beginning of the novel, the young miss writes to her bosom friend Mina that she is the lucky recipient of three marriage proposals. ('THREE proposals in one day! Isn't it awful! I feel sorry, really and truly sorry for two of the poor fellows!'[32]). Lucy settles for the not very bright, utterly English aristocrat Arthur Holmwood, but what she feels 'really and truly sorry about' is that she cannot get her cake and eat it! ('Why can't they let a girl marry three men or as many as want her and save all this trouble'[33]). Later, after being bled by Dracula, she receives transfusions from all three suitors, and also from Van Helsing himself. The sexual nature of these transfusions is explicit. John Seward records that 'No man knows till he experiences it, what it is to feel his own life-blood drawn away into the veins of the woman he loves'.[34] When Seward remarks to Van Helsing that he had taken far more blood from Arthur Holmwood, the professor retorts 'He is her lover, her fiancé', and he then enjoins Seward not to tell Arthur about the second transfusion: 'It would at once frighten him and enjealous him too.'[35] After the four transfusions have been performed he comments: 'Said he not that the transfusion of his blood [i.e. Arthur's] to her veins had made her truly his bride? [. . .] Then this so sweet maid is a polyandrist and me, with my poor wife dead to me but alive by Church's law, though no wits, all gone – even I who am faithful husband to this now-no wife, am bigamist.'[36]

Dracula, in drinking Lucy's blood, also absorbs the blood of Arthur Holmwood, John Seward, Quincy Adams and Van Helsing, providing them with the opportunity to supplant their predecessor. The Count, as well as allowing Lucy to have all her men (plus an extra) at the same time enables the latter to pump themselves into her body. The circulation of blood and the realization of desire are achieved at one and the same stroke. Blood is a potent and dangerous fluid not because it is symbolic (of social rank, of race, of Christ) but because it is libidinal and real, dissolving symbolic and social distinctions in an unstoppable haemorrhage. Resurrected bodies, the Un-Dead, are condemned to immortality on earth because they have violated the transcendent (symbolic) value of blood. It is therefore quite logical that the Holy Water, the flesh made symbol, should prove to be such an effective antidote to vampirism (and that the host should burn its imprint on Mina Harker's forehead, for

Mina has precisely imbued too much of the vampire's asymbolic blood for the symbolic to enter her body and redeem her).

To return to Lucy. When her transformation into vampire finally occurs the men are struck by her carnal, lifelike appearance as well as by her expression of 'voluptuous wantonness'. She is no longer referred to by her name but as 'the foul thing that ha[d] taken Lucy's shape'.[37] Lucy, as the subject of untrammelled lust, has no name because the proper name – she was about to become Lady Godalming – assigns the individual a place within a symbolic hierarchy. Given the abominable nature of her transgressions, Lucy must be both punished and wedded (reassigned her position within the hierarchy and so recovering her name) through what must surely be one of literature's most brutal acts of penetration:

Arthur took the stake and the hammer, [. . .] Then he struck with all his might.

The Thing in the coffin writhed; and a hideous, bloodcurdling screech came from the opened red lips. The body shook and quivered and twisted in wild contortions; [. . .] But Arthur never faltered. He looked like a figure of Thor as his untrembling arm rose and fell, driving deeper and deeper the mercy-bearing stake, whilst the blood from the pierced heart welled and spurted up around it. [. . .]

And then the writhing and quivering of the body became less, and the teeth ceased to champ, and the face to quiver. Finally it lay still. The terrible task was over. [. . .]

There in the coffin lay no longer the foul Thing that we had so dreaded and grown to hate [. . .] but Lucy as we had seen her in her life, [. . .] One and all, we felt that the holy calm that lay like sunshine over the wasted face and form was only an earthly token and symbol of the calm that was to reign for ever.[38]

The blood has completely disappeared from the description, but understandably so, for as Lucy becomes Lucy once more she re-enters the realm of socio-symbolic hierarchies. By sending her to heaven, Arthur has not only saved Lucy's worldly reputation but also rescued his own marriage.

The linked acts of consuming other lives and of dissolving socio-symbolic significations are repeated in the character of John Seward's patient, Renfield, possessed by Dracula: 'What he desires is to absorb as many lives as he can and he has laid himself out to achieve it in a cumulative way',[39] Seward records in his phonographic diary. The lunatic who wants to progress in his zoophagous habits from flies, spiders and rats to kittens and dogs, is also the madman who fails to take crucial social distinctions into consideration: 'His attitude to me [i.e. Seward] was the same as that to the attendant; in his sublime self-feeling the difference between myself and attendant seemed to him as nothing. These infinitesimal distinctions between man and man are too paltry for an Omnipotent being. How these madmen give themselves away.'[40]

Renfield is true to his master, for the Count himself, though a haughty Boyar as far as his historical identity goes, as vampire is an ardent democrat making no distinction between the upper-class Lucy Westerna, the *petite bourgeoise* Mina Harker or even the millions of potential victims thronging the metropolis.

Writing, reading and vampirism: What gives *Dracula* a special interest is that we find exactly the same theme of possessing, of 'digesting' other lives accompanied by the motif of social dissolution in the frequent representations that the novel gives of the acts of writing and reading, acts that assume the utmost importance for the main characters. Indeed, in the case of Jonathan Harker's journal (in which he recounts his sojourn at Castle Dracula), the written word is considered by Mina to be a form of holy sacrament. On her wedding night, Mina

took the book from under his pillow and wrapped it up in white paper, and tied it with a little bit of pale blue ribbon . . . sealed it over the knot with a sealing-wax, and for my seal I used my wedding ring. Then I kissed it and showed it to my husband and told him that I would keep it so, and then it would be an outward and visible sign for us all our lives that we trusted each other; that I would never open it unless it were for his own dear sake or for the sake of some stern duty.[41]

The gift of Mina's body to her husband is compensated by Jonathan's offering of an unviolated text to his wife. But this journal (whose intimacy and secrecy are heightened by the fact that it is written in shorthand, a form of private code) must be broken into if there is to be a narration, i.e., if *Dracula* is to exist. The sense of 'stern duty' commands Mina to read and transcribe it:

I shall take his foreign journal and lock myself up in my room and read it. . . .
 24 *September*. – I hadn't the heart to write last night; that terrible record of Jonathan's upset me so. [. . .] There seems to be through it all some thread of continuity. . . . That fearful Count was coming to London [. . .] There may be a solemn duty; and if it comes we must not shrink from it. . . . I shall be prepared. I shall get my typewriter this very hour and begin transcribing. Then we shall be ready for other eyes if required. And if it be wanted, then perhaps, if I am ready, poor Jonathan may not be upset, for if I can speak for him and never let him be troubled or worried with it all.[42]

Mina, on becoming the transcriber of the first four chapters of *Dracula*, makes the vital transcription without her husband's consent. She has taken possession of Jonathan's journal, with all its intimate revelations, including sexual ones (Jonathan's encounter with the three female vampires) in order to make it available 'for other eyes'. Thanks to Mina, or rather to her typewriter, confessions of unrequited love, of despair, of sexual encounters and of personal weaknesses will circulate between the main (human) characters.

The latter, then, are engaged in a process of mutual absorption and possession. Knowledge of the inner life of other people circulates in exactly the same way as do blood and desire. As Seward says to Mina:

I know you now and let me say that I should have known you long ago. May I make the only atonement in my power? Take the cylinders and hear them – the first half dozen of them are personal to me and they will not horrify you, then you will know me better. In the meantime I shall read over some of those documents [i.e., Mina's and Jonathan's journal].[43]

It is in such a way that the characters become vampires to one another, needing to digest and exchange their inner lives in an unbroken circulation. Van Helsing remarks: 'It is that we become as him; that we henceforward become foul things of the night like him . . . preying on the bodies and the souls of those we love best.'[44] Thanks to Mina's transcriptions, such preying, the possession of other souls, become possible. Mina, in her role as transcriber of part of the text of Dracula enjoys the same relationship to those around her as Count Dracula does to Lucy, John Seward, Quincy Adams and Van Helsing, opening up a breach in other people's lives, breaking down barriers and bringing about the same promiscuity in which an assistant schoolmistress, an aristocrat, a 'genius', a psychiatrist, a junior solicitor and an extrovert Texan comingle and absorb one another. John Seward notes how 'Dame Nature gathers round a foreign body an envelope of some insensitive tissue which can protect from evil that which it would otherwise harm by contact. If this be an ordered selfishness, then we should pause before we condemn any one for the vice of egoism.'[45] It is this insensitive tissue, protecting each individual, that Mina's keyboard causes to disappear.

Garlic, crucifixes, wafers and typewriters: However, and in perfect accordance with Mina's intermediate status of crusader-cum-vampire, the acts of transcribing and circulating knowledge of other lives are ambivalent ones for, if they are a form of vampirism, these acts are also an essential part of the struggle to eliminate Dracula. Indeed, the Count himself realizes how important the narrative is as he destroys a copy of Mina's manuscript. 'Knitting together in chronological order every scrap of evidence in order to show a whole connected narrative'[46] is considered essential for the successful pursuit of the vampire, even when the gang of six are in the wilds of Transylvania. 'I feel so grateful', Mina notes 'to the man who invented the Traveller's typewriter and to Mr Morris for getting this one for me. I should have felt quite astray doing this work if I had to write with a pen'.[47] (It is interesting to note that it is precisely when Mina is not the transcriber, when the men decide to pursue Dracula alone and to let their adventures 'be a closed book to her' that she falls prey to the monster, i.e., once excluded from the 'right' form of vampirism, Mina is a victim of its evil variant.)

Clearly, along with garlic, crucifixes and wafers, the typewriter is part of the panoply of weapons needed to destroy the vampire. Its role should be carefully distinguished from that other modern communication instrument that makes its appearance in *Dracula*, the phonograph. Mina says to Seward after she has typed out his recordings:

I have been more touched than I can say by your grief. That is a wonderful machine but it is cruelly true. It told me, in its very tones, the anguish of your heart. It was like a soul crying out to almighty God. No-one must hear them spoken again. See, I have tried to be useful. I have copied out the words on my typewriter and none other need now hear you heart beat as I did.[48]

The phonograph is to the ear what the photograph is to the eye, representing an unmediated form of duplication. Mina makes it clear that typewriting, on the other hand, is a form of recording that distances the individual from himself and others, in other terms that it is a positive form of dispossession or depersonalization. The individual's heartbeat can no longer be heard, only 'read'.

The ambivalence of the typewriter, which is echoed in Mina's dual nature, is also the ambivalence inherent in the situation of writers like Bram Stoker who type rather than write. As Michel Butor has noted, 'the typewriter challenges the mythology of the writer: 'first of all, due to the very fact that it is a machine, it removes from the act of writing a good deal of its aristocratic prestige. What I am doing at the moment is therefore working with my hands!'[49] This loss of prestige is apparent not only in the subject chosen by Stoker (a horror tale) but also in the social rank and sex of the fictional transcriber of his text.

The typewritten work also differs from the text written with a pen in that it is impossible to inscribe on the paper an individual graphic sign, the expression of a singular personality. The typewritten text appears as if written by someone else, i.e., the individual writer is dispossessed of his own identity in the very act of creation, producing a document theoretically available for immediate circulation and that, visually, could have been the work of any other writer. But it is here that the typewritten page and, by extension, the printed work, also form that 'protective envelope' that, we are told, should defend one from dangerous foreign bodies. Printed characters are like holy wafers, solidified and depersonalized intermediaries that refer to but are not 'living flesh', and make us immune from the 'dangers' that we are absorbing through the act of reading. In other words, the perils of contamination, possession and dissolution evoked by *Dracula* are finally seen to have no material existence. It is 'just' a novel that we have been reading. As Jonathan Harker notes on the last page of his journal (which is the final page of *Dracula*): 'We were struck with the fact that, in all the mass of material of which the record is composed, there is hardly one authentic document! nothing but a mass of type-writing [. . .] We could hardly ask anyone, even did we wish to, to accept these as proofs of so wild a story.'[50]

The Un-Dead novel in which contemporary society is imperilled by a contagious monster from another age is finally made safe, that is, it is destroyed, by the fact that it is simply a printed, and hence mediated, account of desire and transgression. The reader, like Mina when her purity is restored after her release from the vampire's hypnotic hold, will return to another life when the novel is finished, no doubt finding it, as Jonathan Harker notes, 'impossible to believe that the things which we had seen with our own eyes and heard with our own ears were living truths'.[51]

9
The Bread and the Blood

The two great fantastic novels that have proved to be most fertile in supplying scenarios for the cinema declared themselves right at the start as end-games: that is to say, *Frankenstein* and *Dracula* appeared to have arisen without any form of influence from history (dogma or ideology); but at the same time, they disclosed a profound engagement with various kinds of (sacred) ordinance that directly affected the body and the way in which it was organized. They treated the body in terms of the mark left there by the sacred, and, in the same process, they achieved a new level of freedom in historical terms, considering human goals and aspirations from a fresh perspective.

Frankenstein's monster, to begin with, has a soul that will not rest within the frame established for it (this theme is foreshadowed by the extraordinary state of 'ecstasy' that Dr Frankenstein experiences on the Swiss glacier; I see it both as a prefiguration of the 'bedazzlement' of Hans Castorp in Thomas Mann's *The Magic Mountain*, and as a contemporary echo of Michelet's thoughts on the painting of mountain scenery: here we sense for the first time what it is to exist in a less heavy atmosphere). If the frenzy of the test-tube monster suggests that feelings have been pumped into a creature that is not ready for them; if the inhuman triumph of the laboratory comes across less as an approximation to life than as a disorganized or barely containable flow of feelings, words and affects (a way of spelling out his misery that the cinema translates into ugliness, and the visible expression of suffering), then it is also true to say that Dracula marks the return, in a different guise, of this shattered, or unfulfilled, state of equilibrium. Dracula's unearthly slumbers, his continual returns and his insatiable thirst for blood are the very sign and site of a sacred act that has been badly interpreted and brought to no conclusion.

My comparison ends here. Dracula is, beyond any doubt, a monster; that is to say, a man who, from time to time, turns into a thing, and a thing that transgresses the boundaries of the behaviour of the human species, in moral and physiological terms. But Dracula's particular form of disequilibrium, his monstrosity, is not psychological in origin, as it is with Frankenstein's creature, who suffers from a lack of due balance between the moral and the physical realms. As we shall see, my argument is that the disequilibrium of the monster of the Carpathians is of a totally different order: no healing is possible (even the type that expresses itself in terms of the creator's remorse, his intention first to correct his handiwork and then to destroy it: successive impulses that we can follow as they war with one another in the mind of Frankenstein).

Dracula's sickness (his extraordinary propensity to 'bleed the whole universe', like one of Molière's doctors), his fateful and inescapable destiny, his capacity to elucidate the different character types existing in the novel (here we have, one after another, and in no special order, a miserly lawyer out of Marlowe or Shakespeare, a travelling salesman resembling the young Werther, and a Marguerite suffering from consumption); all of this – like a game of 'pass the slipper' incorporating fiction, legend and romance, or a film surgical stitch which binds all the bodies together – eventually comes down to a contagious disease (for vampirism is 'catching') for the very reason that a character from history is coming to life again and does so, precisely, in the form of a sickness. To put it more exactly, because History itself is reliving a sickness *in terms of* a character.

For the fable to be believable, Dracula's sickness has to be hereditary or genealogical. But his race lives on in him alone, as if he alone had been for many centuries all his ancestors and all his descendants. How can this be possible, and what can be the historical basis? In both of his aspects, the civilized and the barbaric, the vegetarian and abstinent (religious in the fashion of the neo-Platonist philosopher Porphyry) as opposed to the cannibalistic, his daytime and his night-time modes of behaviour, Dracula is a creation in which, to a remarkable extent, the traditional legends attaching to the Eucharist succeed in living on.

The lord who eats meat, and devours his own subjects, is a repeated motif in history; as we find in Perrault's fairy-tales, the people eat bread (flour), while the lord makes his everyday diet of the children of the people (these stories get told again and again, with their sexual variants, for example in the Breton legends of Gilles de Rais, or those of the 'bloody countess' Erzebeth Bathory). A really clever variation of the same motif is contrived by Carl Theodor Dreyer in the film *Vampyr*: the two substances running through the work are blood (which is continually named, but never shown: as if it were offstage in a Racinian drama) and flour: the latter being the chosen death instrument for the vampire's assistant. The mill that dispenses the flour is to a certain degree the keeper of both the popular and the symbolic form of nourishment, bread; it also brings about the separation of flesh and bread, as if it were dealing not merely with two alternative forms of human nourishment but with two great principles, two vehicles of the sacred.

The resurrection of the deceased, his presence which remains real in defiance of time, the blood of sacrifice as a means of regeneration, the consecrated bread: all of these themes in Bram Stoker's novel are present in two different ways: they are available for sacred purposes, but also for evil ones, in a devilish form of parody that follows the same ritual. The apparition of the vampire, and the return of the body in defiance of time, suggest a eucharistic rite of conversion that has taken the wrong direction, and can be kept at bay only by utilizing the consecrated Christian symbols (the Cross and the host). It should be borne in mind that, by contrast with what comes through in the 'straight' eucharistic legends (those involved with 'profanation'), the host and the whole principle of the Eucharist are in this case treated in much the same way as they are formulated in the symbolic or intellectualist arguments put forward by figures in the history of the Church such as Ratramme, Berengar of Tours and, at a later date, the Vaudois, all well known as heretics. The abomination of blood (the monstrosity of the real presence and its bloody attestation) are here being transferred to, incarnated by, and given life through, a monster.

The interesting point is that we find here one of the central motifs of the great eucharistic controversies of the ninth and eleventh centuries: it was the Pope's party, supported by the great princes, that always upheld the dogma of the real presence, invoked as a proof in miracles concerning the Eucharist, which involved the bleeding of the altar bread, as opposed to doctrines that claimed to be more in accord with the Gospels and which conceived the Eucharist to be a commemoration of the Last Supper.

It is worth juxtaposing extracts from Bram Stoker's novel with passages from the long essay written by Dom Augustin Calmet, an eighteenth-century scholar, on the various legends concerning vampires. This incidentally brings to light a possible source for Stoker's fiction (but that is not my main concern); in particular, Calmet draws attention in a highly convincing manner to the link between vampirism, legends about the Eucharist and the way in which the heritage of Byzantium was handed down, in defiance of the official policy of the Papacy, with a special regard to issues of ritual. We know that the whole problem of the 'conservatism' of ritual in the East turned on the small degree of symbolic credit that the Eucharist enjoyed in the Byzantine world if compared with the very powerful degree of symbolic weight invested in the icon.

The miracles involving a proof of the reality of the Incarnation that derive from the East are very specific in character: it is the icon that bleeds, not the host. We can easily appreciate that, in such an event, a blow is being struck at a major cultural symbol, one on which (mysterious though it may be) the proof of dogma is founded.

In Dom Calmet's view (*Dissertation sur les revenants en corps, les excommuniés, les oupires ou vampires, brucolaques, etc.*, 1751), the numerous legends he has collated (to prove the impossibility of natural resurrection) demonstrate that the invention of the vampire was a quite recent affair, with no clear precedent in antiquity, which took place exclusively in the Balkans and, more generally, on the territories of the former Byzantine Empire (or those of Byzantium's successors, such as Russia). This invention is thus specific to the 'new Greeks' who are cut off from the Roman Church.

It is not hard to spot the very deep-seated significance of the motif which Calmet sketches out here: at virtually the same moment as the legends of the profaned host (which are also miraculous, since they bleed) are spread around in Latin Europe, the vampire legends are being diffused throughout the Byzantine territories; in each case, the Eucharist, the real presence and the resurrection are brought into play in terms of what comes across to us as an obsession with blood. Around this manifestly eucharistic theme, Latin Europe stages on repeated occasions its demonstrations of the real presence in the sacrificial bread through its miraculous bleeding (in the different legends, the host either bleeds on its own, or the flow of blood is provoked by a non-ritual, or non-Christian, sacrifice, a 'profanation').

Let me mention again the theory advanced earlier: that the *topos* of the eucharistic profanation could well be a transformation of the Byzantine (*iconodule*) *topos* of the profanation of the icon. Both the end product and the process of demonstration are the same in both cases: the sacred object (eucharistic bread or icon) bleeds as a proof of the reality of the Incarnation (Byzantium) or of the real presence (Latin Europe). The profanations appear (and multiply in number) after the schism between the two Churches – they are, however, preceded by a few cases of the spontaneous apparition of the bleeding bread on the altar; this clearly corresponds to the necessity of giving support and popular credence to the ultra-realist thesis of the Eucharist, which the Western Church is maintaining constantly and firmly against any and every symbolic interpretation of the sacrifice; the extraordinary thing here is that the legends pertaining to the profanation of the Host are contemporary with the first stories of vampires (according to Dom Calmet). So we have here a schema that can be seen as the direct inversion of the scenario that proves the real presence.

The point of departure for these legends, in Dom Calmet's view (which is entirely plausible), must be contemporary with the schism between the Eastern and Western Churches; to be precise, it coincides with the long controversy over the Eucharist – from 1048 to 1097 – that captured the attention of Europe (that is to say, France, Germany, Italy and, through Lanfranc, probably England as well). This controversy aimed at settling a particular issue of immense consequence both politically and dogmatically: the realist theory of the Eucharist (deriving from Paschase Radebert), with its axiom of the real presence, was supported by papal authority (and the great princes of Christendom, like the King of France) through the involvement of Lanfranc (at that time Prior of Bec and Abbot of Caen). In opposition was Berengar, Bishop of Tours, the chief heretic and defender of a symbolic theory of the sacrament, who justified himself by reference to the treatise of Ratramme (a monk of Corbie, in the ninth century, like Radebert).

This debate acquired great importance because of its consequences (it provides legitimacy for the symbolic system of the *Corpus mysticum*) and involved numerous participants (six councils were called over a 30-year period to sort out the question). It resulted in a swift clarification of dogmatic thought: a development of the notion of substance which took the place of matter – in terms that anticipated St Thomas Aquinas's resolution of the issue – and a new definition of the 'conversion' operated by the Eucharist which came close to the formula for trans-substantiation as it was later to appear in the first canon of the Fourth Lateran Council. These are the achievements in terms of dogma: the argument vigorously pursued by Berengar is a critique, supported by passages from the scriptures (the Gospels) and the Fathers (both Augustine and Ambrose define the sacrament as a sign: '*sacramentum, id est sacrum signum*') of the 'vulgar' realism of the theses of Paschase Radebert, held to be 'incompatible with the dogma of the Resurrection'. (How can the resurrected Christ, seated in glory for all eternity at the right hand of the Father, be really on the altar, returning in a morsel of flesh that was never his body, etc.?)

This symbolic and intellectual theory (Berengar denies that the conversion of the bread and wine into the body and blood takes place *sensualiter* and defends their conversion *intellectualiter*) involves a real element of danger for the political positions of Pope and King (simply put, it compromises the symbolic basis of the *corpus mysticum*; it is no accident that Berengar was defended at the papal court, and against the King of France, by the Count of Anjou); this is indeed a symbolic dismemberment of the *Corpus Christi* that anticipates the heretical path to be followed in particular by the Vaudois (some of the sixteenth-century Huguenot authors make their reliance on Berengar quite explicit); above all, Berengar's thesis provides a theory of the sacramental sign that is extremely close to the theories held in Byzantium.

We shall see how the Byzantine side of the matter that concerns us here – that which relates to vampire legends – in effect adds up to a distortion or a monstrous compromise between the basic beliefs (and legends) attaching to the cult of icons, and a fairly crude version of the real presence in the Eucharist (the ultra-realist version cherished by the Latin Church). Once this hypothesis is put forward, it becomes obvious that the eucharistic motifs appearing in the Dracula legend (perfectly synthesized in Bram Stoker's novel) are not in any way decorative: they touch on the very essence of the eucharistic debate; they raise exactly the same conflict in interpretation that led to the definition of the dogma of the Eucharist once and for all within the Latin Church. The real issue for Byzantium remained that of the Incarnation, a dogma that the icon illustrates perfectly well, and which inculcated a form of piety based on the mystical status of intelligible objects: for the Byzantines, the Eucharist could only be a feeble variant of icon worship – a significant reason for the failure of the iconoclastic reforms: the Eucharist and the mystique of the State (the juridical and administrative construction of the *Corpus mysticum*) were supposed to supplant the existing cultic practices involving the icon.

Here is how Don Calmet concludes the Preface to his *Dissertation*:

The belief of the new Greeks, who hold that the bodies of the excommunicated do not rot in their tombs, is an opinion without any foundation, either in Antiquity, or in good theology, or indeed in history. This supposition seems only to have been invented by the schismatic new Greeks for the purpose of justifying and consolidating their separation from the Roman Church. Christian Antiquity believed, on the contrary, that the incorruptibility of a body was rather a probable mark of the person's sanctity, and a proof of the particular protection given by God to a body which was during its lifetime a temple of the Holy Spirit, and to a person who maintained in justice and innocence the character of the Christian faith.

There is no real need to argue the point: the 'Middle Ages' still serve as a vast reservoir of fantasies, all the more important in that the institutions of the modern world, the law, art and philosophy of more recent epochs, have their roots there. The very pronounced violence of the ideological and political conflicts that come together there (the memorable combination of myth, legend and regulation by dogma from which the modern world, in many respects, derives) – all of this comes into play in a specially emphatic manner in the vampire legends of Central Europe. There we can find these legends a home and a birth certificate. Their remote and deep-seated causes are religious and political, as were those of the schism between East and West (it was a matter of maintaining the unity of the *Corpus mysticum* being constructed by the states of Latin Europe, which Byzantium had put at risk in ideological, economic and political terms).

So the recurrent basis for the vampire legends is not, as one might think (in line with the choice of themes commonly found in the nineteenth-century novel), just a matter of using any old legend involving devils or demons that appear to be 'typical' of the medieval period. Dom Calmet makes the crucial point that vampirism is the special affair of the 'new Greeks', the Russians (who moreover invented the term *oupire*), Hungarians, Serbs, in short the *inheritors of Byzantium*; he also identifies the confused patterns of dogma that underlie the composition of such legends. The fact that eucharistic legends and vampire tales are mixed up in this way is thus neither accidental nor marginal in relation to our theme. My own view is that the vampire legends are in effect a translation of the issues of dogma involved in defining the formula of the Eucharist, and more specifically, the Roman theory of the Eucharist, which is that of the real presence.

Here two points should be noted: the controversy over iconoclasm did not arise as a result of a dispute over the content of the image; there can be no question of a semiotic controversy (which would have taken on the guise of a civil war). The idea that the crisis was to some extent determined by the pressures of Islam (Yazid II having chosen a Jew as his counsellor) is partly true, but belongs at the same time to the class of arguments advanced and publicized by the *iconodule* faction (who commonly used anti-semitic arguments against their opponents, the iconoclasts, citing them as 'new Jews'). It is both closer to the truth and more sensible (in the light of the historical and political data of the High Middle Ages) to recognize that the conflict which set Leo III and Constantine V against the iconodules did not take on the form of a semiotic dispute in favour of, or against, images, or of a debate about whether to have more or less images (one need only read the *Antirrhetics* of Nicephorus and the *Questions* of Constantine V). Neither is their confrontation primarily – or solely – concerned with the relations of Byzantium to its own East, that is to say, the provinces under Islamic control. The same applies to the great political project of the iconoclasts: the argument about idolatry used in the struggle against the iconodules is a weak argument, and probably a subsidiary one (it is kept going by the iconodules as the only one to which they offer a reply).

The problem which the iconoclast rulers (*Basileis*) are attempting to resolve is that of the dismemberment of the state and the regionalization of powers (the sickness of the state that Hegel associates specifically with Byzantium): the remedy prescribed by the iconoclasts is realistic, subtle and very simple; it is political, but the political model is not Islam, it is the Carolingian state. The *Libri carolini* are full of the reverberations of this whole question: when called on to take sides in the quarrel over images, the Carolingians reply that their problem is of an entirely different order: it is the construction of the state. Now the state is required to have a central symbol and a mystique. As we find in Henri de Lubac and Ernst Kantorowicz, this symbol is the Eucharist, the *Corpus Christi* that ends up by giving its name to the Christian state, and whose mystical definition (body, head and limbs) is to provide a framework for the renewal of the legal system. It is precisely this form of structure, this universal model, that the reforms of the iconoclasts seek to achieve throughout the territories of Byzantium. And it is for this reason, precisely, that the Roman Church and the great Christian princes of Latin Europe consistently defend the most realist theses about the Eucharist, so as to safeguard the efficacity of the symbol, in all its mystical power.

The premises of the schism with Byzantium (which are known to have been political and ritual in character, in other words, of a cultural type) are already implicit in the failure of the attempts to reform the Byzantine State, which was to become decadent as a result of the basic defects in its structure.

To sum up my hypothesis: the problem of Byzantium recurs as a reference point in the whole range of texts produced by the West in the medieval period: the main motif however comes through only in terms of the recognition that the Greeks do not understand the dogma of the Eucharist (important symptoms of this are disputes about unleavened bread, and forms of ritual). The Fourth Lateran Council that tried to establish peace in Christendom did not omit to mention the insolent behaviour of the Greeks and to stigmatize various practices that were offensive to the Latins. St Thomas, not wishing to inflame the quarrels that were dividing Christendom, maintained that all forms of ritual were acceptable. However, he held that there was a greater coherence in the form of consecration used by the Latins: unleavened bread is purer, the leavened bread of the Greeks already holds the seed of corruption.

My suggestion, then, is that traditional legends concerning the Eucharist are making their reappearance, or gaining a new lease of life, in a text like *Dracula*. In so far as the story of Dracula can be illuminated by accounts of the debates and legends concerning the Eucharist, so, in a similar way, the establishment of the eucharistic dogma, and the division of Christendom around questions of ritual, the debate about kinds, and the eucharistic formula, can be seen to reach in *Dracula* a striking form of conclusion: one which is genuinely a resolution of the fantasies entertained since the High Middle Ages with reference to the accidents and proofs of the real presence. Just in the same way as there would have been no reason to produce, or search for, eucharistic miracles ('proofs by blood') if there had not been a need to impose one eucharistic thesis (that of the real presence) in preference to another (that of the symbolic presence), so the vampire legends would be in part incomprehensible if it were not for these themes: regeneration through blood, the sacred host and the Cross being used as weapons against the vampire. (It should be noted that these particular hosts cannot be profaned; or at any rate, they never produce blood; that is because they form a term in a paradigm which also includes a social and political component: as mentioned earlier, the ogres who thirst for blood are the lords – Dracula, Gilles de Rais, Erzebeth Bathory – while the people is bread-eating, flour-consuming.) The legend of Dracula has a natural link to the other vampire stories (as Dom Calmet summarizes them): Dracula's 'real' history is that of a Christian hero who takes the Cross in the war against the Turks. Turkey is at once the enemy of Byzantium and of Rome – the Jews expelled from Spain receive a welcome in their empire: so the issue of 'profanation' is raised once again. The predella commissioned from Uccello by the congregation of the *Corpus Domini* of Urbino, in accordance with the wishes of Pope Pius II, who is planning a Crusade against the Turks, is a revival of the scenario of the sacred objects directly profaned by, or at the instigation of, the Jews. A similar scenario was current at Byzantium: icons had been profaned by, or at the instigation of the Jews (according to the rumours spread by the iconodules). In both cases, the sacred sign 'bleeds' to demonstrate its true character. So we have this extension to the scenario: the monster is a prince of the Balkans (the buffer zone between Byzantium and Rome): he is caught up in the weighty political issues of the region; indeed he epitomizes the distorted relationship between the former Byzantine Empire and the Latin Empire of the West.

This provides further food for thought. Where is the origin of Dracula – in Vlad III? The Christian princes of the Balkans, after the capture of Constantinople by the Turks, figure in the struggle against the Turkish occupier as allies of the House of Austria, which is undertaking a policy of reconquest; they are therefore champions of the papal cause. The cathedral of SS Michael and Gudule in Brussels (Brabant being, at the beginning of the sixteenth century, an Austrian province) commemorates the struggle of Maximilian against the Turks in a series of stained-glass windows: these are, in a sense, in honour of the Balkan princes who are represented kneeling and under the protection of the Emperor of Austria, who is thanking them for their help in the struggle 'against the Barbarians'. The 'allegorical gift' that Austria presents to them in the upper part of the windows is composed out of sequences from a story about a Jewish profanation of the host. This is a reference to a legend that originally arose in Brussels in 1369 and was first given publicity by the Duke of Burgundy, then lord of that province, who stood beside the King of France as champion of the *Corpus mysticum*; it thus formed a direct counterpart to the popular Parisian legend, which had been made public by Philippe Le Bel in 1290. The House of Austria (which put itself forward as the most sure defender of the Catholic faith) thus took up the eucharistic legend current in Brabant; as late as 1720 it was to publicize it yet again, with a Jubilee, triumphal arches, processions and the publication of a detailed account of the miracle of 1369.

This appearance of the princes of Central Europe under the protection of Austria (allies in a combined struggle against Islam, the Jews and the reformed churches) is in any event significant: to the point that my syllogism and my conclusion should not seem too hasty. The extraordinary thing about the lands where the vampires were born and propagated is that, however many different forms the legend may have adopted, these territories were always dominated by pro-eucharistic parties and policies. Austria succeeded in her politics of iconoclasm: the Balkan princes took the Cross under the banner of Catholic Austria against the Turks, who were Islamic, anti-eucharistic and . . . favourable to the Jews expelled from Spain.

I cannot omit including in this web of convergent motifs (which I can only offer as a framework, a 'portrait' sketch, not for that reason any less convincing) the fact that the iconoclast ruler commissioned a provincial visitor (one who left behind a memory no less terrible than the Inquisitor Torquemeda) to enforce the decrees that ordered the icons to be destroyed. This bloodthirsty inquisitor, known for his extermination of monks and devotees of icons, bore the feared, and soon to be legendary, name of Draco. I have no idea why the accounts of the period of iconoclasm have been (and sometimes still are) so superficial in their coverage, being concerned uniquely with the debate over images, summed up in the incredible scenario of a 'Hundred Years' War' over icons, with the case being treated quite obviously from the iconodules' point of view. This is to exclude from consideration two important motifs. The first is political: here we have an existing state attempting a project of reform designed to revive its exhausted and archaic structures. The second is theological (and the symbolic expression of the first): for the State to be effectively organized and regarded as a body, it is necessary for the body to have a symbol and a mystique that will legitimate it – the very things that contribute to the success of Latin Europe – by basing the *Corpus mysticum* on the dogma of the Eucharist (without forcing the metaphor, we can say that the Western states secured their progress through being able to exploit the mobility of this 'body').

The way in which the roles are distributed is thus quite clear, according to this account. The profaners of the host are, for the Latins, the Orientals: Jews and 'new Greeks' from after the schism (the gestures of profanation are described in such terms as to repeat, in a literal fashion, the performance of the orthodox ritual); for the Greeks, the destroyers of icons are the allies of the power of the Eucharist: they even go so far as to re-enact the effects of reincarnation and trans-substantiation. Naturally (and the legend will not pass over this point) it is always possible to pit a good Eucharist against a bad one (the immaculate host that paralyses the body of the vampire, a prodigy that has been resurrected and defies death with its ruby-red blood), in the same way as we can combat (and papal policy had to combat) an intellectual theory of the Eucharist (heretical and as often as not an occasion for schism) that is close to Greek thinking (as featured in the iconodule arguments of Berengar) with an ultra-realist theory: one that follows Paschase Radebert in maintaining the principle that Christ is really present in body and blood on the altar.

I hope that I have not made too much of the conjunction between this theme (the blood-drinking monster) and my present area of research (the

Eucharist); Dom Calmet at any rate provides more than enough hints for us to see the possibility of reformulating the vampire legends in this way. A clear line of argument emerges: the fact that the nations that formed part of the old Byzantine Empire (the 'new Greeks') have deserted the faith and continue as heretics is connected, to a large extent, with the reputed phenomenon of vampirism: this is a feature of their schism, and their misapprehension of the true objects of faith and dogma.

In accord with this interpretation, it is important to note that the vampire (not excluding the one in Stoker's novel, which is a superb synthesis of the various legends) repeats or copies the process of conversion which takes place at the Eucharist, or proposes states of paradox (stages of aporia) deriving from that process: the resurrection, the blood of the dead; the opposition (so commonplace in the ecclesiastical debates of the eleventh century) between bread (flour) and flesh (blood).

The bizarre nature of this scenario leaves us in some amazement: the resuscitated persecutor who must be made a victim (by being pierced and decapitated) is drawn not from any observation of natural phenomena (and in no way infringes such processes: Dom Calmet raises in his critique of the legends, because it strikes a blow at the dogma of the Resurrection, the case of hibernating animals); this monster is not presented as a type which eludes classification – or even as a kind of mixed species. It has no reference to any such divisions and categories, since its monstrosity resides precisely in an unresolved, unstable and disquieting mix between the terrestrial and the supernatural. No doubt the state of schismatic dereliction into which the Latin West considered the Byzantine Empire and its successors to have fallen, since the Middle Ages, explains how such an image arose, and how the principle of heresy became interiorized in such a way (for *all* the elements of mythology involved, all the figurative materials drawn upon, are rooted in the notion eucharistic reincarnation); the picture of intolerance and incomprehension is a stark one (and yet the vampire does come from a specific historical terrain: he is the product of a long, drawn-out struggle): the demoniac is also the sacred form of *the other*, all the more so as it is on the basis of this form of sacredness (on the ritual of the one who is sacrificed: commemoratively *or* effectively) that schism took place, that is to say, political and religious 'continents' became separate from one another, to such an extent that the interplay of alliances was never capable of soldering them together again (this was the great issue of Austrian politics and of the alliances against the Turks, and the only thing holding together the former Byzantine Empire, marking, by the same token, its real degree of isolation).

Translated by Stephen Bann

APPENDIX I
From Bram Stoker, *Dracula* (London, 1897)

From chapter XVI: DR SEWARD'S DIARY:

[. . .] As to Van Helsing, he was employed in a definite way. First he took from his bag a mass of what looked like thin, wafer-like biscuit, which was carefully rolled up in a white napkin; next he took out a double-handful of some whitish stuff, like dough or putty. He crumbled the wafer up fine and worked it into the mass between his hands. This he then took, and rolling it into thin strips, began to lay them into the crevices between the door and its setting in the tomb. I was somewhat puzzled at this, and being closed, asked him what it was that he was doing. Arthur and Quincey drew near also, as they too were curious. He answered: –

'I am closing the tomb, so that the Un-Dead may not enter.'

'And is that stuff you have put there going to do it?' asked Quincey. 'Great Scott! Is this a game?'

'It is.'

'What is that which you are using?' This time the question was by Arthur. Van Helsing reverently lifted his hat as he answered: –

'The Host. I brought it from Amsterdam. I have an Indulgence.' It was an answer that appalled the most sceptical of us, and we felt individually that in the presence of such earnest purpose as the Professor's, a purpose which could thus use the to him most sacred of things, it was impossible to distrust.

[. . .] And so for full half a minute, which seemed an eternity, she remained between the lifted crucifix and the sacred closing of her means of entry.

[. . .] We could hear the click of the closing lantern as Van Helsing held it down; coming close to the tomb, he began to remove from the chinks some of the sacred emblem which he had placed there. We all looked on in horrified amazement as we saw, when he stood back, the woman, with a corporeal body as real at the moment as our own, pass in through the interstice where scarce a knife-blade could have gone. We all felt a glad sense of relief when we saw the Professor calmly restoring the strings of putty to the edges of the door.

From chapter XVIII: MINA HARKER'S JOURNAL:

[. . .] 'There have been from the loins of this very one great men and good women, and their graves make sacred the earth where alone this foulness can dwell. For it is not the least of its terrors that this evil thing is rooted deep in all good; in soil barren of holy memories it cannot rest.'

[. . .] 'We must trace each of these boxes; and when we are ready, we must either capture or kill this monster in his lair; or we must, so to speak, sterilize the earth, so that no more he can seek safety in it. Thus in the end we may find him in his form of man between the hours of noon and sunset, and so engage with him when he is at his most weak.'

From chapter XIX: JONATHAN HARKER'S JOURNAL:

[. . .] 'Keep this near your heart' – as he spoke he lifted a little silver crucifix and held it out to me, I being nearest to him – 'put these flowers round your neck' – here he handed to me a wreath of withered garlic blossoms – 'for other enemies more mundane, this revolver and this knife; and for aid in all, these so small electric lamps, which you can fasten to your breast; and for all, and above all at the last, this, which we must not desecrate needless.' This was a portion of sacred wafer, which he put in an envelope and handed to me.

APPENDIX 2
From Dom Augustin Calmet, *Dissertation sur les Revenants en corps, les Excommuniés, les Oupires ou Vampires, Brucolaques, etc.* (Paris, 1751)

Chapter XIII: 'Account taken from the *Mercure galant* of 1693 and 1694 on the subject of those who return from the dead':

[. . .] This born-again creature or oupire leaves his tomb, or a demon does so under the same face, and goes, by night, to embrace and clasp violently his friends and those close to him, and sucks their blood to the point of enfeebling them, tiring them out and ultimately killing them. This persecution does not confine itself to a single person; it reaches as far as the last member of the family, unless the process is interrupted by cutting off the head or opening the heart of the revenant, whose corpse can be found in his coffin, soft, flexible, swollen and rubicund, despite the fact that he has been dead for a long time. There comes out from his body a great quantity of blood which some people mix with flour to make bread; and this bread, ate in the normal way, preserves them from the vexatiousness of the spirit which comes no more.

Chapter XIV: 'Conjecture of the *Glaneur de Holande* in 1733, no. IX':

The *Glaneur hollandais* [. . .] claims that the peoples in whose lands vampires can be seen are very ignorant and very superstitious [. . .]. The whole thing is occasioned and aggravated by the poor nourishment of these peoples who, for most of the time, eat only bread made of oats, roots and bark of trees, foods which can only engender a gross form of blood, and one which in consequence is very disposed to become corrupt and produce in the imagination sombre and vexing ideas.

Chapter XXII: 'The excommunicated who leave churches':

[. . .] St Gregory tells us that a young monk of [. . .] the order of St Benedict who had left the monastery without the blessing of the holy abbot, died in his disobedience and was buried in holy ground. The next day, his body was found outside the tomb. His parents alerted St Benedict who gave them a consecrated host and told them to put it with all due respect on the breast of the young monk. They placed it there, and the earth no longer cast him out of its protection [. . .].

In certain places there has been no lack of placing hosts in the tombs of people who are remarkable for their sanctity, as in the tomb of St Othmar, Abbot of Saint-Gall, where a number of little round pieces of bread were found under his head, and there was no doubt at all that these were hosts [. . .]. However this may be, we know that Cardinal Humbert, in his reply to the objections of the Patriarch Michael Cerularius, reproaches the Greeks with burying the Holy Eucharist when some is left after the communion of the faithful.

Chapter XLV: 'The dead who masticate like pigs in their tombs, and devour their own flesh':

It is an opinion widely held throughout Germany that certain of the dead masticate in their tombs and devour what is to be found around them; that one can hear them even eating like pigs, with a kind of dull cry, as if they were groaning and growling.

A German author called Michel Rauff has composed a work entitled *De masticatione mortuorum in tumulis*, the dead who masticate in their tombs. He takes it for granted that there are certain of the dead who have devoured all their winding sheets and all that was within range of their mouths, and have even devoured their own flesh in their tombs. He notes that in some places in Germany, to prevent the dead from masticating, people place under their chin, in the coffin, a clod of earth. That elsewhere, they put in their mouths a small piece of silver and a stone. Elsewhere, they bind the throat tight with a handkerchief. The author cites a number of German writers who allude to this ridiculous practice, and he refers to a number of others, who speak of the dead who have devoured their own flesh in their burial place. This work was printed in Leipzig in 1728. It refers to an author called Philip Rehrius who published in 1679 a treatise under the same title, *De masticatione mortuorum*.

He could have added the fact that Henry, Count of Salm, who had been believed dead, was buried while still alive. There was heard during the night, in the church of the Abbey of Haute-Selle where he was buried, a great shouting; and the next day, when the tomb had been opened, he was found upside down with his face underneath, although he had been buried on his back with his face uppermost.

A few years ago at Bar-le-Duc, a man having been buried in the cemetary, a noise was heard in his grave. The next day, it was discovered that he had eaten the flesh of his arms, as we have heard from eyewitnesses. This man had got drunk on *eau-de-vie*, and had been buried as if he was dead. Rauff speaks of a woman of Bohemia who, in 1355, had eaten in her grave half of her winding sheet. In the time of Luther, a man who was dead and buried, and a woman similarly, gnawed their own entrails. Another man, dying in Moravia, devoured the linen of a woman interred next to him.

References

Introduction

1 Cf. Roland Barthes, 'Littérature et discontinu', in *Essais critiques* (Paris, 1964), pp. 175–87.
2 Mary Shelley, *Frankenstein*, edited with an introduction by Maurice Hindle (London, 1992), p. 56.
3 Cf. Michel Foucault, *Les Mots et les choses* (Paris, 1966), p. 33.
4 Ger Luijten *et al.* (eds), *Dawn of the Golden Age: Northern Netherlandish Art 1580–1620*, exh. cat., Amsterdam, Rijksmuseum, 1993, p. 411.
5 Ibid.
6 David Freedberg, 'Ferrari on the Classification of Oranges and Lemons', in Elizabeth Cropper *et al.* (eds), *Documentary Culture: Florence and Rome from Grand-Duke Ferdinand I to Pope Alexander VII* (Bologna, 1992), pp. 304–5.
7 Ibid., pp. 298–9.
8 Krzysztof Pomian, *Collectors and Curiosities: Paris and Venice, 1500–1800*, trans. Elizabeth Wiles-Porter (Cambridge, 1990), p. 64.
9 John Ruskin, *Modern Painters*, III (London, 1897), pp. 110–11.
10 Charles Waterton, *Wanderings in South America* (4th edn, London, 1839), p. 75.
11 Ibid., p. 290.
12 Ibid.
13 Charles Waterton, *Essays on Natural History, chiefly Ornithology* (London, 1838), p. 304.
14 Waterton, *Wanderings*, p. 305.
15 Ibid., p. 306.
16 Ibid., p. 278.
17 Ibid., pp. 87–8.
18 Cf. Julia Blackburn, *Charles Waterton: Traveller and Conservationist*, Foreword by Gerald Durrell (London, 1989).
19 Waterton, *Wanderings*, p. 278.
20 Ibid., pp. 278–9.
21 Blackburn, *Charles Waterton*, pp. 92–3.
22 Waterton, *Wanderings*, p. 166.
23 Quoted in Blackburn, *Charles Waterton*, p. 141.
24 Cf. Bram Stoker, *Dracula*, edited with an introduction and notes by Maurice Hindle (London, 1993), pp. vii–xxx.

1 *Elisabeth Bronfen: Rewriting the Family:*
  Mary Shelley's 'Frankenstein' in its Biological/Textual Context

1 'Family Romances', in *The Standard Edition of the Complete Psychological Works of Sigmund Freud*, ed. J. Strachey *et al.*, 24 vols (London, 1953–74), IX, p. 237.
2 Ibid., p. 239.
3 Ibid., p. 241.
4 Harold Bloom, *The Anxiety of Influence: A Theory of Poetry* (Oxford, 1973).
5 Indeed, as Muriel Spark argues in *Mary Shelley* (London, 1987), while the parents Wollstonecraft and Godwin modified their theories as they put them into practice, the children Mary and Percy Shelley, initially at least, radicalized them. Repeatedly they lived by the books their parents wrote, as Spark notes: 'Mary was to return to her mother's work, as if to find in those pages a glimpse into part of her own nature; she was, moreover, justly proud of her parentage, and sitting on the rock with Shelley it pleased her to hear him talk about her mother's autobiographical romance' (p. 29). See also Anne Mellor, *Mary Shelley: Her Life, her Fiction, her Monsters* (New York, 1988) and Emily W. Sunstein, *Mary Shelley: Romance and Reality* (New York, 1989).
6 See George Levine and U. C. Knoepflmacher, *The Endurance of Frankenstein: Essays on Mary Shelley's Novel* (Berkeley, CA, 1979), and Fred Botting, *Making Monstrous: Frankenstein, Criticism, Theory* (Manchester, 1991).
7 For a biographical reading of *St Leon*, see William St Clair, *The Godwins and the Shelleys: The Biography of a Family* (London, 1989), especially 'The Philosophers Stone', pp. 210–20. All citations from William Godwin's novel are from the reprint *St Leon: A Tale of the Sixteenth Century* (New York, 1972).
8 St Clair, *op. cit.*, repeatedly documents how Percy Shelley copied Godwin in his activities, living out what both he and his wife had written. The parents' texts served as precedents and justification for the socially unconventional lifestyle of the children: 'It scarcely mattered that the books had been written at different times, in different circumstances, and to teach different lessons: it was enough that they had been written by Mary Wollstonecraft and William Godwin. If the books offered encouragement, the runaways were strengthened in their resolution. If they warned of suffering, they were comforted to know that their own lives were conforming to pattern' (p. 366).
9 Spark, *op. cit.*, notes that 'Mary formed the habit of taking her books to her mother's grave in St Pancras Churchyard, there to find some peace after her irksome household duties, and to pursue her studies in an atmosphere of communion with a mind greater than the second Mrs Godwin's' (p. 19). See also 'Horror's Twin: Mary Shelley's Monstrous Eve' in Sandra M. Gilbert and Susan Gubar, *The Madwoman in the Attic: The Woman Writer and the Nineteenth-century Literary Imagination* (New Haven, 1979), pp. 213–47.
10 Cited in St Clair, *op. cit.*, p. 376.
11 Citations will be from the following editions: Mary Shelley, *Frankenstein, or, The Modern Prometheus*, ed. Maurice Hindle (Harmondsworth, 1985); Percy Shelley, 'Alastor, or, The Spirit of Solitude', in *Poetical Works*, ed. Thomas Hutchinson (Oxford, 1970); and Mary Wollstonecraft, *The Wrongs of Woman* (Oxford, 1973).
12 St Leon, p. 211.
13 Ibid., p. 474.
14 Ibid., p. 477.
15 Ibid., p. 3.
16 *Frankenstein*, p. 16.
17 Ibid., p. 17.
18 Ibid., p. 55.

19 Ibid., p. 56.
20 Ibid., p. 54.
21 Ibid.
22 Ibid., p. 56.
23 Ibid., p. 54.
24 For a somewhat different discussion of Mary Shelley's conflation of authorship and monstrosity see Barbara Johnson, 'My Monster/My Self', in *Mary Shelley's Frankenstein*, ed. Harold Bloom (New York, 1987), pp. 55–66. See also Ellen Moers, 'Female Gothic', in *Literary Women: The Great Writers* (New York, 1977).
25 *Frankenstein*, p. 59.
26 Ibid., p. 63.
27 Ibid., p. 69.
28 Ibid., p. 72.
29 Ibid., p. 74.
30 Mary Poovey, ' "My Hideous Progeny": The Lady and the Monster' in *Mary Shelley's Frankenstein*, ed. Harold Bloom (New York, 1987), pp. 81–106, discusses the depiction of Frankenstein's curiosity as full-fledged egotism, as a feeding of his selfish desires, and reads Mary Shelley's emphasis on the anti-social dimension of the imaginative quest as well as her plea for a governing of individual desire and a disciplining of the imagination as her 'growing desire to accommodate her adolescent impulses to conventional propriety'.
31 Margaret Homans, 'Bearing Demons: Frankenstein's Circumvention of the Maternal', in *Mary Shelley's Frankenstein*, ed. Bloom, p. 139.
32 As Homans, *op. cit.*, explains, Mary Shelley wrote her novel when Percy Shelley had completed, besides *Queen Mab*, only this poem, 'the archetypal poem of the doomed Romantic quest' (p. 139), so that it is safe to assume that it is to this poem that she alludes. Mellor, *op. cit.*, also offers a comparative reading between Frankenstein and 'Alastor', emphasizing how Shelley deconstructs her father and her husband's phantasies of human perfectibility and immortality so as to show the rampant egoism underlying these poetic constructions of the poet-saviour: 'Mary Shelley understood that the romantic affirmation of the creative process over its finite products could justify a profound moral irresponsibility on the part of the poet . . . [she] conveyed her conviction that one must take full and lasting responsibility for *all* one's offspring and continue to care for the family one engenders' (p. 80).
33 Harold Bloom, *The Visionary Company: A Reading of English Romantic Poetry* (Ithaca, NY, 1971), p. 285.
34 *Frankenstein*, p. 96.
35 Ibid., p. 97f.
36 Ibid., p. 101.
37 Homans, *op. cit.*, p. 141. Indeed she argues that Frankenstein can be read as a narrative about what it feels like 'to be the undesired embodiment of Romantic imaginative desire', drawing a parallel between the monster, rejected by Victor Frankenstein owing to his body, and Mary Shelley, rejected by Percy, because even as she was to embody the goal of his poetic quest he as poet had to reject any form of embodiment.
38 *Frankenstein*, p. 120.
39 See also Mary Todd, 'Frankenstein's Daughter: Mary Shelley and Mary Wollstonecraft' *Women & Literature*, IV/2 (1976), pp. 18–27.
40 *The Wrongs of Woman*, p. 106.
41 Ibid., p. 162.
42 Ibid., p. 259.
43 Ibid., p. 187.

44 As Homans, *op. cit.*, argues, in the author's introduction, Shelley 'aims to bring the writing of the novel further within the fold of the conventional domestic life Shelley retrospectively substitutes for the radically disruptive life she in fact led' (p. 147); the introduction domesticating her 'hideous idea' serves as a trope for her desire to domesticate a monstrous family life.

45 St Clair, *op. cit.*, p. 492ff. documents the weeding of the Shelley archives of any embarrassing documents, as well as Mary Shelley's attempt, in her publications on William Godwin and Percy Shelley, to sever all explicitly intellectual connections between her father and her husband.

46 Spark, *op. cit.*, p. 129.

2 *Crosbie Smith: Frankenstein and Natural Magic*

I am especially grateful to Ludmilla Jordanova, Ian Higginson, Michael Neal and Michael Griffiths for their comments and assistance during the drafting of this essay. I must also acknowledge a debt to undergraduates at the University of Kent, too numerous to mention individually, who have participated in discussions on *Frankenstein* in my Humanities course 'Literature and Science'.

1 M. W. Shelley, *Frankenstein or The Modern Prometheus. The 1818 Text*, ed., with introduction and notes, Marilyn Butler (London, 1993), p. 34 (references below are to Shelley, *The 1818 Text*);

2 J. B. Porta, *Natural Magick*, ed. D. J. Price (New York, 1957), pp. 3–4. First published as *Natural Magick by John Baptista Porta, a Neapolitane: in Twenty Books . . . Wherein are Set Forth All the Riches and Delights of the Natural Sciences* (London, 1658).

3 Shelley, *The 1818 Text*, p. 192.

4 Marilyn Butler in Shelley, *The 1818 Text*, pp. 199–201 (Appendix A).

5 Shelley, *The 1818 Text*, p. 38.

6 Mario Praz, 'Introductory Essay', in *Three Gothic Novels*, ed. Peter Fairclough (Harmondsworth, 1968), pp. 25–7.

7 See J. A. Secord, 'Extraordinary Experiment: Electricity and the Creation of Life in Victorian England', in *The Uses of Experiment*, ed. David Gooding *et al.* (Cambridge, 1989), pp. 337–83. This stimulating paper examines in the historical context of British science of the 1830s the claims of Andrew Crosse, an eccentric English experimentalist, to have created life in his private laboratory. Located outside the legitimate boundaries set by the British Association for the Advancement of Science, Crosse's 'extraordinary' practices invite comparison with Mary Shelley's earlier positioning of Victor Frankenstein as an isolated genius working well beyond orthodox science.

8 Crosbie Smith, 'From Design to Dissolution: Thomas Chalmers' Debt to John Robison', *British Journal for the History of Science*, XII (1979), pp. 59–70 (on natural history, natural philosophy and natural theology); J. H. Brooke, *Science and Religion: Some Historical Perspectives* (Cambridge, 1991), pp. 192–225 (on the fortunes and functions of natural theology in the early nineteenth century).

9 T. L. Hankins, *Science and the Enlightenment* (Cambridge, 1985), pp. 3–7 (on Reason and natural law); Richard Kieckhefer, *Magic in the Middle Ages* (Cambridge, 1989), p. 9 (on natural magic as a science of hidden powers).

10 M. N. Wise (with the collaboration of Crosbie Smith), 'Work and Waste: Political Economy and Natural Philosophy in Nineteenth-century Britain (I)', *History of Science*, XXVII (1989), pp. 263–301 (pp. 266–8).

11 Ibid., pp. 268–75.

12 Ibid., pp. 272–5, 288.
13 John Locke, *Of Civil Government* (1690), cited in Gerd Buchdahl, *The Image of Newton and Locke in the Age of Reason* (London, 1961), pp. 91–2.
14 Wise (with Smith), *op. cit.*, pp. 278, 281–2.
15 Shelley, *The 1818 Text*, pp. 17, 46.
16 Ibid., pp. 17–19.
17 Ibid., p. 19.
18 Ibid., p. 20.
19 Ibid., p. 21.
20 Ibid., p. 25.
21 Ibid., p. 21.
22 Ibid., pp. 21–3, 260–61 (notes 8–9 by Marilyn Butler).
23 Ibid., p. 23. See, especially, 'Alchemy' in *Dictionary of the History of Science*, ed. W. F. Bynum, E. J. Browne and Roy Porter, pp. 9–10 (a summary of alchemical goals and practices); Kieckhefer, *Magic in the Middle Ages*, pp. 133–39 (on alchemy); pp. 151–75 (on demonic magic).
24 Shelley, *The 1818 Text*, pp. 23–4.
25 Cited in Simon Schaffer, 'Natural Philosophy and Public Spectacle in the Eighteenth Century', *History of Science*, XXI (1983), pp. 1–43 (8).
26 Cited in Schaffer, *op. cit.*, p. 9.
27 Shelley, *The 1818 Text*, p. 24.
28 Ibid., p. 26.
29 Ibid., p. 27.
30 Ibid., p. 28.
31 Ibid.
32 Ibid., pp. 28–9.
33 Schaffer, *op. cit.*, pp. 9–15.
34 Hankins, *op. cit.*, pp. 7–8.
35 Shelley, *The 1818 Text*, p. 30.
36 Ibid., pp. 30–31. See, especially, C. E. Perrin, 'The Chemical Revolution', in *Companion to the History of Modern Science*, ed. R. C. Olby, G. N. Cantor, J.R.R. Christie and M.J.S. Hodge (London, 1990), pp. 264–77.
37 Schaffer, *op. cit.*, pp. 28–9.
38 Ibid., pp. 6–15 (on electricity); pp. 15–21 (on earthquake imitation).
39 Ibid., p. 21; Shelley, *The 1818 Text*, p. 31.
40 Simon Schaffer, 'Genius in Romantic Natural Philosophy', in *Romanticism and the Sciences*, ed. A. Cunningham and N. Jardine (Cambridge, 1990), pp. 82–98 (82–3).
41 Shelley, *The 1818 Text*, pp. 21, 30–31.
42 Ibid., pp. 31–2.
43 Ibid., pp. 32–3, 186.
44 Ibid., pp. 33–4.
45 Ibid.
46 Ibid., p. 35.
47 Ibid.
48 Ibid., pp. 99–100. On Condorcet, see Hankins, *op. cit.*, pp. 188–90. On radical political contexts for Mary Shelley, see Lee Sterrenburg, 'Mary Shelley's Monster: Politics and Psyche in *Frankenstein*', in *The Endurance of Frankenstein*, ed. G. Levine and U. C. Knoepflmacher (Berkeley, 1979), pp. 143–71.
49 Shelley, *The 1818 Text*, p. 7.
50 Ibid., pp. 35–6.
51 Ibid., p. 37.
52 Ibid., pp. 37–9.

53 Ibid., pp. 39–44, 48.
54 Ibid., p. 55.
55 Ibid., pp. 55–7.
56 Ibid., p. 59.
57 Ibid., pp. 74–81, 170–71.
58 Ibid., pp. 95, 108–10.
59 Ibid., pp. 111, 115, 196, 117.
60 Ibid., pp. 194–5.
61 Ibid., p. 73.
62 Ibid., pp. 72, 127.
63 Ibid., pp. 142–4.
64 Ibid., p. 162.
65 Ibid., p. 178.
66 Ibid., pp. 162, 166.
67 Ibid., pp. 16, 185.
68 Ibid., pp. 4, 9, 12, 41. British public enthusiasm for the search for a North-west passage linking the Atlantic and the Pacific was rekindled in 1817 when the whaling captain William Scoresby reported finding whales in the Atlantic with harpoons of a type characteristic of Pacific whalers embedded in them. A year later Captain John Ross led two ships on a scientific expedition that made extensive measurements of terrestrial magnetism in Arctic regions. But they failed to find a North-west passage. See Brendan Lehane, *The North-West Passage* (Amsterdam, 1981), especially pp. 94–100.

3 *Ludmilla Jordanova: Melancholy Reflection:*
   Constructing an Identity for Unveilers of Nature

This essay was presented, in a slightly different form, to an interdisciplinary seminar at the University of Victoria, BC, in January 1994. I am most grateful to my hosts, Paul Wood and Carol Gibson Wood, and to the participants, for their helpful comments. I owe a particular debt to Gregory Dart, not only for his detailed responses to my draft, but also for his support and encouragement in preparing the finished essay.

1 Mary Shelley, *Frankenstein* (Harmondsworth, 1985), p. 89. All subsequent references to Shelley's text are from this edition, edited by Maurice Hindle, hereafter cited as *Frankenstein*.
2 Robert Morris, James Kendrick and others, *Edinburgh Medical and Physical Dictionary* (Edinburgh, 1807); the definition of 'melancholia' is in volume II, not paginated. Definitions of melancholy and its cognates in the *OED* are also illuminating. On melancholy see W. Lepenies, *Melancholy and Society* (Cambridge, MA, 1992). Some paintings by Joseph Wright of Derby could be said to touch on 'melancholy' in their exploration of the relationships between natural knowledge, the boundaries between life and death, contemplation and introspection. Indeed, Wright's *Hermit Studying Anatomy* of 1771–3 was used for the cover of the Penguin edition of *Frankenstein*. Equally interesting are *The Alchemist, in Search of the Philosopher's Stone, Discovers Phosphorus* (exh. 1771; reworked and dated '1791'), *Miravan Opening the Tomb of his Ancestors* (1772), the portrait *Brooke Boothby* (1781), and *The Indian Widow* (1785); see B. Nicolson, *Joseph Wright of Derby: Painter of Light*, 2 vols (London, 1968), and *Wright of Derby*, exh. cat. ed. J. Egerton; London, Tate Gallery; Paris, Grand Palais; New York, Metropolitan Museum of Art; 1990. It is perhaps significant that Wright painted Erasmus Darwin, who is so often mentioned in connection with *Frankenstein*, five times.

3 L. S. Jacyna, 'Images of John Hunter in the Nineteenth Century', *History of Science*, XXI (1983), pp. 85–108; S. Schaffer, 'Genius in Romantic Natural Philosophy', in *Romanticism and the Sciences*, ed. A. Cunningham and N. Jardine (Cambridge, 1990), pp. 82–98; D. Knight, 'The Scientist as Sage', *Studies in Romanticism*, VI (1967), pp. 65–88. See also A. Desmond, *The Politics of Evolution: Morphology, Medicine and Reform in Radical London* (Chicago, 1989).

4 *Frankenstein*, p. 73.

5 It is sometimes said that Coleridge coined the term 'scientist' in 1833; for example in T. Levere, 'Coleridge and the Sciences', in *Romanticism and the Sciences* (Cambridge, 1990), pp. 295–306, especially p. 296, but see also R. Williams, *Keywords: A Vocabulary of Culture and Society* (revd edn London, 1983), pp. 276–80, especially p. 279, where Williams attributes it to Whewell in 1840. Williams notes that the word 'scientist' was used very occasionally in the late eighteenth century.

6 Richard Walker, *Regency Portraits* (London, 1985), I, pp. 605–8; II, plates 516–24, NPG nos. 1075, 1075a, 1075b and 1383a.

7 *Frankenstein*, p. 86.

8 The most important source for scientific and medical portraits is Renate Burgess, *Portraits of Doctors and Scientists in the Wellcome Institute of the History of Medicine* (London, 1973); my impression is that signatures were particularly likely to be added to portraits when prints were published as frontispieces to be collected works of medical authors or as illustrations to obituaries. Recent work on French eulogies is also relevant: Dorinda Outram, 'The Language of Natural Power: The "Eloges" of Georges Cuvier and the Public Language of Nineteenth Century Science', *History of Science*, XVI (1978), pp. 153–78; Daniel Roche, 'Talent, Reason, and Sacrifice: The Physician during the Enlightenment', in *Medicine and Society in France*, ed. R. Forster and O. Ranum (Baltimore, 1980), pp. 66–88; C. Paul, *Science and Immortality: The Eloges of the Paris Academy of Sciences (1699–1791)* (Berkeley, 1980).

9 Humphry Davy, *Elements of Chemical Philosophy* (London, 1812), p. 503; the 'Historical View of the Progress of Chemistry' is pp. 1–60. On Mary Shelley's reading see N. White, *Shelley* (London, 1947), II, pp. 539–45, and P. Feldman and D. Scott-Kilvert, eds, *The Journals of Mary Shelley 1814–1844* (Oxford, 1987), I, pp. 85–103. Hindle comments on her reading of Davy: *Frankenstein*, pp. 24–5.

10 *Frankenstein*, p. 91.

11 Ibid.

12 Ibid., p. 92.

13 C. Webster, 'The Historiography of Medicine' in *Information Sources in the History of Science and Medicine* (London, 1983), pp. 29–43; J. Christie, 'The Development of the Historiography of Science', in *Companion to the History of Modern Science*, ed. R. Olby, G. Cantor, J. Christie and M. Hodge (London, 1990), pp. 5–22.

14 L. Rosner, *Medical Education in the Age of Improvement: Edinburgh Students and Apprentices, 1760–1850* (Edinburgh, 1991), conveys most effectively the ways in which medical students encountered the ancients and the more modern masters.

15 L. Jordanova, 'The Art and Science of Seeing in Medicine: Physiognomy 1780–1820', in *Medicine and the Five Senses*, ed. W. Bynum and R. Porter (Cambridge, 1993), pp. 122–33; R. Darnton, *Mesmerism and the End of the Enlightenment in France* (Cambridge, MA, 1968); R. Porter, *Health for Sale: Quackery in England, 1660–1850* (Manchester, 1989).

16 D. Allen, 'The Women Members of the Botanical Society of London, 1836–56', *British Journal for the History of Science*, XIII (1981), pp. 240–54; L. Schiebinger, *The Mind Has No Sex? Women in the Origins of Modern Science* (Cambridge, MA, 1989); L. Davidoff and C. Hall, *Family Fortunes: Men and Women of the English*

Middle Class, 1780–1850 (London, 1987), especially pp. 289–93; A. Morrison-Low, 'Women in the Nineteenth-century Scientific Instrument Trade', in *Science and Sensibility: Gender and Scientific Enquiry, 1780–1945* (Oxford, 1991), pp. 89–117.

17 W. Lefanu, *British Periodicals of Medicine, 1640–1899* (Oxford, 1984); I. Inkster and J. Morrell, eds, *Metropolis and Province: Science in British Culture, 1780–1850* (London, 1983); R. Emerson, 'The Organisation of Science and its Pursuit in Early Modern Europe', and J. Morrell, 'Professionalisation', both in *Companion to the History of Modern Science*, pp. 960–79 and 980–89; T. Gelfand, 'The History of the Medical Profession', in the *Companion Encyclopedia of the History of Medicine*, ed. W. Bynum and R. Porter (London, 1993), II, pp. 1119–50; J. Morrell and A. Thackray, *Gentlemen of Science: Early Years of the British Association for the Advancement of Science* (Oxford, 1981).

18 For example, S.A.A.D. Tissot, *De la santé des gens de lettres* (Lausanne, 1758); *Avis aux gens de lettres et aux personnes sédentaires sur leur santé* (Paris, 1767); *An Essay on Diseases Incidental to Literary and Sedentary Persons* (London, 1768); and *An Essay on the Disorders of People of Fashion* (London, 1771). See also R. Porter, 'Diseases of Civilization', in the *Companion Encyclopedia of the History of Medicine*, I, pp. 584–600, especially 589–92.

19 S.A.A.D. Tissot, *Onanism* (London, 1766); Ludmilla Jordanova, 'The Popularisation of Medicine: Tissot on Onanism', *Textual Practice*, I (1987), pp. 68–79.

20 Details of these two pairs of prints may be found in the *Catalogue of Prints and Drawings in the British Museum* (London, 1877 and 1935). The 'Benevolent Physician' prints are discussed in volume V covering 1771–83 (nos 6347 and 6350, c. 1783), the 'Rapacious Quack' ones in volume III covering 1751–60 (nos. 3797 and 3798, c. 1760). Since the 'Physician' and the 'Quack' were pendants, the implication is that the prints were issued twice, once c. 1760 and again c. 1783. Despite the titles, these two pairs are quite different in design.

21 On this point it is suggestive that, in the preface he wrote for the 1818 edition, Percy Shelley specifically insisted that no 'inference [was] justly to be drawn from the following pages as prejudicing any philosophical doctorine of whatever kind' (*Frankenstein*, p. 58).

22 This was published in 1986, by New Orchard Editions, and is accompanied by wood engravings by Lynd Ward.

23 *Frankenstein*, p. 98.

24 J. McManners, *Death and the Enlightenment: Changing Attitudes to Death among Christians and Unbelievers in Eighteenth-century France* (Oxford, 1981); P. Ariès, *The Hour of Our Death* (Harmondsworth, 1983); R. Maulitz, *Morbid Appearances: the Anatomy of Pathology in the Early Nineteenth Century* (Cambridge, 1987); R. Richardson, *Death, Dissection and the Destitute* (London, 1987).

25 D. Ramsay, *A Review of the Improvements, Progress and State of Medicine in the XVIIIth Century* (Charleston, 1801), p. 15.

26 Ramsay, *Review*, p. 16.

27 Ibid., p. 34.

28 *Frankenstein*, p. 96.

29 K. Garlick, *Sir Thomas Lawrence. A Complete Catalogue of Oil Paintings* (Oxford, 1989).

30 Biographies of all these medical men may be found in the *DNB*, which in a significant sense constitutes a primary source, since the entries were written in the idiom of nineteenth-century heroism. Cf. the *Dictionary of Scientific Biography*, the first volume of which appeared in 1970.

31 Richardson, *op. cit.*

32 James Hall, *Dictionary of Subjects and Symbols in Art* (revd edn, London, 1979), pp. 94 ('Death'); pp. 130–1 ('Four Temperaments'); p. 285 ('Skull'). Hall stresses the direct links between melancholy, contemplation, books and a skull. (See also note 2.)

33 A. Cunningham and N. Jardine, eds, *Romanticism and the Sciences* (Cambridge, 1990).

34 Cunningham and Jardine, *op. cit.*, especially pp. 13–22 and 213–27.

35 Marten Hutt in the Wellcome Unit for the History of Medicine, University of Oxford, is currently completing a doctoral dissertation on medical biographies in the late eighteenth and early nineteenth centuries. See, for example, John Aikin, *A Specimen of the Medical Biography of Great Britain; with an Address to the Public* (London, 1775) and *Biographical Memoirs of Medicine of Great Britain* (London, 1780); Joseph Towers, *British Biography; or, an Accurate and Impartial Account of the Lives and Writings of Eminent Persons in Great Britain and Ireland*, 10 vols (London, 1766–1780).

36 For example, Thomas Garnett (1766–1802) and John Haighton (1755–1823) in the *DNB* (Oxford, 1949–50), volumes VII and VIII respectively (first published 1889–90).

37 A particularly clear example of such histories is W. Black, *An Historical Sketch of Medicine and Surgery, from their Origin to the Present Time* (London, 1782).

38 R. Baker, 'The History of Medical Ethics', in *Companion Encyclopedia of the History of Medicine*, pp. 852–87, especially pp. 861–8. These themes emerged particularly clearly in the early nineteenth-century medical reform movement: A. Desmond, *The Politics of Evolution: Morphology, Medicine and Reform in Radical London* (Chicago, 1989); I. Loudon, 'Medical Practitioners 1750–1850, and the Period of Medical Reform in Britain', in *Medicine in Society: Historical Essays*, ed. A. Wear (Cambridge, 1992), pp. 219–47; R. French and A. Wear, eds, *British Medicine in an Age of Reform* (London, 1991).

39 L. Jordanova, *Sexual Visions: Images of Gender in Science and Medicine between the Eighteenth and Twentieth Centuries* (Hemel Hempstead, 1989), ch. 5.

40 For example, Marie Roberts, 'The Male Scientist, Man-Midwife and Female Monster: Appropriation and Transmutation in *Frankenstein*', in *A Question of Identity: Women, Science and Literature*, ed. M. Benjamin (New Brunswick, 1993), pp. 59–74. For a very different view of man-midwifery see W. Bynum and R. Porter, eds, *William Hunter and the Eighteenth-century Medical World* (Cambridge, 1985), part IV.

41 S. W. Fores, *Man-Midwifery Dissected; or, The Obstetric Family Instructor* (London, 1793).

42 P. Feldman and D. Scott-Kilvert, eds, *The Journals of Mary Shelley, 1814–1844* (Oxford, 1987), p. 100. N. Hampson, *The Enlightenment* (Harmondsworth, 1968). Buffon is still widely read as a stylist in France, and as a result today remains available in cheap editions.

43 S. Schaffer, 'States of Mind: Enlightenment and Natural Philosophy', in *The Languages of Psyche: Mind and Body in Enlightenment Thought* (Berkeley, 1990), pp. 233–90; R. Porter, *Health for Sale: Quackery in England 1660–1850*.

44 P. Feldman and D. Scott-Kilvert, eds, *The Journals of Mary Shelley, 1814–1844*, e.g. pp. 26, 39, 47, 55, 65, 67, 124, 180.

45 Nigel Leask, 'Shelley's "Magnetic Ladies": Romantic Mesmerism and the Politics of the Body', in *Beyond Romanticism: New Approaches to Texts and Contexts, 1780–1832*, ed. S. Copley and J. Whale (London, 1992), pp. 53–78.

46 Brian Easlea, *Fathering the Unthinkable: Masculinity, Scientists and the Nuclear Arms Race* (London, 1983), pp. 28–39; Maurice Hindle makes a similar point in his introduction, *Frankenstein*, pp. 41–2.

4 *Louis James: Frankenstein's Monster in Two Traditions*

This essay was originally planned as a joint venture with Dr Jan Shepherd, who provided key material on the drama. She died tragically before the piece could be completed, and this essay is dedicated to her memory.

1 Chris Baldick, *In Frankenstein's Shadow* (Oxford, 1987), pp. 75–84.
2 In Fred Botting, *Making Monstrous* (Manchester, 1991).
3 George Levine, *The Realistic Imagination* (Chicago and London, 1981), p. 47.
4 Franco Moretti, *Signs Taken as Wonders* (London, 1983), p. 85.
5 Moretti, *op. cit.*, p. 91.
6 Fred Botting, *Making Monstrous*, pp. 7–12.
7 Paul Sherwin, 'A Psychoaesthetic Reading of Mary Shelley's *Frankenstein*,' in *English Forum*, ed. Sam Brody and Harold Schechter (New York, 1985), pp. 199–210.
8 Gilliam Beer, *Darwin's Plots* (London, 1983), pp. 110–11; *idem, Forging the Missing Link* (Cambridge, 1991), pp. 32–3.
9 Robert B. Pollin, 'Philosophical and literary sources of *Frankenstein*', *Comparative Literature*, XVII (1965), pp. 97–108.
10 'Pgymalion' in Robert Buchanan, *Poetical Works* (London, 1874), II, pp. 248–58.
11 Mrs Gaskell, *Mary Barton* (1848), ch. 15.
12 See Chris Baldick, *In Frankenstein's Shadow*, ch. 5.
13 Charles Dickens, *Great Expectations* (1860–1), ch. 27.
14 Ibid., ch. 40.
15 Rousseau's *Pygmalion* (1770) was the first work to be identified as a 'melodrame'. The experiment belongs strictly to the evolution of opera rather than drama: however it does have relevance to the development of stage melodrama. See, for example, Peter Brooks, *The Melodramatic Imagination* (New Haven and London, 1976), and Janet Shepherd, 'Music, Text and Performance in English Popular Theatre, 1790–1840' (University of London thesis, 1991).
16 This is discussed in Brooks, *op. cit.*, pp. 66, 87. Brooks's chapters 3 and 4 are relevant here.
17 Playbill in the Pettingell Collection, Templeman Library, University of Kent at Canterbury.
18 From a playbill for the Royal City of London Theatre, 1 February 1843, in Pettingell Collection, Templeman Library, University of Kent at Canterbury.
19 Henry Saxe Wyndham, *The Annals of Covent Garden* (1906), p. 316.
20 C.I.M. Dibdin, *The Wild Man* (1809), II, vi.
21 From a playbill in Louis James's collection.
22 H. M. Milner, *Frankenstein: or, The Man and the Monster!* (London, n.d.), p. 10.
23 Milner, *Frankenstein*, II, ii.
24 Ibid., I, iii.
25 Ibid.
26 Ibid., p. 24.
27 Ibid., I, vii.
28 A frame-by-frame exposition of the film is available in Richard J. Anobile, ed., *James Whale's Frankenstein* (London, 1974).
29 Anobile, *op. cit.*, p. 96.
30 Ibid., p. 5.
31 George Speaight, *Juvenile Drama: The History of the English Toy Theatre* (London, 1946), p. 208.
32 Anobile, *op. cit.*, p. 6.

5 *Michael Fried: Impressionist Monsters: H. G. Wells's 'The Island of Dr Moreau'*

1 Rudyard Kipling, 'A Matter of Fact', in *Many Inventions* (New York, 1893), pp. 190–91.
2 Ibid., pp. 192–4.
3 Published Chicago: University of Chicago Press, 1987.
4 *Critical Inquiry*, XVII (1990), pp. 193–235.
5 It may be useful to have that passage in mind throughout what follows:

> Once the line encountered the body of a dead soldier. He lay upon his back staring at the sky. He was dressed in an awkward suit of yellowish brown. The youth [the novel's protagonist, Henry Fleming] could see that the soles of his shoes had been worn to the thinness of writing paper, and from a great rent in one the dead foot projected piteously. And it was as if fate had betrayed the soldier. In death it exposed to his enemies that poverty which in life he had perhaps concealed from his friends.
> The ranks opened covertly to avoid the corpse. The invulnerable dead man forced a way for himself. The youth looked keenly at the ashen face. The wind raised the tawny beard. It moved as if a hand were stroking it. He vaguely desired to walk around and around the body and stare; the impulse of the living to try to read in dead eyes the answer to the Question. (Stephen Crane, *Prose and Poetry*, ed. J. C. Levenson, New York, 1984, pp. 101–2.)

6 See his *The Gold Standard and the Logic of Naturalism: American Literature at the Turn of the Century* (Berkeley, CA, 1987). This is as good a place as any to thank Michaels, Stephen Bann, James Conant, Frances Ferguson, and Ruth Leys for helpful conversations about particular points in the present essay.
7 H. G. Wells, *The Island of Dr Moreau: A Variorum Text*, ed. R. M. Philmus (1896; Athens, GA, and London, 1993); hereafter cited as *Moreau*. Page references to this edition will be given in parentheses in the text. I might add that I am currently at work on a book to be called 'Almayer's Face: Rewriting Literary Impressionism' in which the present essay, or the material in it, will be subsumed.
8 See Philmus, 'Introducing *Moreau*', ibid., p. xxxii.
9 Maps, charts and diagrams, with their elision of the distinction between writing and drawing (or imaging), are a basic impressionist motif. *Heart of Darkness*, again, is an obvious example, as is *Kim*, which juxtaposes mapmaking in the service of imperialism to the lama's novel-long labours on his religious chart/diagram. Significantly, the latter is torn in two, disfigured, in the climactic encounter with the enemy agents, in the course of which the lama is also struck in the face (an action the reader registers as one of shocking violence). The mention of *Kim* leads me to add that *spying* – a special case of *seeing* – is another impressionist motif, as in *Under Western Eyes*, *The Fifth Queen*, and Childers's *The Riddle of the Sands*. In the last of these, maps printed in the body of the text play a crucial role; I shall have more to say about all these works in 'Almayer's Face'.
10 See Fried, *Realism, Writing, Disfiguration*, p. 123.
11 See ibid., p. 96 and *passim*.
12 See Philmus, 'Introducing *Moreau*', p. xix. Philmus notes that Wells actually referred to *Frankenstein* twice in the opening chapter of his first draft for the novel.
13 It hardly needs stating that Prendick's horrified, disgusted description of the 'black-faced creature' and the other beast-men trades on contemporary racialist discourse to achieve some portion of its effect. What is less obvious is Wells's attitude towards that discourse: as Philmus remarks, the first draft of the novel contains more blatantly

racialist passages than the final version, and even in that draft 'there are signs of Wells's growing consciousness of the prejudices to which his class background rendered him particularly liable' (ibid., p. xxii). Philmus also finds in both versions the suggestion of a satire or at least a commentary on the colonial enterprise (ibid.).

14 See 'Almayer's Face' (as cited in n.4), for a discussion of these and other motifs of disfigured faces.

15 Rudyard Kipling, 'The Mark of the Beast', in *Life's Handicap* (1891; Harmondsworth, 1987), pp. 195–207. Two other passages in Kipling are worth citing in this connection. In the first, the artist-journalist Dick Heldar in a skirmish in the desert is said to have 'fired his revolver into a black, foam-flecked face which forthwith ceased to bear any resemblance to a face', and of another dead Arab we are told that 'His upturned face lacked one eye' (*The Light that Failed*, 1891; Harmondsworth, 1970, pp. 27–8). (The eye had been gouged out by Dick's friend Torpenhow.) The second is the scene in which Dan and Harvey retrieve from the sea 'the body of the dead Frenchman buried two days before! The hook had caught him under the right armpit, and he swayed, erect and horrible, head and shoulders above water. His arms were tied to his side, and – he had no face. The boys fell over each other in a heap at the bottom of the dory, and there they lay while the thing bobbed alongside, held on the shortened line' (*Captains Courageous*, 1896; New York, 1982, p. 98).

16 On the significance of Mergenthaler's invention, see, for example, S. H. Steinberg, *Five Hundred Years of Printing* (1955; Harmondsworth, 1974), pp. 288–9; Warren Chappell, *A Short History of the Printed Word* (New York, 1970), pp. 190–92; and the privately printed *New Wings for Intelligence. Being A Tribute to the Life and Work of Ottmar Mergenthaler . . .* (Baltimore, 1954). In the words of Justin Kaplan: 'The London *Times* was using a rotary type caster, patented in 1881, which worked so fast . . . that instead of distributing type at the end of the run the printers simply melted t down and started all over again with fresh type. This bypass of the human analogy was the basic principle of Ottmar Mergenthaler's Linotype machine [1884], which cast its own type from its own matrices in single slugs of a line's length which were afterwards thrown back into the melting pot. Mergenthaler was to sweep the field' (*Mr Clemens and Mark Twain*, New York, 1966, p. 282). Twain, of course, staked his entire fortune in a rival machine, the Paige typesetter, which unlike the Mergenthaler Linotype machine was based on the movements of a human typesetter and largely for that reason continually broke down. The implicit relation of 'the human analogy' and its 'bypass' to the thematics of monstrosity in Wells's novel invites further reflection.

17 See Fried, *Realism, Writing, Disfiguration*, pp. 151–5. There is also a suggestive detail in the first draft's version of 'Doctor Moreau Explains'. Before commencing his explanation, Moreau insists that Prendick join him in smoking a cigar; and after reporting Moreau's account of the discovery of the dead Kanaka and the rifle barrel curved into an S-shape, Prendick writes: 'He became silent. I sat in silence watching his face, with my dead cigar in my fingers' (*Moreau*, p. 134). Sometimes a cigar is just a pen.

18 See H. G. Wells, *Experiment in Autobiography* (New York, 1934), p. 250, where a Miss Healey criticizes the young Wells's verse for lacking *feet*.

19 But never merely to *simple* brutes: when Moreau concedes that he might just as well have made sheep into llamas or llamas into sheep, he is in effect expressing a commitment to *difference* (or say *representation*) within beasthood itself. As I read this, it is another marker of a thematics of writing, which Michaels and I understand as crucially involving difference-from-itself in that writing *to be* writing must in some sense be different from its material basis. See Michaels's introduction, 'The Writer's Mark', to *The Gold Standard and the Logic of Naturalism*, as well as all of 'Stephen Crane's Upturned Faces'.

20 R. B. Cunninghame Graham, 'Progress', in *Progress and Other Sketches* (London, 1905), pp. 1–61.

21 Rudyard Kipling, 'Wireless', in *Traffics and Discoveries* (1904; Harmondsworth, 1987), pp. 181–99. Kipling's 'The Mark of the Beast', cited in n.15, is also pertinent here. Its climax comes when the narrator and a friend, Strickland, torture the faceless Silver Man with heated gun-barrels to force him to cure a case of 'hydrophobia' that he had caused. The narrator writes:

> I understand then how men and women and little children can endure to see a witch burnt alive; for the beast was moaning on the floor, and though the Silver Man had no face, you could see horrible feelings passing through the slab that took its place, exactly as waves of heat play across red-hot iron – gun-barrels for instance.
>   Strickland shaded his eyes with his hands for a moment and we got to work. This part is not to be printed. (p. 205.)

The last sentence is not exactly a case of regression from print to writing but together with the blank space between paragraphs that follows (the only such space in the text) it invites us to imagine the deliberate elision of a written description too horrible to lend itself to print.

22 As Philmus remarks ('Introducing *Moreau*', pp. xxx, xlvii, n.65), Moreau's views are very close to those expressed by Wells himself in 'Province of Pain', an article published in *Science and Art* (February 1894), pp. 58–9. The article concludes with Wells saying that 'the province of pain is after all a limited and transitory one; a phase through which life must pass on its evolution from the automatic to the spiritual; and, so far as we can tell, among all the hosts of space, pain is found only on the surface of this little planet' (*H. G. Wells: Early Writings in Science and Science Fiction*, ed. R. M. Philmus and D. Y. Hughes, Berkeley, CA, and London, 1975, pp. 198–9). But Wells's identification with Moreau in this regard only underscores the problematic status of pain in the novel as distinct from the article.
    Note, by the way, the curious connection Wells draws between the province of pain and the *surface* of the earth. Earlier in the article he writes: 'The province of pain . . . in man . . . is merely the surface of his body, with "spheres of influence", rather than proper possessions in the interior, and the centre seat of pain is in the mind' (p. 196). The concept of surface, of course, played a considerable role in contemporary discussions of literary impressionism, and its prominence in Wells's article suggests that writerly considerations may have been entangled with strictly scientific ones.

23 Thus the Grand Lunar's brain is described by Cavor as 'very much like an opaque, featureless bladder with dim, undulating ghosts of convolutions writhing visibly within' (H. G. Wells, *The First Men in the Moon*, 1901; London and Glasgow, 1954, p. 238).

24 In *Experiment in Autobiography* Wells reports that in response to Miss Healey's criticism that his poem had no feet (see n.18 above), he had replied: 'The humming bird has no feet, the cherubim round the Mater Dolorosa have no feet. The ancients figured the poetic afflatus as a horse *winged* to signify the poet was sparing of his feet' (p. 251).

25 H. G. Wells, *Tono-Bungay* (1908 and 1909; Lincoln, NB, and London, 1978), p. 247.

26 See, for example, Ford Madox Ford, *Return to Yesterday* (1932; New York, 1972), where he explains: 'The trouble . . . with Conrad and myself was this: we could not get our own prose keyed down enough. We wanted to write, I suppose, as only Mr W. H. Hudson writes – as simply as the grass grows. We desired to achieve a style – the *habit* of a style – so simple you would notice it no more than you notice the unostentatious covering of the South Downs. The turf has to be there, or the earth would not be

green. . . . We wanted the reader to forget the writer – to forget that he was reading' (p. 216).

27 More broadly, it perhaps expresses the same sort of critique not just of Hudsonian but also of Conradian impressionism (as understood by Wells, not by Ford) that Wells develops in one of the most interesting sections of *Experiment in Autobiography* (pp. 525–32): 'This incessant endeavour to keep prose bristling up and have it "vivid" all the time defeats its end', Wells argues. 'I find very much of Conrad oppressive, as overwrought as an Indian tracery, and it is only in chosen passages and some of his short stories that I would put his work on a level with the naked vigour of Stephen Crane' (p. 531). The larger question of Wells's particular slant on impressionism requires to be dealt with at greater length.

28 H. G. Wells, *The Invisible Man* (1897; New York, 1983), p. 136.

6 *Michael Grant: James Whale's 'Frankenstein':*
The Horror Film and the Symbolic Biology of the Cinematic Monster

1 Gregory A. Waller, ed., *American Horrors* (Urbana and Chicago, 1987), p. 4.
2 Andrew Tudor, *Monsters and Mad Scientists* (Oxford, 1989), p. 178.
3 J. L. Schefer, 'Schefer on Schefer', *Wide Angle*, VI (1982), pp. 54–63. This article consists of translations from *L'homme ordinaire du cinéma* (Paris, 1980). Schefer's arguments should be sharply distinguished from those of 'apparatus theorists' such as Jean-Louis Comolli, Jean-Louis Baudry and Stephen Heath. Unlike these thinkers, Schefer is not concerned to address issues of 'subject positioning' or ideology.
4 As Donald Davie has argued in a very different context; see *The Poet in the Imaginary Museum* (Manchester, 1977), p. 98. I am deeply indebted to Davie's arguments throughout the first section of this paper.
5 Ibid., p. 194.
6 Ibid., p. 103.
7 T. R. Ellis, *A Journey Into Darkness: The Art of James Whale's Horror Films* (Ann Arbor, 1984), pp. 61–2.
8 Noël Carroll, 'Nightmare and the Horror Film: The Symbolic Biology of Fantastic Beings', *Film Quarterly*, XXXIV (Spring 1981), pp. 16–25. Carroll's later treatment of the nightmare theme is in *The Philosophy of Horror* (London, 1990), pp. 168–78.
9 Carroll, p. 17.
10 Ibid.
11 Ibid.
12 Ernest Jones, *On the Nightmare* (London, 1971), p. 78. Cited by Carroll, p. 17.
13 John Mack, *Nightmares and Human Conflict* (Boston, 1970). Cited by Carroll, p. 18.
14 Carroll, p. 19.
15 Ludwig Wittgenstein, *Remarks on Frazer's 'Golden Bough'*, ed. Rush Rhees (Doncaster, 1979), p. 4e.
16 P.M.S. Hacker, 'Developmental Hypotheses and Perspicuous Representations: Wittgenstein on Frazer's "Golden Bough"', *Iyyun: The Jerusalem Philosophical Quarterly*, XLI (1992), p. 296.
17 Hacker, p. 288.
18 Ibid., p. 289.
19 Ibid.
20 Hacker, p. 296. A relation between two objects is 'internal' (in Wittgenstein's sense) if it is inconceivable that *these* two objects should not stand in *this* relation. Wittgenstein writes in the *Remarks* on Frazer: 'one might illustrate the internal relation of a circle to an ellipse by gradually transforming the ellipse into a circle; *but not in order to assert that a given ellipse in fact, historically, came from a circle* (hypothesis of development)

but only to sharpen our eye for a formal connection' (p. 9e). For a further discussion of the significance of the *Remarks*, see Paul Johnston, *Wittgenstein and Moral Philosophy* (London, 1989), pp. 26–51.

21 Wittgenstein, *Remarks*, p. 4e.
22 Wittgenstein, *Philosophical Investigations* (Oxford, 1986), I, §531.
23 Ibid.
24 Ibid., I, §533.
25 Stanley Cavell, *Must We Mean What We Say?* (Cambridge, 1989), p. 81.
26 Carroll, p. 21.
27 Ibid.
28 Ibid.
29 R.H.W. Dillard, *Horror Films* (New York, 1976), p. 18. Cited by Ellis, *A Journey Into Darkness*, p. 64.
30 Ellis, p. 48.
31 Ibid.
32 Dillard, *Horror Films*, p. 27. Cited by Ellis, p. 67.
33 Cited by Ellis, p. 68, n. 80.
34 Cited by Ellis, p. 64.
35 Mary Shelley, *Frankenstein*, ed. Maurice Hindle (London, 1992), p. xxii.
36 Earl R. Wasserman, *The Subtler Language: Critical Readings of Neoclassic and Romantic Poems* (Baltimore, 1968), p. 11.
37 Wasserman, p. 26.
38 Cited by Wasserman, p. 203.
39 Ellis, *A Journey Into Darkness*, p. 63.
40 Georges Bataille, *Literature and Evil*, trans. Alastair Hamilton (London, 1973), p. 66.
41 Wittgenstein, *Remarks*, p. 6e.
42 Hacker, 'Developmental Hypotheses', p. 297.
43 Frank Cioffi, 'Wittgenstein and Obscurantism', *Proceedings of the Aristotelian Society*, suppl. vol. LXIV (1990), p. 12. It is this article that occasioned Hacker's essay of 1992. Cioffi has also written on Frazer and Wittgenstein in 'Wittgenstein and the Fire-Festivals' in *Ludwig Wittgenstein: Critical Assessments*, IV, ed. Stuart Shanker (Beckenham, 1986), pp. 312–33. In this article, Cioffi concludes 'that what [is] called for by the notion of human sacrifice [is] neither an historical nor a causal enquiry, but rather an attempt to unravel the web of associations wound round the subject by nature and the unavoidable conditions of humanity' (p. 331).
44 Hacker, p. 281.
45 Wittgenstein, *Remarks*, p. 18e.
46 Ibid., p. 6e.
47 Hacker, p. 298.

7 Jasia Reichardt: Artificial Life and the Myth of Frankenstein

1 R. M. Fox, *The Triumphant Machine* (London, 1928), p. 26.
2 Throughout this essay, therefore, I shall refer to Victor Frankenstein as Victor and to the creature he makes as 'Frankenstein'.
3 Alexander M. Capron, cited in *The New York Times* (9 June 1987), section C, p. 8.
4 Philip M. Boffey, in 'Concern over Genetics Prompts a New Coalition of Critics', *The New York Times* (9 June 1987), section C, p. 8.
5 Reported in *Time* magazine (24 January 1994), p. 11.
6 See 'Applications for Gene Patents "thrown on bonfire" ', *New Scientist* (19 February 1994), p. 4.
7 *Time* (14 February 1994), p. 11.

8 Andy Warhol, *From A to B and Back Again* (London, 1975), p. 96.
9 Published in *Mind*, LIX/236 (October 1950), pp. 433–60.
10 Ibid., p. 442.
11 Norbert Wiener, *God & Golem Inc.* (Cambridge, MA, 1964), p. 48.
12 Steven J. Heims, *John von Neumann and Norbert Wiener* (Cambridge, MA, 1980), p. 212.
13 Vidal, in an Arena television interview for 'In Search of OZ', BBC2, 1994.

8 *Robert Olorenshaw: Narrating the Monster: From Mary Shelley to Bram Stoker*

1 Tzvetan Todorov, *Introduction à la littérature fantastique* (Paris 1970), p. 29.
2 Roland Barthes, *S/Z* (Paris, 1970), p. 24.
3 Percy Shelley, 'Preface' to the first edition of *Frankenstein*, in Mary Shelley, *Frankenstein* (Harmondsworth, 1992), p. 11.
4 Bram Stoker, *Dracula* (Harmondsworth, 1993), p. 17.
5 Mary Shelley, *Frankenstein* (Harmondsworth, 1993), p. 40.
6 Ibid., p. 51.
7 John Locke, 'Anatomie', published in full in K. Dewhurst, ed., 'Locke and Sydenham on the Teaching of Anatomy', *Medical History*, II (1958); see pp. 11–12.
8 Michel Foucault, *Les mots et les choses* (Paris, 1966), p. 142 (my translation).
9 Ibid., p. 280.
10 *Frankenstein*, p. 47.
11 Ibid., p. 50.
12 Ibid., p. 52.
13 Immanuel Kant, *Critique of Pure Reason*, trans. N. Kemp-Smith (London 1964), p. 320.
14 Percy Shelley, 'Speculations on Morals' (1815), cited in M. M. Bhalla, *Studies in Shelley* (New Delhi, 1973), pp. 3–4.
15 Mary Wollstonecraft, *A Vindication of the Rights of Woman*, in *The Works*, vol. V, ed. J. Todd and M. Butler (London, 1989), pp. 156–7.
16 *Frankenstein*, p. 56.
17 Ibid., p. 8.
18 Ibid., p. 100.
19 Ibid., p. 110.
20 Ibid., p. 125.
21 William Godwin, *An Enquiry Concerning Political Justice* (London 1793), II, pp. 855–6.
22 *Frankenstein*, p. 124.
23 Ibid., p. 121.
24 Godwin, *op. cit.*, p. 380.
25 Wollstonecraft, *op. cit.*, p. 243.
26 *Frankenstein*, p. 134.
27 Peter Brook, 'Godlike Science, Unhallowed Arts', in *The Endurance of Frankenstein* (Los Angeles, 1979), pp. 207–8.
28 *Frankenstein*, p. 5.
29 *Dracula*, p. 147.
30 Ibid., p. 246.
31 Voltaire, 'Dictionnaire Philosophique', *Oeuvres complètes* (Paris 1879), XX, p. 547.
32 *Dracula*, p. 77.
33 Ibid., p. 81.
34 Ibid., p. 159.
35 Ibid., p. 168.

36 Ibid., p. 227.
37 Ibid., p. 271.
38 Ibid., p. 277.
39 Ibid., p. 95.
40 Ibid., p. 133.
41 Ibid., p. 139
42 Ibid., pp. 231–2.
43 Ibid., p. 285.
44 Ibid., p. 305.
45 Ibid., p. 158.
46 Ibid., p. 220.
47 Ibid., p. 450.
48 Ibid., pp. 285–6.
49 Michel Butor, 'Eloge de la machine à écrire', *Répertoire IV* (Paris, 1974), p. 425.
50 *Dracula*, p. 486.
51 Ibid., pp. 485–6.

Select Bibliography

COMPILED BY BRANISLAV DIMITRIJEVIĆ

Anobile, Richard J. ed., *James Whale's 'Frankenstein'* (London, 1974).

Baldick, Chris, *In Frankenstein's Shadow: Myth, Monstrosity, and Nineteenth-century Writing* (Oxford, 1987).

Beer, Gillian, *Darwin's Plots: Evolutionary Narrative in Darwin, George Eliot, and Nineteenth-century Fiction* (London, 1983).

Bennet, Betty T. ed., *The Letters of Mary Wollstonecraft Shelley* (Baltimore, 1980).

Bloom, Harold, 'Frankenstein or the New Prometheus', *Partisan Review*, XXXII (1965), pp. 611–18.

——, *The Anxiety of Influence: A Theory of Poetry* (Oxford, 1973).

——, ed., *Mary Shelley's Frankenstein* (New York, 1987).

Botting, Fred, *Making Monstrous: Frankenstein, Criticism, Theory* (Manchester, 1991).

Brooke, J. H., *Science and Religion: Some Historical Perspectives* (Cambridge, 1991).

Burton, Pollin R., 'Philosophical and Literary Sources for Frankenstein', *Comparative Literature* XVII/2 (Spring 1965), pp. 97–108.

Butor, Michel, 'Eloge de la machine écrire', *Répertoire IV* (Paris 1974).

Cantor, Paul, *Creature and Creator: Myth-making and English Romanticism* (Cambridge, 1984).

Carroll, Noël, 'Nightmare and the Horror Film: The Symbolic Biology of Fantastic Beings', *Film Quarterly* XXXIV/3 (Spring 1981), pp. 16–25.

Clemit, Pamela, *The Godwinian Novel: The Rational Fictions of Godwin, Brockden Brown, Mary Shelley* (Oxford, 1993).

Cooter, Roger, *The Cultural Meaning of Popular Science: Phrenology and the Organization of Consent in Nineteenth-century Britain* (Cambridge, 1984).

Cunningham, Andrew, and Nicholas Jardine, eds, *Romanticism and the Sciences* (Cambridge, 1990).

Dunn, Jane, *Moon in Eclipse: A Life of Mary Shelley* (London, 1978).

Freud, Sigmund, 'Family Romances', *Standard Edition*, IX (London, 1959).

Feldman, Paula R., and Diana Scott-Kilvert, eds, *The Journals of Mary Shelley* (Oxford, 1987).

Fisch, Audrey A., Anne K. Mellor and Esther H. Schor, eds, *The Other Mary Shelley: Beyond Frankenstein* (Oxford, 1993).

Forry, Steven Earl, *Hideous Progenies: Dramatizations of Frankenstein from Mary Shelley to the Present* (Philadelphia, 1990).

Fried, Michael, *Realism, Writing, Disfiguration: On Thomas Eakins and Stephen Crane* (Chicago, 1987).

Friedman, Lester D., 'Sporting with Life: "Frankenstein" and the Responsibility of Medical Research', *Medical Heritage*, I/3 (May/June 1985), pp. 181–5.

Gilbert, Sandra M. and Susan Gubar, *The Madwoman in the Attic: The Woman Writer and the Nineteenth-century Literary Imagination* (New Haven, 1979).

Gillispie, Charles Coulston, *Genesis and Geology: A Study in the Relations of Scientific Thought, Natural Theology, and Social Opinion in Great Britain, 1790–1850* (New York, 1959).

Homans, Margaret, 'Bearing Demons: Frankenstein's Circumvention of the Maternal', in Harold Bloom, ed., *Mary Shelley's Frankenstein* (New York, 1987), pp. 133–53.

Johnson, Barbara, 'My Monster/My Self', in Harold Bloom, ed., *Mary Shelley's Frankenstein* (New York, 1987), pp. 55–66.

Jordanova, Ludmilla, *Lamarck* (Oxford, 1984).

——, ed., *Languages of Nature: Critical Essays on Science and Literature* (London, 1986).

Lecercle, Jean-Jacques, *Frankenstein: mythe et philosophie* (Presses universitaires de France, 1988).

Levine, George, *The Realistic Imagination: English Fiction from Frankenstein to Lady Chatterley* (Chicago, 1981).

—— and U. C. Knoepflmacher, eds, *The Endurance of Frankenstein: Essays on Mary Shelley's Novel* (Berkeley, 1982).

Mellor, Anne, *Mary Shelley: Her Life, her Fictions, her Monsters* (New York and London, 1988).

Michaels, Walter Benn, *The Gold Standard and the Logic of Naturalism: American Literature at the Turn of the Century* (Berkeley, 1987).

Miyoshi, Masao, *The Divided Self: A Perspective on the Literature of the Victorians* (New York, 1969).

Moers, Ellen, *Literary Women: The Great Writers* (New York, 1977).

Moretti, Franco, *Signs Taken as Wonders* (London, 1983).

O'Flinn, Paul, 'Production and Reproduction: The Case of Frankenstein', *Literature and History* (Autumn 1983), pp. 194–213.

Musselwhite, David E., *Partings Welded Together: Politics and Desire in the Nineteenth-century English Novel* (London, 1987).

Philmus, Robert M., *Into the Unknown: The Evolution of Science Fiction from Francis Godwin to H.G. Wells* (Berkeley, 1970).

Praz, Mario, 'Introductory Essay', *Three Gothic Novels*, ed. Peter Fairclough (Harmondsworth, 1968).

Poovey, Mary, 'My Hideous Progeny: Mary Shelley and the Feminization of Romanticism', *Publications of the Modern Language Association of America*, xcv (1980), pp. 332–47.

——, *The Proper Lady and the Woman Writer: Ideology as Style in the Works of Mary Wollstonecraft, Mary Shelley and Jane Austen* (Chicago, 1984).

Reed, T. R., *A Journey Into Darkness: The Art of James Whale's Horror Films* (Ann Arbor, 1984).

Secord, J. A., 'Extraordinary Experiment: Electricity and the Creation of Life in Victorian England', in David Gooding *et al.*, eds, *The Uses of Experiment* (Cambridge, 1989), pp. 337–83.

Schaffer, Simon, 'Natural Philosophy and Public Spectacle in the Eighteenth Century', *History of Science*, xxi (1983), pp. 1–43.

Shelley, Mary, *Frankenstein; or, The Modern Prometheus*, ed. Maurice Hindle, with the 'Preface' to the first edition by Percy Shelley (Harmondsworth, 1992).

Shelley, Percy, *Poetical Works*, ed. Thomas Hutchinson (Oxford 1970).

Sherwin, Paul, 'A Psychoaesthetic Reading of Mary Shelley's Frankenstein', in Sam Brody and Harold Schechter, eds., *English Forum* (New York, 1985), pp. 199–210.

Spark, Muriel, *Mary Shelley* (London, 1987).

St Clair, William, *The Godwins and the Shelleys: The Biography of a Family* (London, 1989).

Sterrenburg, Lee, 'Mary Shelley's Monster: Politics and Psyche in "Frankenstein" ', in

G. Levine and U. C. Knoepflmacher, eds, *The Endurance of Frankenstein: Essays on Mary Shelley's Novel* (Berkeley, 1982).

Stoker, Bram, *Dracula*, ed. Maurice Hindle (Harmondsworth, 1993).

Stoker, John, *The Illustrated Frankenstein* (Newton Abbot, 1980).

Sunstein, Emily W., *Mary Shelley: Romance and Reality* (Baltimore, 1991).

Thornburn, Mary, *The Monster in the Mirror: Gender and the Sentimental/Gothic Myth in Frankenstein* (Ann Arbor, 1987).

Todd, Mary, 'Frankenstein's Daughter: Mary Shelley and Mary Wollstonecraft' *Women & Literature*, IV/2 (Fall 1976), pp. 18–27.

Todorov, Tzvetan, *Introduction à la littérature fantastique* (Paris, 1970).

Vasbinder, Samuel Holmes, *Scientific Attitudes in Mary Shelley's 'Frankenstein'* (Ann Arbor, 1976).

Veeder, William, *Mary Shelley and Frankenstein: The Fate of Androgyny* (Chicago, 1986).

Wells, H. G., *The Island of Dr Moreau: A Variorum Text*, ed. Robert M. Philmus (Athens, GA, and London, 1993).

Wise, M. N., 'Work and Waste: Political Economy and Natural Philosophy in Nineteenth-century Britain', *History of Science*, XXVII (1989), pp. 263–301.

Wollstonecraft, Mary, *The Wrongs of Woman* (Oxford, 1973).

——, *A Vindication of the Rights of Woman*, ed. M. B. Kramnick (Harmondsworth, 1992).

Index